ACTIVE LEARNING:

Cooperation in the College Classroom

DAVID W. JOHNSON

ROGER T. JOHNSON

KARL A. SMITH

Interaction Book Company

7208 Cornelia Drive
Edina, MN 55435

(612) 831-9500

Johnson, Johnson, & Smith

This book is dedicated to the college professors who have taken our training in how to implement cooperative learning and have used it to create classrooms where students care about each other and about each other's learning.

ISBN 0-939603-14-4

Table of Contents

 Preface

This book is about how college faculty can use cooperative learning to increase student achievement, create positive relationships among students, and promote healthy student psychological adjustment to college. It is about how you, the reader, can ensure that students in your courses actively create their knowledge rather than passively listening to yours. Your challenge is to inspire and motivate your students toward a common purpose of maximizing each other's learning. Your students have to be friends with each other. Students cannot care for someone they never interact or work with. Structuring learning situations so that students do in fact interact with each other is a prerequisite for creating a cohesive class striving to achieve mutual goals.

How students interact with each other as they learn has been relatively ignored, despite its powerful effects. Student relationships may be structured so that teachers compete to see who is best, ignore each other and work independently, or work together cooperatively. The extensive research comparing these interaction patterns clearly suggests that cooperation among students produces greater achievement and higher-level reasoning, more positive relationships among students, greater acceptance of differences, higher self-esteem, increased psychological health, and a number of other outcomes than do competition or working individualistically. At the same time, faculty have been taught and encouraged to prevent students from helping each other, talking to each other, or encouraging each other.

This book is about structuring learning situations cooperatively, so that students work together to achieve shared goals. Cooperation is an old idea. Shifting the emphasis from working alone to working together and caring about whether classmates are working productively is a relatively simple idea. Implementing it is not. This book contains a set of practical strategies for structuring cooperative learning. Gaining a high level of expertise in implementing cooperative strategies is not easy. It takes training, perseverence, and support. The training that has been planned to go with these chapters should provide a good start, but it may take a year or two of experience before structuring cooperative efforts becomes integrated and natural. Persisting until you can use cooperative procedures and strategies at a routine-use level will benefit your students in numerous ways. It is well worth your efforts.

It has taken us nearly 25 years to build the theory, research, and practical experience required to write this book. In the 1960's we began by reviewing the research, conducting our initial research studies, and training teachers in the classroom use of cooperation (Johnson, 1970). Since then our work has proliferated. Our more recent writings on cooperative learning include **Cooperation in the Classroom** (Johnson, Johnson, & Holubec, 1984/1991), **Learning Together and Alone** (Johnson & Johnson, 1975/1991) and **Circles of Learning** (Johnson, Johnson, & Holubec, 1984/1990). Related work on interpersonal skills may be found in our books such as **Reaching Out** (Johnson, 1990), and **Joining Together** (Johnson & F. Johnson, 1991). **Creative Conflict** (Johnson & Johnson, 1987a) focuses on the classroom use of conflict to teach students how to challenge each other's reasoning and manage conflicts within cooperative learning groups constructively. Yet the concept of cooperative learning is much, much older than our work. Our roots reach back to Morton Deutsch and then to Kurt Lewin. We wish to acknowledge our indebtedness to the work of both of these social psychologists.

Many professors have taught us procedures for implementing cooperative learning and have field tested our ideas in their classrooms with considerable success. We have been in their classrooms and we have taught beside them. We appreciate their ideas and celebrate their successes. In addition, we have had many talented and productive graduate students who have conducted research studies that have made significant contributions to our understanding of cooperation. We feel privileged to have worked with them.

Our debt to Judy Bartlett is unmeasurable. Her talents, her dedication, and her work beyond the call of duty have all contributed to the completion of this book. We are continually impressed with and are grateful for her work. She also believes in cooperative learning and often works beyond the call of duty to ensure that it is shared with students in the classroom.

College Teaching And Cooperative Learning

Introduction

Beginning in 1492 with the discovery of America, Spain acquired an empire that was one of the most vast and richest the world has ever known. The royal standard of Spain was proudly flown from California and Florida in the north to Chile in the south, in the Philippine Islands across the Pacific, and at scattered outposts along the coast of Africa. Never before had a country controlled such far-flung territories or gained such great wealth. Spain was able to build such an empire through being the greatest naval power in the world.

In 1588 Spain decided to invade England, conquer it, and end its challenge to Spain's dominance of the seas. An armada of more than 130 ships sailed into the English Channel. A naval battle ensued, Spain suffered heavy casualties and retreated, and a storm came up and sank several more Spanish ships. Only about half of the great Armada returned home to Spain and the back of Spain's empire was broken. Amazingly, the English ships suffered almost no damage. The question is, "How did the English sink all those Spanish ships while suffering very little damage to their ships?"

A number of hypotheses have been advanced to answer this question. One hypothesis was that the armada ships were too large and slow. In fact, the largest and slowest ship in the battle was the Triumph, an English ship. A second hypothesis was that the Armada was too lightly armed. In fact, they did have one-third fewer cannons than the English, but all the cannons were of equivalent size and power and there were lots of them on the Spanish ships. A third hypothesis was that the armada ran out of ammunition. In fact, the research indicates that the Spanish had plenty of ammunition. The most interesting finding is that the Spanish cannons were fired on an average of one to two times a day during the battle.

Here is a sufficient explanation for the Spanish's remarkable failure to inflict serious damage on the English fleet. The Spanish simply did not fire their cannons, especially their heaviest cannons, often enough. Why? The answer appears to be that the Spanish had not planned to fire their cannon at sea. The cannons were to be used primarily for land artillery once the Spanish had landed in England.

Until that fateful day, naval battles consisted mostly of capturing enemy ships by maneuvering close, tying the two ships together, firing one round of grape-shot to clear the deck of the enemy ship, and then boarding and fighting it out hand-to-hand until the enemy ship was captured. The last thing you would want to do is blow a hole in the side of the enemy ship because if it sank while you were tied to it, it would take you down with it. The English changed the rules. Instead of tying their ships to Spanish ships, the English kept their distance and blew holes in the sides of Spanish ships, which then sank.

The Spanish did not know what to do. They could not adapt quickly enough to save themselves due to their highly specialized procedures and battle drills. They had no procedure for disciplined reloading on board ship: The cannons could not be withdrawn and run out, reloading crews were drawn from many different stations, cannons of different calibers and metrics were on the same ship which made it difficult to load the right cannon ball in the right cannon, and the Spanish crews were largely captured sailors pressed into service who spoke many different languages and could not understand each other. Given these problems, the Spanish could not respond to the English's change of paradigms of naval warfare.

The lesson to learn from the armada's failure is not to hang onto the past, trying to make do with slight modifications in the status quo, when faced with a need to change paradigms. And sometimes paradigms have to change quickly.

Changing Nature Of College Teaching

Changing Paradigms Of College Teaching

A **paradigm** is a theory, perspective, or frame of reference that determines how you perceive, interpret, and understand the world. It is a **map** of certain aspects of the world. To deal with the world effectively, you need the right map. Suppose, for example, you wanted to find a specific location in central Minneapolis. If you were given a map of Seattle by mistake, you would be frustrated and your efforts would be futile. You might decide that the problem is your **behavior**. You could try harder, be more diligent, or double your speed. But your efforts would still be ineffective. You might decide that the problem is your **attitude**. You could think more positively. But you still would not find your destination.

The fundamental problem has nothing to do with your behavior or your attitude. It has everything to do with having a wrong map. Your behavior and attitude only affect your outcomes when you have the right map.

Almost every significant breakthrough in the field of scientific endeavor is first a break with traditional old ways of thinking--with old paradigms (Kuhn, 1970). There are a number of classic examples. For Ptolemy, the great Egyptian astronomer, the earth was the center of the universe. But Copernicus created a paradigm shift (and a great deal of resistance and persecution as well) by placing the sun at the center. Suddenly, everything took on a different interpretation. Until the germ theory was developed, a high percentage of women and children died during childbirth, and no one could understand why. In military skirmishes, more men were dying from small wounds and diseases than from the major traumas on the front lines. No one knew what to do. But as soon as the germ theory was developed, dramatic medical improvement became possible due to the paradigm shift.

In college teaching a paradigm shift is taking place. Minor modifications in current teaching practices will not solve the current problems with college instruction. Teaching success in today's world requires a new approach to instruction.

History Of College Teaching

American higher education has moved through three distinct, yet overlapping, phases (Boyer, 1990). The colonial college focused on teaching students to build their character and prepare them for civic and religious leadership. Teaching was viewed as a sacred calling honored as fully as the ministry. Students were entrusted to faculty tutors responsible for their intellectual, moral, and spiritual development. Faculty were employed with the understanding that they would be educational mentors, both in the classroom and beyond.

The second phase focused on service to help the building of the nation. The mission of the university moved toward the practical serving of the democratic community. The service-oriented patriot was the ideal product. Professors were expected to (a) spread knowledge that would improve agriculture, manufacturing, and democracy, and (b) conduct applied research to help them do so.

The third phase began in the early 1900's and focused on the advancement of knowledge through research. Teaching and service began to be deemphasized. Creating new knowledge through conducting research to test theory was seen as fueling human progress. Faculty were hired to teach, but they were evaluated as published researchers. The highest status and most rewarded responsibility of the professor became conducting basic research and publishing results in reputable journals.

First came teaching, then service, and finally the challenge of basic research. In more recent years, faculty have paid lip service to blending the three, but when it comes to making judgments about professional performance, the three are rarely assigned equal merit. Research and publication dominate. Ideally, research leads to teaching valid knowledge and applying it in the real world. Yet the process is not linear. Causality frequently is bidirectional. Theory surely leads to practice, but practice also leads to theory. And teaching can shape both research and practice.

The deemphasis on teaching is based partially on the misperception that teaching is a routine function that anyone can do. If a faculty member has a PhD it is assumed that he or she is qualified to teach. The view that those who know can teach is part of a paradigm of teaching that is labeled as the "old" paradigm. It is discussed below.

Old Paradigm

> *Pardon him, Theodotus: he is a barbarian, and thinks that the customs of his tribe and island are the laws of nature.*
>
> G. B. Shaw, **Caesar and Cleopatra**

The old paradigm of college teaching is based on John Locke's assumption that the untrained student mind is like a blank sheet of paper waiting for the instructor to write on it. Student minds are viewed as empty vessels into which instructors pour their wisdom. Because of these and other assumptions, faculty think of teaching in terms of these principal activities:

1. **Transferring knowledge from faculty to students.** The faculty's job is to give it. The student's job to is get it. Faculty transmit information that students are expected to memorize and then recall.

2. **Filling passive empty vessels with knowledge.** Students are passive recipients of knowledge. The faculty **own** the knowledge that students memorize and recall.

3. **Classifying students** by deciding who gets which grade and **sorting students into categories** by deciding who does and does not meet the requirements to be graduated, go on to graduate school, and get a good job.

4. **Conducting education within a context of impersonal relationships among students and between faculty and students.** Based on the Taylor model of industrial organizations, students and faculty are perceived to be interchangeable and replaceable parts in the "education machine."

5. **Maintaining a competitive organizational structure** in which students work to outperform their classmates and faculty work to outperform their colleagues.

6. **Assuming that anyone with expertise in their field can teach without training to do so.** This is sometimes known as the content premise--if you have a PhD in the field, you can teach.

The **old paradigm** is to transfer the faculty's knowledge to a passive student so that faculty can classify and sort students in a norm-referenced, competitive way. The assumption was that if you have content expertise, you can teach.

Many faculty members consider the old paradigm the only alternative. They have no vision of what could be done instead. Lecturing while requiring students to be passive, silent, isolated, and in competition with each other seems the only way to teach. For such instructors it may be helpful to review Hans Christian Andersen's tale of **The Emperor's New Clothes.** An emperor invests substantial time and money in order to be well- dressed. One day two dishonest men arrive at court. Pretending to be weavers, they claim that they are able to create garments so fine that they are not visible to people who are either unfit for the office that they hold, or stupid. The emperor's vanity and desire to test the competence of his staff leads him to be duped. The weavers are supplied with silk, gold thread, and money, all of which they keep for themselves while pretending to weave the emperor's new clothes.

When the weavers announce that the clothes are ready the emperor sends a succession of trusted ministers to see them. Not wanting to appear unfit for office or stupid, they all report that the new clothes are lovely. Finally, the emperor himself goes to see the clothes which were so heartily praised by his subordinates. Although he sees nothing, he proclaims, "Oh! The cloth is beautiful! I am delighted with the clothes!"

Johnson, Johnson, & Smith

On the day of a great procession the emperor disrobes, dons his "new clothes," and marches through his kingdom, warmed only by the ooh's and ah's emitted by his subjects. Never before had any of the emperor's clothes caused so much excitement! Then, with an innocent persistence, a small child said, "But the emperor has nothing on at all!" The child was not yet constrained by the forces that silenced the adult crowd and caused them, despite the evidence of their senses, to validate their superior's false judgment.

This story is an example of events that all too often occur in colleges: **Not wanting to appear unfit or stupid, faculty members conform to the current consensus about instruction and are afraid to challenge the collective judgment of how best to teach.** The tradition of the old paradigm is carried forward by sheer momentum, while almost everyone persists in the hollow pretense that all is well.

All is not well. Students often do not learn what faculty think they are teaching. Student performance on exams or students' questions may indicate that they do not understand the material in the way or to the extent that faculty would like them to. Furthermore, students often ask boring questions, such as "What do I have to do to get an A?" or "Will it be on the final exam?" Students ask the latter question to determine if the material is important. What matters, of course, is not whether or not it will be on the exam but rather do professionals in practice use the concept or procedure regularly. Such problems wear professors down. There is a way to break out of the old paradigm of teaching and define in more creative ways what it means to be an instructor. The way is known as the new paradigm of teaching.

New Paradigm Of Teaching

It is time for us to reaffirm that education--that is, teaching all its forms--is the primary task of higher education.

Stanford University President Donald Kennedy

College teaching is changing. We are dropping the old paradigm of teaching and adopting a new paradigm based on theory and research that has clear applications to instruction. Faculty ought to think of teaching in terms of several principal activities.

First, knowledge is constructed, discovered, transformed, and extended by students. Faculty create the conditions within which students can construct meaning from the material studied by processing it through existing cognitive structures and then retaining it in long-term memory where it remains open to further processing and possible reconstruction.

Table 1.1 Comparison of Old and New Paradigms of Teaching

	Old Paradigm	**New Paradigm**
Knowledge	Transferred From Faculty To Students	Jointly Constructed By Students And Faculty
Students	Passive Vessel To Be Filled By Faculty's Knowledge	Active Constructor, Discoverer, Transformer Of Own Knowledge
Faculty Purpose	Classify And Sort Students	Develop Students' Competencies And Talents
Relationships	Impersonal Relationships Among Students And Between Faculty And Students	Personal Transaction Among Students And Between Faculty And Students
Context	Competitive/ Individualistic	Cooperative Learning In Classroom And Cooperative Teams Among Faculty
Assumption	Any Expert Can Teach	Teaching Is Complex And Requires Considerable Training

Second, students actively construct their own knowledge. Learning is conceived of as something a learner does, not something that is done to a learner. Students do not passively accept knowledge from the instructor or curriculum. Students activate their existing cognitive structures or construct new ones to subsume the new input. The failure of colleges and universities to involve students actively in the learning process has been consistently criticized by recent national commissions and scholarly reports (Association of American Colleges, 1985; Bok, 1986; Boyer, 1987; National Institute of Education, 1984; Task Group on General Education, 1988). College instruction is criticized as being focused on transmitting fixed bodies of information while ignoring (a) the preparation of students to engage in a continuing acquisition of knowledge and understanding and (b) the careful supervision of students reasoning about challenging problems. The contining acquisition of knowledge and monitoring reasoning require students to be active participants in discussions with classmates.

Despite the academic advantages of involving students in active discussions, many instructors do not do so. Probably the most frequent strategy used is to involve students in whole-class discussions. Frequently, however, students are so socialized into a "spectator" role that it is difficult to get them to participate in class. Barnes (1980) found in an observational study of instructor-student interaction that even when instructors attempted to solicit student participation through whole-class questioning, students responded only 50 percent of the time. Even when teachers manage to obtain student participation, a very small minority of students tends to dominate. Karp and Yoels (1988) documented that in classes of less than 40 students, four to five students accounted for 75 percent of all interactions and, in classes with more than 40 students, two to three students accounted for over half of the exchanges. Stones (1970) surveyed over 1,000 college students and found that 60 percent stated that a large number of classmates listening would deter them from asking questions, even if the instructor encouraged them to do so.

Third, faculty effort is aimed at developing students' competencies and talents. Student effort should be inspired and colleges must "add value" by cultivating talent. James Duderstadt, President of the University of Michigan, noted that colleges and universities have focussed on selection processes in the recruitment of students and faculty and have given little or no attention to developing human potential (Sheahan & White, 1990). Astin (1985) has challenged the four traditional models of excellence in higher education--reputation, content, resources, outcome--and advocated a talent-development model in which the development of student and faculty talent is primary. Within colleges and universities, a "cultivate and develop" philosophy must replace a "select and weed out" philosophy.

In the old paradigm of college teaching, students are classified and sorted into categories that are considered more or less permanent. In the new paradigm, the emphasis is on the development of student competencies and talents which are considered dynamic and always susceptible to change. The implications of this difference may be seen in the history of the IQ test (Davison, 1991). When Benet built his IQ test, he conceived of a measure that would facilitate student development through the promotion of effort. Just as children matured physically, Benet was convinced that children matured mentally. He wanted to be able to

show students through IQ scores that they are smarter this year than they were last year. Each year a student's IQ score would increase, and the teacher could say, "If you work hard and learn a great deal, next year you will have an even higher IQ." What Terman at Stanford University did to the IQ was to reverse the emphasis from effort and development to classifying and sorting students. By dividing IQ by chronological age, Terman created a situation in which IQ does not change. Thus, a teacher says to a student, "No matter how hard you work, no matter how much you learn, your IQ will stay the same. You will never get smarter." In the new paradigm, with its emphasis on student development, it is important for students to associate effort with achievement and intelligence. Colleges want students to go to bed each night celebrating the fact that they are smarter today than they were yesterday.

The colleges that produce the most knowledgeable graduates are not necessarily doing the best job in educating their students. Why? Because under the old paradigm the management of quality within American colleges has generally focused on (a) selecting only the most intelligent students for admission and then (b) inspecting continually to weed out defective students. Under such a system, the "value added" by some colleges is questionable. Colleges may produce the most knowledgeable graduates because they attracted and admitted the highest achieving students and provided a holding ground. Quality is managed in the admission process, not in the educational process. Little or no attention is given to the developing human potential. Marginal students who, with a little development effort, could be transformed into superstars are ignored. Similarly, when only the most productive faculty members are hired the college can ignore the faculty-development process. Thus, the true "value added" by the college or university must be questioned.

The second part of quality control under the old paradigm is constant inspection to "weed out" any defective students. One of the mistakes that American industry made was trying to "inspect" quality into its products by identifying and throwing out all defective parts. The ineffective practices were left in place while more and more effort was put into better inspection procedures. American colleges are making the same mistake by using entrance exams, tests and final exams in courses, qualifying exams, comprehensive exams, and dissertation defenses to "inspect" quality into the college's product. Those students who fail and, therefore, who are obviously defective, are weeded out so that only the most high quality students are graduated. The educational practices that resulted in the failure are not questioned and only the student pays the penalty. Quality control in American industry is changing. The new focus is on curing the cause of defects rather than to continue to reject defective parts. Likewise, academia may wish to focus its attention on identifying the source of its "failures." Under the new paradigm, (a) student performance is monitored and when students falter, help and support is provided and (b) when a student fails the educational practices are examined and modified to prevent such a failure occurring again in the future.

The old paradigm classifies and sorts students into categories under the assumption that ability is fixed and unaffected by effort and education. The new paradigm develops students' competencies and talents under the assumption that with effort and education they can be improved. The old paradigm controls quality through emphasizing selection and weeding-out processes. The new paradigm controls quality through continually refining the educational process to cultivate and develop students' competencies and talents. Under the old paradigm colleges are holding grounds for carefully selected students. Under the new paradigm colleges add value by developing students' potential and transforming students into more knowledgeable and committed individuals.

Fourth, education is a personal transaction among students and between the faculty and students as they work together. All education is a social process that cannot occur except through interpersonal interaction (real or implied). Learning is a personal but social process that results when individuals cooperate to construct shared understandings and knowledge. Faculty must be able to build positive relationships with students and to create the conditions within which students build caring and committed relationships with each other. The college then becomes a learning community of committed scholars in the truest sense.

Within the new paradigm, faculty recognize that (a) long-term, hard, persistent efforts to achieve come from the heart, not the head, and (b) the fastest way to reach a student's heart is through peer relationships (Johnson & Johnson, 1989b). Students work together to construct their knowledge and as they succeed in doing so, they become committed to and care about each other's learning and each other as people. Caring about how much a person achieves and caring about him or her as a person go hand-in-hand; academic and personal support tend to be closely related (Johnson & Johnson, 1989a). Within learning situations, it is acts of caring that draw students together and move them forward. Love of learning and love of each other (as well as the faculty) are what inspire students to commit more and more of their energy to their studies.

Striving for increased expertise is an arduous and long-term enterprise. Individuals become exhausted, frustrated, and disenchanted. They are tempted to give up. Caring relationships encourage the heart to continue improving expertise year after year after year. What sustains students' efforts is the knowledge that classmates care about, and are depending on, their progress. Students' commitment to learning is nurtured by their knowing that (a) their contributions to classmates' learning and (b) their own progress in gaining knowledge and expertise, are perceived, recognized, appreciated, and celebrated by their classmates and the faculty. Caring and committed relationships provide meaning and purpose to learning. They contribute to achievement and productivity, physical health, psychological health, and constructive management of stress (Johnson & Johnson, 1989a).

The more difficult and complex the learning, the harder students have to struggle to achieve, the more important the social support students need. There is a general rule of instruction: **The more pressure placed on students to achieve and the more difficult the** material to be learned, the more important it is to provide social support within the learning situation. Challenge and social support must be balanced if students are to cope successfully with the stress inherent in learning situations.

In summary, learning is a social process that occurs through interpersonal interaction within a cooperative context. Individuals, working together, construct shared understandings and knowledge. Learning proceeds more fruitfully when relationships are personal as well as professional. Long-term, persistent efforts to achieve come from the heart, not the head, and the heart is reached through relationships with peers and faculty. Love of learning and love of each other are what inspire students to commit more and more of their energy to their studies. The more difficult and complex the learning, the more important are caring relationships to provide the needed social support.

Seven Principles For Good Practice In Undergraduate Education

1. *Encourage student-faculty contact.*

2. *Encourage cooperation among students.*

3. *Encourage active learning.*

4. *Give prompt feedback.*

5. *Emphasize active learning.*

6. *Communicate high expectations.*

7. *Respect diverse talents and ways of learning.*

Chickering, A., & Gamson, Z. (1987). Seven principles for good practice in undergraduate education. *Wingspread*, 9, 1-8.

Fifth, all of the above can only take place within a cooperative context. When students interact within a competitive context communication is minimized, misleading and false information is often communicated, helping is minimized and viewed as cheating, and classmates and faculty tend to be disliked and distrusted. Competitive and individualistic learning situations, therefore, discourage active construction of knowledge and the development of talent by isolating students and creating negative relationships among classmates and with instructors. Classmates and faculty need to be viewed as collaborators rather than as obstacles to students' own academic and personal success. Faculty, therefore, structure learning situations so that students work together cooperatively to maximize each other's achievement. Ideally, administrators would in turn create a cooperative, team-based organizational structure within which faculty work together to ensure each other's success. There is considerable data indicating that higher achievement, more positive relationships, and better psychological adjustment results from cooperative than from competitive or individualistic learning (Johnson & Johnson, 1989a). That data is reviewed in Chapter 2.

Ensuring that students are active in class usually requires the use of cooperative learning groups. It takes two or more people interacting within a cooperative context to think creatively in divergent ways so that **new** ideas, solutions and procedures are generated and conceptual frameworks are constructed (i.e., process gain) (Johnson & Johnson, 1989a). McKeachie and his associates (1986, 1988) have recently reviewed the research on methods of college teaching and found that students were more likely to acquire critical thinking skills and meta-cognitive learning strategies such as self-monitoring and learning-how-to-learn skills from discussions with groupmates. Bligh (1972) reviewed close to 100 studies of college teaching that were conducted over 50 years. He found that students who participated in active discussions of their ideas with classmates had fewer irrelevant or distracting thoughts and spent more time synthesizing and integrating concepts than students who listened to lectures. Bligh concluded that during discussion students tended to be more attentive, active, and thoughtful than during lectures. Kulik and Kulik (1979) concluded from a review of research on college teaching that student discussion groups were more effective than lectures in promoting students' problem-solving abilities. Smith (1977, 1980) conducted an observation study of college classes in a variety of academic subjects and found student-student interaction to be related to critical thinking outcomes and study habits characterized by more active thinking and less rote memorization.

Sixth, teaching is assumed to be a complex application of theory and research that requires considerable instructor training and continuous refinement of skills and procedures. Becoming a good teacher takes at least one life time of continuous effort to improve.

The **new paradigm of teaching** is to help students construct their knowledge in an active way while working cooperatively with classmates so that students' talents and competencies are developed. The assumption is that teaching requires training and skill in and of itself.

Implementing The New Paradigm: Cooperative Learning

The primary means of achieving the new paradigm of teaching in the college classroom is to use cooperative learning. Cooperative learning provides the means of operationalizing the new paradigm of teaching and provides the context within which the development of student talent is encouraged. Carefully structured cooperative learning ensures that students are cognitively, physically, emotionally, and psychologically actively involved in constructing their own knowledge and is an important step in changing the passive and impersonal character of many college classrooms.

The intent of this book is to provide instructors with the knowledge required for beginning the journey of gaining expertise in using cooperative learning. To gain this expertise faculty must **first** understand what cooperative learning is and how it differs from competitive and individualistic learning. **Second,** they must be confident that using cooperative learning is the most effective thing to do. Confidence in the use of cooperative learning in the college classroom is based on the 90 years of research that has produced over 600 studies demonstrating that cooperative learning experiences result in higher achievement, more positive relationships among students, and healthier psychological adjustment than do competitive or individualistic learning experiences. **Third,** faculty must realize that simply placing students in discussion groups will **not** magically produce these outcomes. For cooperation to be effective, five essential elements must be structured within the learning situation. **Fourth,** faculty must know that there are many different ways to use cooperative learning within the college classroom. The various operationalizations of cooperative learning may be subsumed under formal cooperative learning groups, informal cooperative learning groups, and base groups. **Fifth,** one of the most powerful ways to use formal cooperative learning groups is through the use of structured academic controversies, which promotes higher-level reasoning, deeper-level understanding, and long-term retention of what is learned. **Sixth,** probably the most essential aspect of cooperative learning is positive interdependence, which may be operationalized a variety of ways within all three types of cooperative learning groups. **Finally,** what is good for students is even better for faculty. It is just as important to structure the college so faculty work in cooperative teams as it is to use cooperative learning within the classroom. In essence, the organizational structure of colleges must change from competitive-individualistic to cooperative.

Student-Student Interaction

In every college classroom, no matter what the subject area, instructors may structure lessons so that students:

1. Work cooperatively in small groups, ensuring that all members master the assigned material.

2. Engage in a win-lose struggle to see who is best.

3. Work independently on their own learning goals at their own pace and in their own space to achieve a preset criterion of excellence.

There are three ways student-student interaction may be structured in college classes: competitively, individualistically, and cooperatively. When students are required to **compete** with each other for grades, they work against each other to achieve a goal that only one or a few students can attain. Students are graded on a norm-referenced basis, which requires them to work faster and more accurately than their peers. In doing so, they strive to be better than classmates, work to deprive others (*My winning means you lose*), to celebrate classmates' failures (*Your failure makes it easier for me to win*), view resources such as grades as limited (*Only a few of us will get "A's"*), recognize their negatively linked fate (*The more you gain, the less for me; the more I gain, the less for you*), and believe that the more competent and hard-working individuals become "haves" and the less competent and deserving individuals become the "have nots" (*Only the strong prosper*). In **competitive situations** there is a negative interdependence among goal achievements; students perceive that they can obtain their goals if and only if the other students in the class fail to obtain their goals (Deutsch, 1962; Johnson & Johnson, 1991). Unfortunately, most students perceive college classes as predominantly competitive enterprises. Students either work hard to do better than their classmates, or they take it easy because they do not believe they have a chance to win.

When students are required to work **individualistically** on their own, they work by themselves to accomplish learning goals unrelated to those of the other students. Individual goals are assigned and students' efforts are evaluated on a criteria-referenced basis. Each student has his or her own set of materials and works at his or her own speed, ignoring the other students in the class. Students are expected and encouraged to focus on their strict self-interest (*How well can I do*), value only their own efforts and own success (*If I study hard, I may get a high grade*), and ignore as irrelevant the success or failure of others (*Whether my classmates study or not does not affect me*). In **individualistic learning situations,** students' goal achievements are independent; students perceive that the achievement of their learning goals is unrelated to what other students do (Deutsch, 1962; Johnson & Johnson, 1991).

Cooperation is working together to accomplish shared goals. Within cooperative activities individuals seek outcomes that are beneficial to themselves **and** beneficial to all other group members. **Cooperative learning** is the instructional use of small groups so that students work together to maximize their own and each other's learning. The idea is simple.

Class members are split into small groups after receiving instruction from the teacher. They then work through the assignment until all group members have successfully understood and completed it. Cooperative efforts result in participants striving for mutual benefit so that all group members benefit from each other's efforts (*Your success benefits me and my success benefits you*), recognizing that all group members share a common fate (*We all sink or swim together here*), recognizing that one's performance is mutually caused by oneself and one's colleagues (*We can not do it without you*), and feeling proud and jointly celebrating when a group member is recognized for achievement (*You got an A! That is terrific!*) In cooperative learning situations there is a positive interdependence among students' goal attainments; students perceive that they can reach their learning goals if and only if the other students in the learning group also reach their goals (Deutsch, 1962; Johnson & Johnson, 1991).

In summary, students' learning goals may be structured to promote cooperative, competitive, or individualistic efforts. In every classroom, instructional activities are aimed at accomplishing goals and are conducted under a goal structure. A **learning goal** is a desired future state of demonstrating competence or mastery in the subject area being studied. The **goal structure** specifies the ways in which students will interact with each other and the teacher during the instructional session. Each goal structure has its place (see Johnson & R. Johnson, 1991). In the ideal classroom, all students would learn how to work collaboratively with others, compete for fun and enjoyment, and work autonomously on their own. The teacher decides which goal structure to implement within each lesson.

After half a century of relative neglect, cooperative learning procedures are increasingly being used throughout public and private colleges. Cooperative learning is the most important of the three types of learning situations, yet currently it is the least used in college classrooms. This has not always been the case. Cooperative learning is a tradition within education.

History Of Cooperative Learning

> *Two are better than one, because they have a good reward for toil. For if they fall, one will lift up his fellow; but woe to him who is alone when he falls and has not another to lift him up...And though a man might prevail against one who is alone, two will withstand him. A threefold cord is not quickly broken.*
>
> Ecclesiastics 4:9-12

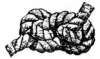

Cooperative learning is an old idea. The capacity to work cooperatively has been a major contributor to the survival of our species. The **Talmud** clearly states that in order to learn one must have a learning partner. As early as the first century, **Quintillion** argued that students could benefit from teaching one another. The Roman philosopher, **Seneca** advocated cooperative learning through such statements as, "Qui Docet Discet" (when you teach, you learn twice). **Johann Amos Comenius** (1592-1679) believed that students would benefit both by teaching and being taught by other students. In the late 1700's **Joseph Lancaster** and Andrew Bell made extensive use of cooperative learning groups in England, and the idea was brought to America when a Lancastrian school was opened in New York City in 1806. Within the **Common School Movement** in the United States in the early 1800's there was a strong emphasis on cooperative learning. Certainly, the use of cooperative learning is not new to American education. There have been periods in which cooperative learning had strong advocates and was widely used to promote the educational goals of that time.

One of the most successful advocates of cooperative learning in America was **Colonel Francis Parker**. In the last three decades of the 19th Century, Colonel Parker brought to his advocacy of cooperative learning enthusiasm, idealism, practicality, and an intense devotion to freedom, democracy, and individuality in the public schools. His fame and success rested on the vivid and regenerating spirit that he brought into the schoolroom and on his power to create a classroom atmosphere that was truly cooperative and democratic. When he was superintendent of the public schools at Quincy, Massachusetts (1875-1880), he averaged more than 30,000 visitors a year to examine his use of cooperative learning procedures (Campbell, 1965). Parker's instructional methods of structuring cooperation among students dominated American education through the turn of the century. Following Parker, **John Dewey** promoted the use of cooperative learning groups as part of his famous project method in instruction (Dewey, 1924). In the late 1930's, however, interpersonal competition began to be emphasized in public schools and colleges (Pepitone, 1980).

In the 1960's the authors began their work on cooperative learning which resulted in the formation of the **Cooperative Learning Center** at the University of Minnesota. We concentrated on five coordinated activities:

1. Synthesizing existing knowledge concerning cooperative, competitive, and individualistic efforts (Johnson, 1970; Johnson & Johnson, 1974, 1978, 1983, 1989; Johnson, Johnson, & Maruyama, 1983; Johnson, Maruyama, Johnson, Nelson, & Skon, 1981). Most recently, we have conducted a series of meta-analyses of all available research through 1989 (Johnson & Johnson, 1989a).

2. Formulating theoretical models concerning the nature of cooperation and its essential components.

3. Conducting a systematic program of research to test the proposed theory. We have conducted and published over 85 research studies on cooperative, competitive, and individualistic efforts.

4. Translating the validated theory into a set of concrete strategies and procedures to use cooperation in the classroom (e.g., cooperative learning), in schools (e.g., colleagial support groups and school-based decision making), and within school districts (e.g., administrator teams) (Johnson, Johnson, & Holubec, 1984/1990; Johnson & Johnson, 1975/1991, 1989b).

5. Orchestrating and assisting a network of schools and colleges a long-term commitment to implementing cooperative strategies and procedures. The network includes school districts and colleges the United States and Canada and in various countries in Europe, Central and South America, the Middle East, Africa, and Asia. The training includes teachers, administrators, and faculty in preschool, elementary, secondary, vocational, college, and adult education programs.

There are several groups of researchers and practitioners scattered throughout the United States and Canada and in several other countries engaged in the study and implementation of cooperative learning lessons, curriculums, strategies, and procedures.

In addition to the history of the practical use of cooperative learning, there is a history of the theorizing about and research on cooperative, competitive, and individualistic efforts. The research studies began in the late 1800's when Triplett (1898) in the United States, Turner (1889) in England, and Mayer (1903) in Germany conducted a series of studies on the factors associated with competitive performance. May and Doobs (1937) conducted an initial review of the research. In the 1940's **Morton Deutsch**, building on the theorizing of **Kurt Lewin**, proposed a theory of cooperative and competitive situations that has served as the primary foundation on which subsequent research on and discussion of cooperative learning has been based. Our own theorizing and research is directly based on Deutsch's work (Johnson & Johnson, 1989a).

Morton Deutsch

Basic Elements Of Cooperative Learning

Together we stand, divided we fall.

Watchword Of The American Revolution

In a classroom the instructor is trying out learning groups. "This is a mess," she thinks. In one group students are bickering over who is going to do the writing. In another group a member sits quietly, too shy to participate. Two members of a third group are talking about football while the third member works on the assignment. "My students do not know how to work cooperatively," the instructor concludes.

What is an instructor to do in such a situation? Simply placing students in groups and telling them to work together does not mean that they know how to cooperate or that they will do so even if they know. Many instructors believe that they are implementing cooperative learning when in fact they are missing its essence. **Putting students into groups to learn is not the same thing as structuring cooperation among students.** Cooperation is **not**:

1. Having students sit side by side at the same table and talk with each other as they do their individual assignments.

2. Having students do a task individually with instructions that the ones who finish first are to help the slower students.

3. Assigning a report to a group where one student does all the work and others put their name on it.

Cooperation is much more than being physically near other students, discussing material with other students, helping other students, or sharing materials with other students, although each of these is important in cooperative learning.

In order for a lesson to be cooperative, five basic elements are essential (Johnson, Johnson, & Holubec, 1990). In a math class, for example, an instructor assigns her students a set of math problems to solve. Students are placed in groups of three. The **instructional task** is for students to solve each story problem correctly and understand the correct strategy for doing so. The instructor must now implement five basic elements. The first element of a cooperative lesson is **positive interdependence**. Students must believe that they are linked with others in a way that one cannot succeed unless the other members of the group succeed (and vice versa), that is, they "sink or swim together." Within the math lesson, the instructor creates positive goal interdependence by requiring group members to agree on the answer and the strategies for solving each problem. Positive role interdependence is structured by assigning each student a role. The **reader** reads the problems aloud to the group. The **checker** makes sure that all members can explain how to solve each problem correctly. The **encourager** in a friendly way encourages all members of the group to participate in the discussion, sharing their ideas and feelings. Resource interdependence is created by giving each group one copy of the problems to be solved. All students work the problems on scratch paper and share their insights with each other. Positive reward interdependence is structured by giving each group five points if all members score above 90 percent correct on the test given at the end of the unit. The most important is goal interdependence. All cooperative learning starts with a mutually shared group goal.

The second element of a cooperative lesson is **face-to-face promotive interaction** among students, which exists when students help, assist, encourage, and support each other's efforts to learn. Students promote each other's learning by orally explaining to each other how to solve problems, discussing with each other the nature of the concepts and strategies being learned, teaching their knowledge to each other, and explaining to each other the connections between present and past learning. In the math lesson, the instructor must provide the time, knee-to-knee seating arrangement, and instructor encouragement for students to exchange ideas and help each other learn.

The third element is **individual accountability**, which exists when the performance of each individual student is assessed and the results given back to the group and the individual. It is important that group members know (a) who needs more assistance in completing the assignment and (b) they cannot "hitch-hike" on the work of others. Common ways of structuring individual accountability include giving an individual test to each student and randomly selecting one student's work to represent the efforts of the entire group.

The fourth element is **social skills**. Groups cannot function effectively if students do not have and use the needed leadership, decision-making, trust-building, communication, and conflict-management skills. These skills have to be taught just as purposefully and precisely as academic skills. Many students have never worked cooperatively in learning situations and, therefore, lack the needed social skills for doing so. In the math lesson the instructor emphasizes the skill of "checking to make sure everyone understands." The instructor defines the skill as the phrases and the accompanying nonverbal behaviors to be used by the checker. The group roles are rotated each day. When the instructor sees students engaging in the skill, she verbally praises the group and/or records the instance on an observation

sheet. Procedures and strategies for teaching students social skills may be found in Johnson (1990, 1991), Johnson and F. Johnson (1991), and Johnson, Johnson, and Holubec (1990).

Finally, the instructor must ensure that **groups process** how well they are achieving their goals and maintaining effective working relationships among members. At the end of the math period the groups **process** their functioning by answering two questions: (1) What is something each member did that was helpful for the group and (2) What is something each member could do to make the group even better tomorrow? Such processing enables learning groups to focus on group maintenance, facilitates the learning of social skills, ensures that members receive feedback on their participation, and reminds students to practice the small group skills required to work cooperatively. Some of the keys to successful processing are allowing sufficient time for it to take place, making it specific rather than vague, varying the format, maintaining student involvement in processing, reminding students to use their social skills while they process, and ensuring that clear expectations of the purpose of processing have been communicated. Often, each group is required to turn in a summary of their processing that is signed by all group members.

These five elements are what differentiates (a) cooperative learning groups from traditional discussion groups and (b) a well-structured cooperative learning lesson from a poorly structured one. The five elements are discussed in detail in Chapter 3. There are three broad types of cooperative learning groups that are structured through the use of the five basic elements. They are discussed in Chapters 4, 5, and 6.

Types of Cooperative Learning Groups

These problems are endemic to all institutions of education, regardless of level. Children sit for 12 years in classrooms where the implicit goal is to listen to the teacher and memorize the information in order to regurgitate it on a test. Little or no attention is paid to the learning process, even though much research exists documenting that real understanding is a case of active restructuring on the part of the learner. Restructuring occurs through engagement in problem posing as well as problem solving, inference making and investigation, resolving of contradictions, and reflecting. These processes all mandate far more active learners, as well as a different model of education than the one subscribed to at present by most institutions. Rather than being powerless and dependent on the institution, learners need to be empowered to think and learn for themselves. Thus, learning needs to be conceived of as something a learner does, not something that is done to a learner.

Catherine Fosnot (1989)

Students often feel helpless and discouraged, especially when facing a difficult class or when they have just entered college. Giving them cooperative learning partners provides hope and opportunity. Perhaps the most important aspect of college faculty life is empowering students by organizing them into cooperative teams. It is social support from and accountability to valued peers that motivates committed efforts to achieve and succeed. Cooperative learning groups empower their members by making them feel strong, capable, and committed. If classrooms are to be places where students care about each other and are committed to each other's success in academic endeavors, a cooperative structure must exist. A cooperative structure consists of the integrated use of three types of cooperative learning groups.

Cooperative learning groups may be used to teach specific content (**formal cooperative learning groups**), to ensure active cognitive processing of information during a lecture (**informal cooperative learning groups**), and to provide long-term support and assistance for academic progress (**cooperative base groups**). Any assignment in any curriculum may be done cooperatively. In **formal cooperative learning groups** the instructor structures the learning groups (deciding on group size and how to assign students to groups); teaches the academic concepts, principles, and strategies that the students are to master and apply; assigns a task to be completed cooperatively; monitors the functioning of the learning groups and intervenes to (a) teach collaborative skills and (b) provide assistance in academic learning when it is needed; and then evaluates student learning and guides the processing by learning groups of their effectiveness.

During a lecture **informal cooperative learning groups** can be used to focus student attention on the material to be learned, set a mood conducive to learning, help set expectations as to what will be covered in a class session, ensure that students cognitively process the material being taught, and provide closure to an instructional session. Students can summarize in three-to-five minute discussions what they know about a topic in focused discussions before and after a lecture. Short three-to-five minute discussions in cooperative pairs can be interspersed throughout a lecture. In this way the main problem of lectures can be countered: The information passes from the notes of the professor to the notes of the student without passing through the mind of either one.

Finally, **cooperative base groups** can be used to provide each student the support, encouragement, and assistance he or she need to make academic progress. Base groups meet daily (or whenever the class meets). They are permanent (lasting from one to several years) and provide the long-term caring peer relationships necessary to influence members consistently to work hard in college. The use of base groups tends to improves attendance, personalizes the work required and the school experience, and improve the quality and quantity of learning. The larger the class or college and the more complex and difficult the subject matter, the more important it is to have base groups.

When used in combination, cooperative formal, informal, and base groups provide an overall structure for college learning.

Using Cooperative Learning In College Courses

The coordinated use of all three types of cooperative learning groups provides a structure to courses. A typical class period, for example, may start with a base group meeting, move to a short lecture utilizing informal cooperative learning groups, give an assignment that is completed in formal cooperative learning groups, and end with a base group meeting. A sample course syllabus may be found in Appendix A. In Chapters 4, 5, and 6 the three types of cooperative learning groups are explained in detail and practical suggestions given as to how they may be used. In Chapter 8 the integrated use of the three will be discussed.

Leaving The Ivy Tower And Preparing Students For The "Real World"

Preparing students to live in the real world includes making classroom experiences (a) more similar to career situations, (b) more reflective of the increased interdependence in the world, and (c) more realistically aimed at building a high quality of life within and after college.

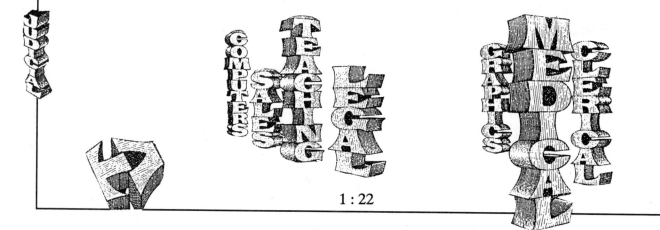

Career Success

Everyone has to work together; if we can't get everybody working toward common goals, nothing is going to happen.

Harold K. Sperlich, President, Chrysler Corporation

For an individual, piloting a Boeing 747 is impossible. For the three-person crew, it is straightforward. The crew, furthermore, does not work in isolation. Large numbers of mechanics, service personnel, cabin attendants, air traffic controllers, pilot educators (who keep crew members abreast of the latest developments and sharp in their responses to problem situations), and many others are necessary to the flying of the plane. From the demands of repairing a flat tire on a dark highway ("You hold the light while I...") to the complex requirements of flying a modern passenger jet, teamwork is the most frequent human response to the challenges of coping with otherwise impossible tasks.

The importance of cooperative learning goes beyond maximizing outcomes such as achievement, positive attitudes toward subject areas, and the ability to think critically, although these are worthwhile outcomes. Knowledge and skills are of no use if the student cannot apply them in cooperative interaction with other people. It does no good to train an engineer, accountant, or teacher if the person does not have the cooperative skills needed to apply the knowledge and technical skills in cooperative relationships on the job.

Much of what students have traditionally learned in school is worthless in the real world. Schools teach that work means performing tasks largely by oneself, helping and assisting others is cheating, technical competencies are the only things that matter, attendance and punctuality are secondary to test scores, motivation is up to the teacher, success depends on performance on individual tests, and promotions are received no matter how little one works. In the real world of work, things are altogether different. Most employers do not expect people to sit in rows and compete with colleagues without interacting with them. The heart of most jobs, especially the

Workplace Basics

A recent survey of major businesses and industrial firms concluded that the workplace basics to learn in school are:

1. *Learning to learn.*

2. *Listening and oral communications.*

3. *Competence in reading, writing and computation.*

4. *Adaptability based on creative thinking and problem solving.*

5. *Personal management characterized by self-esteem, goal-setting motivation, and personal/career development.*

6. *Group effectiveness characterized by interpersonal skills, negotiation skills and teamwork.*

7. *Organizational effectiveness and leadership.*

American Society for Training and Development and the U.S. Department of Labor (1988) higher-paying more interesting jobs, is teamwork. Teamwork involves getting others to cooperate, leading others, coping with complex power and influence issues, and helping solve people's problems in working with each other. Teamwork involves communication, effective coordination, and divisions of labor.

Within the real world, cooperation is pervasive on many levels. Individuals join together in a group that is structured around a mutual goal. The group fits into the larger mosaic of groups working toward a larger goal. Those groups also form a mosaic working toward even a larger superordinate goal. Thus, there are individuals who work within teams that work within departments that work within divisions that work within organizations that work within a societal economic system that works within the global economic system.

Life in the real world is characterized by layers of positive interdependence that stretch from the interpersonal to the international. Current life in colleges is dominated by competitive and individualistic activities that ignore the importance of positive interdependence. It is time for colleges to leave the ivy tower of working alone to see who is best and ensure that classroom experiences realistically reflect the realities of adult life.

World Interdependence

Students increasingly live in a world characterized by interdependence, pluralism, conflict, and rapid change. Because of technological, economic, ecological, and political interdependence, the solution to most problems cannot be achieved by one country alone. The major problems faced by individuals (e.g., contamination of the environment, global warming, world hunger, violence toward women and children, international terrorism, nuclear war) are increasingly ones that cannot be solved by actions taken only at the national level. Our students will live in a complex, interconnected world in which cultures collide every minute and dependencies limit the flexibility of individuals and nations. The internationalization of problems will increase so that there will be no clear division between domestic and international problems. Students need to learn the competencies involved in managing interdependence, resolving conflicts within cooperative systems made up of parties from different countries and cultures, and personally adapting to rapid change.

Quality Of Life

Quality of life depends on having close friends who last a lifetime, building and maintaining a loving family, being a responsible parent, caring about others, and contributing to the well-being of the world. These are things that make life worthwhile. Grades in school do not predict which students will have a high quality of life after they are graduated. The ability to work cooperatively with others does. The ability of students to work collaboratively with others is the keystone to building and maintaining the caring and committed relationships that largely determine quality of life.

Summary

In college teaching a paradigm shift is taking place. Minor modifications in current teaching practices will not solve the current problems with college instruction. Teaching success in today's world requires a new approach to instruction. In planning the new approach, it may be helpful to review the history of college teaching in America. There have been three general definitions of the faculty's role in American colleges. In colonial America, the emphasis was on teaching. In the latter half of the 19th-Century, the emphasis was on practical service to promote America's economic and political strength. In the early 20th-Century, faculty were given the challenge of basic research. In more recent years, faculty have paid lip service to blending the three, but when it comes to making judgments about professional performance, the teaching, service, and research are rarely assigned equal merit. Research and publication dominate. It is time for the pendulum to swing back to include an emphasis on teaching and service as well as research. In doing so, teaching and service must be matched to the modern world. Teaching in the old way harder and faster with more bells and whistles will not do. The "select and weed out" approach to teaching must be replaced with the "development" approach. While academia has a number of purposes, including discovering and formulating knowledge through research and theory, teaching is one of their most important activities. Colleges must refocus on teaching in order to develop student potential and talents. College faculty must "add value" through their teaching. The new paradigm of teaching may only be operationalized and implemented through the use of cooperative learning procedures.

Cooperative learning is the instructional use of small groups so that students work together to maximize their own and each other's learning. There is considerable research demonstrating that cooperative learning produces higher achievement, more positive relationships among students, and healthier psychological adjustment than do competitive or individualistic experiences. These effects, however, do not automatically appear when students are placed in groups. To be cooperative, learning groups must be carefully structured to include five basic elements. There are, furthermore, many different ways to structure cooperative learning. Three broad categories of cooperative learning strategies are formal cooperative learning groups, informal cooperative learning groups, and cooperative base groups. Finally, cooperation is just as powerful among faculty as it is among students. There needs to be an organizational restructuring from the existing competitive-individualistic college structure to a cooperative team-based college structure. Each of these topics is discussed in this book. Cooperative learning was defined in this chapter. Chapter Two focuses on the research and theory underlying the engineering of cooperation within colleges. In Chapter Three the five basic elements will be explicated. Chapters Four, Five, and Six deal specifically with the three types of cooperative learning groups. Chapter Seven describes encouraging critical thinking through structured academic controversy. Chapter Eight discusses positive interdependence in more depth. Chapter Nine discusses cooperation among faculty. Chapter Ten gives a summary and conclusion.

Final Note

Reorganizing a college is like reorganizing a graveyard.

Warren Bennis

The recent Carnegie Foundation study of student life revealed growing social separations and divisions on campus, increased acts of incivility, and a deepening concern that the spirit of community has diminished. In response, colleges and universities from coast to coast are searching for ways to affirm diversity while strengthening the loyalties on campuses. Issues like the quality of campus life for students, however, are not considered by the old paradigm. The work of the faculty needs to be defined in ways that enrich, rather than restrict, the quality of campus life. Cooperative learning provides a procedure for doing so. In choosing between the old and new paradigms of teaching, faculty may wish to remember how to broil a frog.

If you place a frog in a pot of boiling water, it will immediately jump out with little damage to itself. But if you place a frog in a pot of cold water, and slowly raise the temperature, the frog seems to adapt well to the new conditions, and stays in the pot until the water reaches 212 degrees Fahrenheit - boiling - and then the frog quickly dies. The frog does not have the sensors needed to detect the gradual rise in water temperature. Colleges and universities may be in danger of making the same mistake. They may make incremental changes to their dynamic environment until they suddenly realize that there has been a fundamental change and they are obsolete and out of date.

DEFINITIONS

A learning **goal** is a desired future state of competence or mastery in the subject area being studied. A **goal structure** specifies the type of interdependence among students as they strive to accomplish their learning goals. Interdependence may be positive (cooperation), negative (competition), or none (individualistic efforts).

Cooperation: We Sink Or Swim Together

Teachers structure lessons so that students work together to maximize their own and each other's learning. Students work together to achieve shared goals.

- Work in small, often heterogeneous groups
- Strive for all group members' success
- What benefits self benefits others
- Joint success is celebrated
- Rewards are viewed as unlimited
- Evaluated by comparing performance to preset criteria

Competition: I Swim, You Sink; I Sink, You Swim

Teachers structure lessons so that students work against each other to achieve a goal only one or a few can attain.

- Work alone
- Strive to be better than classmates
- What benefits self deprives others
- Own success and others' failure is celebrated
- Rewards are limited
- Graded on a curve or ranked from "best" to "worst"

Individualistic: We Are Each In This Alone

Students work by themselves to accomplish learning goals unrelated to those of other students.

- Work alone
- Strive for own success
- What benefits self does not affect others
- Own success is celebrated
- Rewards are viewed as unlimited
- Evaluated by comparing performance to preset criteria

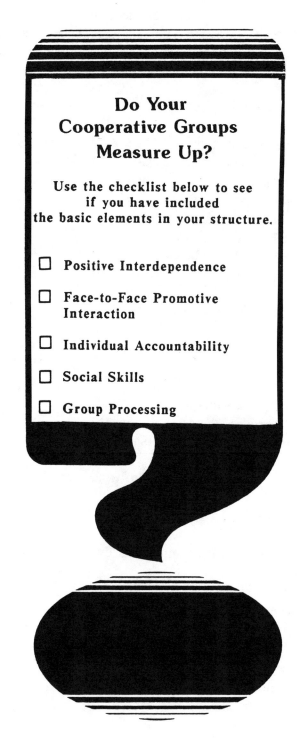

**Do Your
Cooperative Groups
Measure Up?**

Use the checklist below to see
if you have included
the basic elements in your structure.

☐ Positive Interdependence

☐ Face-to-Face Promotive
Interaction

☐ Individual Accountability

☐ Social Skills

☐ Group Processing

Research On Cooperative Learning

Introduction

On July 15, 1982, Don Bennett, a Seattle businessman, was the first amputee ever to climb Mount Rainier (reported in Kouzes & Posner, 1987). He climbed 14,410 feet on one leg and two crutches. It took him five days. When asked to state the most important lesson he learned from doing so, without hesitation he said, "You can't do it alone."

If you ask individuals like Don Bennett who have made remarkable achievements during their lifetimes, they would say their success came from cooperative efforts. Not only is cooperation connected with success, generally competitiveness has been found to be detrimental to career success (Kohn, 1986). The more competitive a person is, the less chance they have of being successful. Perhaps the most definitive research on this issue has been conducted by Robert L. Helmreich and his colleagues (Helmreich, 1982; Helmreich, Beane, Lucker, & Spence, 1978; Helmreich, Sawin, & Carsrud, 1986; Helmreich Spence, et al., 1980). They first determined that high achievers, such as scientists, MBA's, and pilots tend **not** to be very competitive individuals. Then Helmreich and his associates examined the relationship between the competitive drive within individuals and career success. They conceptualized the **desire to achieve** as consisting of **competitiveness** (desire to win in interpersonal situations, where one tends to see that success depends on another's failure), **mastery** (desire to take on challenging tasks), and **work** (positive attitudes toward hard work). A sample of 103 male PhD scientists was rated on the three factors based on a questionnaire. Achievement was defined as the number of times their work was cited by colleagues. The result was that the most citations were obtained by those high on the Work and Mastery but low on the Competitiveness scale. Startled by these results, Helmreich and his associates conducted follow-up studies with academic psychologists, businessmen working in "cut-throat" big business (measuring achievement by their salaries), undergraduate male and female students (using grade-point average as the achievement measure), fifth- and sixth-grade students (measuring achievement by performance on standardized achievement tests), airline pilots (measuring achievement by performance ratings), airline reservation agents (measuring achievement by performance ratings), and super-tanker crews. In all cases they found a negative correlation between achievement and competitiveness. With regard to the faculty members, the researchers proposed that competitive individuals focused so heavily on outshining others and putting themselves forward that they lose track of the scientific issues and produce research that is more superficial and less sustained in direction. As yet Hemreich and his colleagues have not been able to identify a single professional arena where highly competitive individuals tended to be more successful.

Given that competitiveness seems to be detrimental to career success, why has it been so prevalent in college classrooms? One answer may be that the above evidence is not enough. Interesting, but not conclusive. In this chapter, therefore, the research directly comparing the relative effects of competitive, individualistic, and cooperative efforts is reviewed.

Research On Social Interdependence

Learning together to complete assignments can have profound effects on students, teaching assistants, and professors. A great deal of research has been conducted comparing the relative effects of cooperative, competitive, and individualistic efforts on instructional outcomes (Johnson & Johnson, 1974, 1978, 1983, 1989; Johnson, Johnson, & Maruyama, 1983; Johnson, Maruyama, Johnson, & Skon, 1981; Pepitone, 1980; Sharan, 1980; Slavin, 1983). These research studies began in the late 1800's when Triplett (1897) in the United States, Turner (1889) in England, and Mayer (1903) in Germany conducted a series of studies on the factors associated with competitive performance. The amount of research that has been conducted since is staggering. During the past 90 years over 575 experimental and 100 correlational studies have been conducted by a wide variety of researchers in different decades with different age subjects, in different subject areas, and in different settings (see Johnson & Johnson, 1989a for a complete listing of these studies). In our own research program at the Cooperative Learning Center (University of Minnesota) over the past 25 years we have conducted over 85 studies to refine our understanding of how cooperation works. We know far more about the efficacy of cooperative learning than we know about lecturing, departmentalization, the use of technology, or almost any other facet of education. A comprehensive review of all studies and meta-analyses of their results may be found in Johnson and Johnson (1989a).

In this chapter we will summarize the basic results from the meta-analyses on all the studies conducted up to 1989. In addition, we have conducted separate meta-analyses on the results of the 137 experimental studies that compared cooperative, competitive, and individualistic efforts at the college and adult levels. In most cases, references to individual studies are not included in this chapter. Rather, the reader is referred to the reviews that contain the references to the specific studies that corroborate the point being made.

Figure 2.1 Outcomes Of Cooperative Efforts

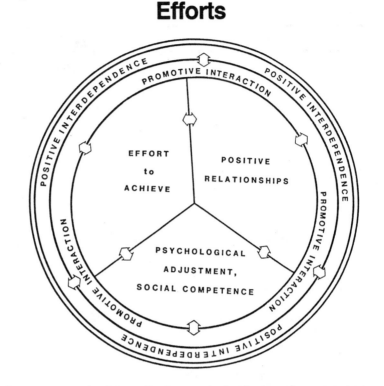

Building on the theorizing of Kurt Lewin and Morton Deutsch, the premise may be made that the type of interdependence structured among students determines how they interact with each other which, in turn largely determines instructional outcomes. This chapter is organized around this progression from goal structure to interaction pattern to outcomes. Structuring situations cooperatively results in promotive interaction, structuring situations competitively results in oppositional interaction, and structuring situations individualistically results in no interaction among students. These interaction patterns affect numerous variables, which may be subsumed within the three broad and interrelated outcomes of effort exerted to achieve, quality of relationships among participants, and participants' psychological adjustment and social competence (see Figure 2.1) (Johnson & Johnson, 1989a).

Interaction Patterns

Two heads are better than one.

Heywood

Simply placing students near each other and allowing interaction to take place does not mean that learning will be maximized, high quality peer relationships will result, or student

Table 2.1 Characteristics of Social Interdependence

Characteristic	Interdependence		
	Positive	Negative	None
Fate	Mutual	Opposite	Individual
Benefit	Mutual	Differential	Self
Time Perspective	Long-Term	Short-Term	Short-Term
Identify	Shared	Relative	Individual
Causation	Mutual	Relative	Self
Affiliation Motives	Enhance	Oppose	Oppose

psychological adjustment, self-esteem, and social competencies will be maximized. Students can obstruct as well as facilitate each other's learning. Or they can ignore each other. The way students interact depends on how faculty members structure interdependence in the learning situation.

Positive interdependence results in students promoting each other's learning and achievement. **Promotive interaction** may be defined as individuals encouraging and facilitating each other's efforts to achieve, complete tasks, and produce in order to reach the group's goals. While positive interdependence in and of itself may have some effect on outcomes, it is the face-to-face promotive interaction among individuals fostered by the positive interdependence that most powerfully influences efforts to achieve, caring and committed relationships, and psychological adjustment and social competence. Students focus both on increasing their own achievement **and** on increasing the achievement of their groupmates. Promotive interaction is characterized by individuals (Johnson & Johnson, 1989a):

1. Providing each other with efficient and effective help and assistance.

2. Exchanging needed resources such as information and materials and processing information more efficiently and effectively.

3. Providing each other with feedback in order to improve the subsequent performance of their assigned tasks and responsibilities.

4. Challenging each other's conclusions and reasoning in order to promote higher quality decision making and greater insight into the problems being considered.

5. Advocating the exertion of effort to achieve mutual goals.

6. Influencing each other's efforts to achieve the group's goals.

7. Acting in trusting and trustworthy ways.

8. Being motivated to strive for mutual benefit.

9. Having a moderate level of arousal characterized by low anxiety and stress.

Negative interdependence typically results in students opposing and obstructing each other's learning. **Oppositional interaction** occurs as students discourage and obstruct each other's efforts to achieve. Students focus both on increasing their own achievement **and** on preventing any classmate from achieving higher than they do. **No interaction** exists when students work independently without any interaction or interchange with each other. Students focus only on increasing their own achievement and ignore as irrelevant the efforts of others.

Giving And Receiving Assistance And Help

Within most task situations, productivity is enhanced when individuals give each other relevant task-related help and assistance (see Johnson & Johnson, 1989a). There are consistent perceptions of more frequent helping and tutoring (including cross-ethnic and cross-handicap helping) in cooperative than in competitive or individualistic situations. In both social-psychological and applied behavior research, cooperative structures have enhanced helping and assistance among group members while competitive structures have resulted in individuals obstructing each other's efforts to achieve, refusing to help and share, and engaging in antisocial behaviors. These effects of competition are exacerbated by losing. Observational studies of actual learning groups consistently find more giving and receiving of help in cooperative than in competitive or individualistic situations.

Information Exchange And Cognitive Processes

More efficient and effective exchange and processing of information takes place in cooperative than in competitive or individualistic situations (Johnson, 1974; Johnson & Johnson, 1989a). While a wide variety of material resources may need to be exchanged in order to complete tasks and accomplish goals, the most common resource shared and exchanged within cooperative efforts is information.

Compared with competitive and individualistic situations, students working cooperatively (Johnson & Johnson, 1989a):

1. Seek significantly more information from each other than do students working within a competitive goal structure.

2. Are less biased and have fewer misperceptions in comprehending the viewpoints and positions of other individuals.

3. More accurately communicate information by verbalizing ideas and information more frequently, attending to others' statements more carefully, and accepting others' ideas and information more frequently.

4. Are more confident about the value of their ideas.

5. Make optimal use of the information provided by other students.

In cooperative situations, students are bound together by their mutual fate, shared identity, and mutual causation and, therefore, celebrate (and feel benefited by) each other's successes. Relevant ideas, information, conclusions, and resources tend to be made available, exchanged, and utilized in ways that promote collective and individual insights and increase energy to complete the task. Such **oral discussion** of relevant information has at least two dimensions: oral explanation and listening. Both benefit the giver and receiver. The **giver benefits** from the cognitive organizing and processing, higher level reasoning, insights, and personal commitment to achieving the group's goals derived from orally explaining, elaborating, and summarizing information and teaching one's knowledge to others. The **receiver benefits** from the opportunity to utilize others' resources in their goal accomplishment efforts.

Information exchange and stimulation of cognitive processes may not occur in competitive or individualistic situations. In **competitive situations** communication and information exchange tends to be nonexistent or misleading and competition biases a person's perceptions and comprehension of viewpoints and positions of other individuals. **Individualistic situations** are usually deliberately structured to ensure that individuals do not communicate or exchange information at all.

Survey research indicates that fear of public speaking is quite common among the general population of adolescents and adults (Motley, 1988). College students, in particular, frequently experience communication apprehension in the classroom (Bowers, 1986). Such

speech anxiety, however, can be significantly reduced if students are given the opportunity to first express themselves in the more comfortable social context of a small group of peers (Neer, 1987). Students whose primary language is not English may especially find their anxiety reduced by working in cooperative learning groups in college classes.

Peer Feedback

An important aspect of promotive interaction is the opportunity for group members to provide each other with feedback as to how they are fulfilling their responsibilities and completing their work. **Feedback** is information made available to individuals that makes possible the comparison of actual performance with some standard of performance. **Knowledge of results** is information provided to the person about his or her performance on a given effort. It may be in the form of qualitative information in which the person is informed that a performance is either correct or incorrect. Or it may be quantitative information about how much discrepancy exists between the person's response and the correct response. Usually, quantitative information (i.e., process feedback) about (a) the size of the discrepancy existing between actual performance and some standard of performance or (b) how to improve one's reasoning or performance promotes achievement more effectively than does qualitative information (i.e., terminal feedback) about being right or wrong or what the correct answer is. Receiving personalized feedback from another person increases performance to a greater extent than does receiving impersonal feedback and peer feedback from collaborators may be especially vivid and personalized. Frequent and immediate feedback serves to increase student's motivation to learn (Mackworth, 1970).

Challenge And Controversy

An important aspect of promotive interaction is **controversy**, the conflict that arises when involved group members have different information, perceptions, opinions, reasoning processes, theories, and conclusions, and they must reach agreement. When controversies arise, they may be dealt with constructively or destructively, depending on how they are managed and the level of interpersonal and small group skills of the participants. When managed constructively, controversy promotes uncertainty about the correctness of one's views, an active search for more information, a reconceptualization of one's knowledge and conclusions and, consequently, greater mastery and retention of the material being discussed. Individuals working alone in competitive and individualistic situations do not have the opportunity for such a process and, therefore, their productivity, quality of decision making, and achievement suffer.

Public Advocacy And Commitment

Promotive interaction includes advocating that cooperators increase their efforts to accomplish the group's goals and publicly committing oneself to do the same. **Commitment** may be defined as the binding or pledging of the individual to an act or decision. To the extent that people act in the absence of coercion, commit themselves to act in front of others, or invest time, money, or personal prestige in an activity, they come to see themselves as believers in that sort of activity and develop a personal interest in it. Individuals become more committed to attitudes that are made public than to attitudes that remain private. People are particularly prone to increase their commitment to actions that they have attempted to persuade another to adopt.

Mutual Influence

During the information-exchange process individuals share ideas and information and utilize each other's resources in order to maximize their productivity and achievement. This entails mutual influence in which cooperators consider each other's ideas and conclusions and coordinate their efforts. Participants must be open to influence attempts aimed at facilitating the accomplishment of shared goals, must trust each other **not** to use the resources being shared in detrimental ways, and must form emotional bonds that result in commitment to each other's welfare and success. There are three ways in which influence takes place within social situations: direct influence, social modeling, and situational norms. Students will be receptive to the **direct influence** attempts of others to the extent that they perceive a cooperative relationship among goal attainments. In cooperative situations, students benefit from groupmates' **modeling** effective and committed behaviors, skills, and attitudes. Visible and credible models who demonstrate the recommended attitudes and behavior patterns and who directly discuss their importance are powerful influences. Finally, achievement is influenced by whether or not **group norms** favor high performance. Within cooperative situations everyone benefits from the efforts of cooperators and, therefore, group norms support efforts to achieve. There is evidence, furthermore, that in the generally competitive climate of most schools, success at academic tasks has little value for many individuals and may even be a deterrent to popularity with peers (see Johnson & Johnson, 1989a).

Achievement Motivation

Achievement is a **we** *thing, not a* **me** *thing, always the product of many heads and hands.*
                                                                        J. W. Atkinson

Motivation to achieve is reflected in the effort individuals commit purposely to strive to acquire increased understandings and skills they perceive as being meaningful and worthwhile. While humans may be born with a motivation to increase their competencies, achievement motivation is basically induced through interpersonal processes, either through internalized relationships or current interaction patterns within the learning situation. Depending on whether interaction takes place within a context of positive, negative, or no interdependence, different interaction patterns result, causing different motivational systems, which in turn affect achievement differentially, which determines expectations for future achievement. The motivational system promoted within **cooperative situations** includes intrinsic motivation, high expectations for success, high incentive to achieve based on mutual benefit, high epistemic curiosity and continuing interest in achievement, high commitment to achieve, and high persistence. The motivational system promoted within **competitive situations** includes extrinsic motivation to win, low expectations for success by all but the highest ability individuals, an incentive to learn based on differential benefit, low epistemic curiosity and a lack of continuing interest to achieve, a lack of commitment to achieving, and low task persistence by most individuals. The motivational system promoted within **individualistic situations** includes extrinsic motivation to meet preset criteria of excellence, low expectations for success by all but the highest ability individuals, an incentive to achieve based on self- benefit, low epistemic curiosity and continuing interest to achieve, low commitment to achieving, and low task persistence by most individuals.

Motivation is most commonly viewed as a combination of the perceived likelihood of success and the perceived incentive for success. The greater the likelihood of success and the more important it is to succeed, the higher the motivation. Success that is intrinsically rewarding is usually seen as being more desirable for learning than is having students believe that only extrinsic rewards are worthwhile. There is greater perceived likelihood of success and success is viewed as more important in cooperative than in competitive or individualistic learning situations (Johnson & Johnson, 1989a). Striving for mutual benefit results in an emotional bonding with collaborators liking each other, wanting to help each other succeed, and being committed to each other's well-being. These positive feelings toward the group and the other members may have a number of important influences on **intrinsic motivation to achieve** and actual productivity. In many cases, the relationships among group members may become more important than the actual rewards given for the work being done. Consequences provided by group members (e.g., respect, liking, blame, rejection) may supplement or replace those produced by task performance (e.g., salary or grades). Such consequences might be important in sustaining behavior during periods in which no task-based reinforcement is received.

Interpersonal Trust

To disclose one's reasoning and information, one must trust the other individuals involved in the situation to listen with respect. Trust is a central dynamic of promotive interaction. Trust tends to be developed and maintained in cooperative situations and it tends to be absent and destroyed in competitive and individualistic situations (Deutsch, 1958, 1960, 1962; Johnson, 1971, 1973, 1974; Johnson & Noonan, 1972). Trust includes the following elements (Deutsch, 1962):

1. Risk--the anticipation of beneficial or harmful consequences.

2. Realization that others have the power to determine the consequences of one's actions.

3. Expectation that the harmful consequences are more serious than are the beneficial consequences.

4. Confidence that the others will behave in ways that ensure beneficial consequences for oneself.

Interpersonal trust is built through placing one's consequences in the control of others and having one's confidence in the others confirmed. Interpersonal trust is destroyed through placing one's consequences in the hands of others and having one's confidence in the others disconfirmed through their behaving in ways that ensure harmful consequences for oneself. Thus, trust is composed of two sets of behaviors. **Trusting** behavior is the willingness to risk beneficial or harmful consequences by making oneself vulnerable to another person. **Trustworthy** behavior is the willingness to respond to another person's risk-taking in a way that ensures that the other person will experience beneficial consequences. In order to establish trust two or more people must be trustworthy and trusting. Within cooperative situations, individuals tend to be both trusting and trustworthy. Within competitive situations, individuals tend to be distrusting and untrustworthy as they use information to promote their own success and the other's failure.

Anxiety And Performance

Cooperation typically produces (a) less anxiety and stress and (b) more effective coping strategies used to deal with the anxiety than does competition. Anxiety is one of the most pervasive barriers to productivity and positive interpersonal relationships. Anxiety generally leads to an egocentric preoccupation with oneself, disruption of cognitive reasoning, and an avoidance of the situation one fears. This can mean skipping school or work, cutting classes or taking long breaks, or avoiding challenging learning and work situations. A continued experience of even moderate levels of anxiety over a number of years, furthermore, can produce psychological and physiological harm. Especially for individuals with a chronic high state of anxiety, cooperation promotes a better learning and work climate.

Summary Of Promotive Interaction

Positive interdependence results in promotive interaction which, in turn, promotes efforts to achieve, positive interpersonal relationships, and psychological health. **Promotive interaction** may be defined as individuals encouraging and facilitating each other's efforts to achieve, complete tasks, and produce in order to reach the group's goals. Promotive interaction is characterized by individuals providing each other with efficient and effective help and assistance, exchanging needed resources such as information and materials and processing information more efficiently and effectively, providing each other with feedback in order to improve their subsequent performance of their assigned tasks and responsibilities, challenging each other's conclusions and reasoning in order to promote higher quality decision making and greater insight into the problems being considered, advocating the exertion of effort to achieve mutual goals, influencing each other's efforts to achieve the group's goals, acting in trusting and trustworthy ways, being motivated to strive for mutual benefit, and a moderate level of arousal characterized by low anxiety and stress. Oppositional interaction results in the opposite pattern of interaction. Promotive interaction results in a number of important outcomes that may be subsumed under three broad categories.

Learning Outcomes

Different learning outcomes result from the student-student interaction patterns promoted by the use of cooperative, competitive, and individualistic goal structures (Johnson & Johnson, 1989a). The numerous outcomes of cooperative efforts may be subsumed within three broad categories: effort to achieve, positive interpersonal relationships, and psychological adjustment. Since research participants have varied as to economic class, age, sex, and cultural background, since a wide variety of research tasks and measures of the dependent variables have been used, and since the research has been conducted by many different researchers with markedly different orientations working in different settings and in different decades, the overall body of research on social interdependence has considerable generalizability.

Effort To Achieve

Achievement

Over 375 studies have been conducted over the past 90 years to give an answer to the question of how successful competitive, individualistic, and cooperative efforts are in promoting productivity and achievement (Johnson & Johnson, 1989a). The results are summarized in Table 2.2. When all of the studies were included in the analysis, the average student cooperating performed at about 2/3 a standard deviation above the average student learning within a competitive (effect size = 0.67) or individualistic situation (effect size = 0.64). When only high-quality studies were included in the analysis, the effect sizes were 0.88 and 0.61, respectively. When only the college and adult studies were included in the analysis, the results were essentially the same. Cooperative learning promotes higher achievement than does competitive or individualistic learning (effects sizes = 0.59 and 0.62 respectively). Interestingly, competition promotes higher achievement than does individualistic learning (effect size = 0.67). Cooperative learning, furthermore, resulted in more higher-level reasoning, more frequent generation of new ideas and solutions (i.e., **process gain**), and greater transfer of what is learned within one situation to another (i.e., **group to individual transfer**) than did competitive or individualistic learning.

Some cooperative learning procedures contained a mixture of cooperative, competitive, and individualistic efforts while others were "pure." The original jigsaw procedure (Aronson, 1978), for example, is a combination of resource interdependence (cooperative) and individual reward structure (individualistic). Teams-Games-Tournaments (DeVries & Edwards, 1974) and Student-Teams-Achievement-Divisions (Slavin, 1980) are mixtures of cooperation and intergroup competition. Team-Assisted-Instruction (Slavin, Leavey, & Madden, 1982) is a mixture of individualistic and cooperative learning. When the results of "pure" and "mixed" operationalizations of cooperative learning were compared, the "pure" operationalizations produced higher achievement (cooperative vs. competitive, pure = 0.71 and mixed = 0.40, cooperative vs. individualistic, pure = 0.65 and mixed = 0.42).

Table 2.2 Social Interdependence and Achievement

	mean	s.d.	n
Total Studies			
Cooperative vs. Competitive	0.67	0.93	129
Cooperative vs. Individualistic	0.64	0.79	184
Competitive vs. Individualistic	0.30	0.77	38
High Quality Studies			
Cooperative vs. Competitive	0.88	1.13	51
Cooperative vs. Individualistic	0.61	0.63	104
Competitive vs. Individualistic	0.07	0.61	24
Mixed Operationalizations			
Cooperative vs. Competitive	0.40	0.62	23
Cooperative vs. Individualistic	0.42	0.65	12
Pure Operationalizations			
Cooperative vs. Competitive	0.71	1.01	96
Cooperative vs. Individualistic	0.65	0.81	164
College And Adult			
Cooperative vs. Competitive	0.59	0.86	52
Cooperative vs. Individualistic	0.62	0.90	96
Competitive vs. Individualistic	0.67	0.90	17

The potential value of cooperative learning in large college classes is highlighted by a recent study designed to identify what specific factors contributed to student learning in large classes. Wulff, Nyquist, and Abbott (1987) surveyed 800 college students and found that the second-most frequently cited factor contributing to their learning in large classes was "other students." The researchers concluded that faculty may wish to use cooperative learning within the large-class context. Levin, Glass, and Meister (1984) concluded from a comparison of the cost effectiveness of four academic strategies that working with class-mates is the most cost-effective support system for increasing student achievement at the college level.

That working together to achieve a common goal produces higher achievement and greater productivity than does working alone is so well confirmed by so much research that it stands as one of the strongest principles of social and organizational psychology. Coop-erative learning is indicated whenever the learning goals are highly important, mastery and retention is important, the task is complex or conceptual, problem solving is desired, divergent thinking or creativity is desired, quality of performance is expected, and higher level reasoning strategies and critical thinking are needed.

Why does cooperation result in higher achievement--what mediates? The critical issue in understanding the relationship between cooperation and achievement is specifying the variables that mediate the relationship. Simply placing students in groups and telling them to work together does not in and of itself promote higher achievement. It is only under certain conditions that group efforts may be expected to be more productive than individual efforts. Those conditions are clearly perceived positive interdependence, considerable promotive (face- to-face) interaction, felt personal responsibility (individual accountability) to achieve the group's goals, frequent use of relevant interpersonal and small group skills, and periodic and regular group processing (Johnson & Johnson, 1989a).

Critical Thinking Competencies

In many subject areas the teaching of facts and theories is considered to be secondary to the development of students' critical thinking and use of higher level reasoning strategies. The aim of science education, for example, has been to develop individuals "who can sort sense from nonsense," or who have the critical thinking abilities of grasping information, examining it, evaluating it for soundness, and applying it appropriately. The application, evaluation, and synthesis of knowledge and other higher-level reasoning skills, however, are often neglected in college classes. **Cooperative learning promotes a greater use of higher level reasoning strategies and critical thinking than do competitive or individualistic learning strategies** (Gabbert, Johnson, & Johnson, 1986; Johnson & Johnson, 1981a; Johnson, Skon, & Johnson, 1980; Skon, Johnson, & Johnson, 1981). Cooperative learning experiences, for example, promote more frequent insight into and use of higher-level cognitive and moral reasoning strategies than do competitive or individualistic learning experiences (effect sizes = 0.93 and 0.97 respectively).

In addition to the research directly relating cooperative learning with critical thinking, there are lines of research linking critical thinking and cooperative learning. McKeachie (1988) concludes that at least three elements of teaching make a difference in college students' gains in thinking skills: (1) student discussion, (2) explicit emphasis on problem-solving procedures and methods using varied examples, and (3) verbalization of methods and strategies to encourage development of metacognition. He states, "Student participation, teacher encouragement, and student-to-student interaction positively relate to improved critical thinking. These three activities confirm other research and theory stressing the importance of active practice, motivation, and feedback in thinking skills as well as other skills. This confirms that discussions, especially in small classes, are superior to lectures in improving thinking and problem solving." Ruggiero (1988) argues that the explicit teaching of higher-level reasoning and critical thinking does not depend on **what** is taught, but rather on **how** it is taught. He states, "The only significant change that is required is a change in teaching **methodology** (p. 12). Cooperative learning is such a methodological change.

Research conducted by Schoenfeld (1985, 1989), Brown, Collins and Duguid (1988), Lave (1988), and others indicates that cooperative learning is an important procedure for involving students in meaningful activities in the classroom and engaging in situated cognition. Higher-level writing assignments may also best be done by cooperative peer response groups (DiPardo and Freedman, 1988).

Attitudes Toward Subject Area

Cooperative learning experiences, compared with competitive and individualistic ones, promote more positive attitudes toward the subject area, more positive attitudes toward the instructional experience, and more continuing motivation to learn more about the subject area being studied (Johnson & Johnson, 1989a). Guetzkow, Kelley, and McKeachie (1954) and McKeachie (1951) found in a study comparing group discussion and lecturing that students in discussion sections were significantly more favorable than the other groups in attitude toward psychology and a follow-up of the students three years later revealed that seven men each from the tutorial and discussion groups majored in psychology, whereas none of those in the recitation group did so. Bligh (1972) found that students who had in-class opportunities to interact actively with classmates and the instructor were more satisfied with their learning experience than were students who were taught exclusively by the lecture method. Kulik and Kulik (1979) reported from their comprehensive literature review on college teaching that students who participated in discussion groups in class were more likely to develop positive attitudes toward the course's subject matter. One of the major conclusions of the Harvard Assessment Seminars was that the use of cooperative learning groups resulted in a large increase in satisfaction with the class (Light, 1990). These findings have important implications for influencing female and minority students to enter science and math oriented careers.

Interpersonal Relationships

Interpersonal Attraction And Cohesion

Cooperative learning experiences, compared with competitive, individualistic, and "traditional instruction," promote considerably more liking among students (effect sizes = 0.66 and 0.60, respectively) (Johnson & Johnson, 1989a; Johnson, Johnson, & Maruyama, 1983) (see Table 2.3). This is true regardless of individual differences in ability level, sex, handicapping conditions, ethnic membership, social class differences, or task orientation. Students who studied cooperatively, compared with those who studied competitively or individualistically, developed considerably more commitment and caring for each other no matter what their initial impressions of and attitudes toward each other were. When only the high quality studies were included in the analysis the effect sizes were 0.82 (cooperative vs. competitive) and 0.62 (cooperative vs. individualistic) respectively. The effect sizes are higher for the studies using pure operationalizations of cooperative learning than for studies using mixed operationalizations (cooperative vs. competitive, pure = 0.79 and mixed = 0.46, cooperative vs. individualistic, pure = 0.66 and mixed = 0.36). Students learning cooperatively also liked the instructor better and perceived the instructor as being more supportive and accepting academically and personally. For the college and adult studies, cooperative experiences resulted in greater interpersonal attraction than did competitive or individualistic experiences (effect sizes = 0.83 and 0.40 respectively). Competition promoted greater interpersonal attraction than did individualistic efforts (effect size = 0.84).

In order to be productive, a class of students has to cohere and have a positive emotional climate. As relationships within the class or college become more positive, absenteeism decreases, and increases may be expected in student commitment to learning, feeling of personal responsibility to do the assigned work, willingness to take on difficult tasks, motivation and persistence in working on learning tasks, satisfaction and morale, willingness to endure pain and frustration to succeed, willingness to defend the college against external criticism or attack, willingness to listen to and be influenced be peers, commitment to peers' success and growth, and productivity and achievement (Johnson, & F. Johnson, 1991; Johnson & Johnson, 1989a; Watson & Johnson, 1972).

Table 2.3 Social Interdependence and Interpersonal Attraction

	mean	s.d.	n
Total Studies			
Cooperative vs. Competitive	0.67	0.49	93
Cooperative vs. Individualistic	0.60	0.58	60
Competitive vs. Individualistic	0.08	0.70	15
High Quality Studies			
Cooperative vs. Competitive	0.82	0.40	37
Cooperative vs. Individualistic	0.62	o.53	44
Competitive vs. Individualistic	0.27	0.60	11
Mixed Operationalizations			
Cooperative vs. Competitive	0.46	0.29	37
Cooperative vs. Individualistic	0.36	0.45	10
Pure Operationalizations			
Cooperative vs. Competitive	0.79	0.56	54
Cooperative vs. Individualistic	0.66	0.60	49
College And Adult			
Cooperative vs. Competitive	0.83	0.47	34
Cooperative vs. Individualistic	0.40	0.73	15
Competitive vs. Individualistic	0.84	0.21	2

In addition, when students are heterogeneous with regard to ethnic, social class, language, and ability differences, cooperative learning experiences are a necessity for building positive peer relationships. This is especially relevant for contemporary higher education since colleges are now witnessing an increasing number of international students on their campuses (Scully, 1981), and an increasing number of black students are attending predominantly white colleges (National Center for Educational Statistics, 1984). Studies on desegregation indicated that cooperation promoted more positive cross-ethnic relationships than did competition (effect size = 0.54) or individualistic (effect -size = 0.44) learning experiences (Johnson & Johnson, 1989a). Cross-handicapped relationships were also more positive in cooperative than in competitive (effect size = 0.70) or individualistic (effect size = 0.64) learning experiences.

Social Support

From Table 2.4 it may be seen that cooperation resulted in greater social support than did competitive or individualistic efforts (effect sizes of 0.62 and 0.70, respectively). For the high-quality studies the results were comparable (effect sizes = 0.83 and 0.72 respectively). The pure operationalizations of cooperation promoted greater social support (compared with competition) than did the mixed operationalizations (effect sizes = 0.73 and 0.45 respectively). When cooperative and individualistic learning experiences were compared the results were even more extreme (effect sizes = 0.77 and 0.02 respectively). When only the college and adult samples were included, the effect sizes were 0.70 and 0.40. Competitive experiences promoted less social support than did individualistic experiences (effect size = -0.45). Social support tends to be related to (see Johnson & Johnson, 1989a):

1. Achievement, successful problem solving, persistence on challenging tasks under frustrating conditions, lack of cognitive interference during problem solving, lack of absenteeism, academic and career aspirations, more appropriate seeking of assistance, retention, job satisfaction, high morale, and greater compliance with regimens and behavioral patterns that increase health and productivity.

2. Living a longer life, recovering from illness and injury faster and more completely, and experiencing less severe illnesses.

3. Psychological health and adjustment, lack of neuroticism and psychopathology, reduction of psychological distress, coping effectively with stressful situations, self-reliance and autonomy, a coherent and integrated self-identity, greater psychological safety, higher self-esteem, increased general happiness, and increased interpersonal skills.

4. Effective management of stress by providing the caring, information, resources, and feedback individuals need to cope with stress, by reducing the number and severity of stressful events in an individual's life, by reducing anxiety, and by helping one appraise the nature of the stress and one's ability to deal with it constructively.

5. The emotional support and encouragement individuals need to cope with the risk that is inherently involved in challenging one's competence as striving to grow and develop.

The importance of social support has been ignored within education over the past 30 years. **A general principle to keep in mind is that the pressure to achieve should always**

be matched with an equal level of social support. Challenge and security must be kept in balance (Pelz & Andrews, 1976). Whenever increased demands and pressure to be productive are placed on students (and faculty), a corresponding increase in social support should be structured.

Student Retention

> *Traditional classroom teaching practices in higher education favor the assertive student. But our analysis indicates that instructors should give greater attention to the passive or reticent student...Passivity is an important warning sign that may reflect a lack of involvement that impedes the learning process and leads to unnecessary attrition.*
>
> National Institute of Education (1984)

Approximately one-half of all students who leave their college will do so during their freshman year (Terenzini, 1986). Many of the student departures will take place during their first semester (Blanc, Debuhr, & Martin, 1983). The major reasons for such dropping out of college may be failure to establish a social network of friends and classmates and to become academically involved in classes.

Tinto (1975, 1987), synthesizing the retention research, concluded that the greater the degree of students' involvement in their college learning experience, the more likely they were to persist to graduation. The social-networking processes of social involvement, integration, and bonding with classmates are strongly related with higher rates of student retention. Astin (1985), on the basis of research conducted over 10 years, found that student involvement academically and socially in the college experience was the "cornerstone" of persistence and achievement. Astin and his associates (1972) had earlier concluded that active involvement in the learning experience was especially critical for "withdrawal-prone" students, such as disadvantaged minorities, who have been found to be particularly passive in academic settings.

Cooperative learning experiences tend to lower attrition rates in college. Students working on open-ended problems in small groups of four to seven members were more likely to display lower rates of attrition and higher rates of academic achievement than those not involved in the group learning approach (Wales & Stager,

Table 2.4 Social Interdependence and Social Support

	mean	s.d.	n
Total Studies			
Cooperative vs. Competitive	0.62	0.44	84
Cooperative vs. Individualistic	0.70	0.45	72
Competitive vs. Individualistic	-0.13	0.36	19
High Quality Studies			
Cooperative vs. Competitive	0.83	0.46	41
Cooperative vs. Individualistic	0.72	0.47	62
Competitive vs. Individualistic	-0.13	0.36	19
Mixed Operationalizations			
Cooperative vs. Competitive	0.45	0.23	16
Cooperative vs. Individualistic	0.02	0.35	6
Pure Operationalizations			
Cooperative vs. Competitive	0.73	0.46	58
Cooperative vs. Individualistic	0.77	0.40	65
College And Adult			
Cooperative vs. Competitive	0.70	0.58	29
Cooperative vs. Individualistic	0.36	0.37	16
Competitive vs. Individualistic	-0.45	0.25	5

1978). Treisman (1985) found that the five-year retention rate for black students majoring in math or science at Berkeley who were involved in cooperative learning was 65 percent (compared to 41 percent for black students not involved). The percentage of black students involved in cooperative learning experiences who graduated in mathematics-based majors was 44 percent (compared to only 10 percent for a control group of black students not participating in cooperative learning groups).

College students report greater satisfaction with courses that allow them to engage in group discussion (Bligh, 1972; Kulik & Kulik, 1979). Students are more likely to stay in college if they are satisfied with their learning experiences (Noel, 1985). Cooperative learning allows for significant amounts of meaningful student discussion that enhances students' satisfaction with the learning experience and, in so doing, promotes student retention.

Faculty Relationships With Students

Many college faculty report that when cooperative learning groups are used they get to know their students better. The process of observing students work in small groups and then intervening seems to create more personal and informal interactions between the instructor and the students than does lecture and whole-class discussion. The instructor's opportunity to interact with students within small groups, for example, gives the instructor a chance to learn and address students by their names. Murray (1985) found that "addressing students by name" correlates significantly with students' overall satisfaction with the course and the instructor. Astin (1977) found that such informal interactions have a positive impact on student retention. When faculty get to know students better in class, they may be more likely to interact with the students informally outside of the classroom. Pascarella (1980) has found that the quantity and quality of out-of-class contact with faculty is strongly associated with student retention.

Importance Of Peer Relationships

There are numerous ways in which peer relationships contribute to (1) social and cognitive development and (2) socialization. Some of the more important consequences correlated with peer relationships are (the specific supporting evidence may be found in Johnson, 1980, and Johnson & Johnson, 1989a):

1. **In their interaction with peers, individuals directly learn attitudes, values, skills, and information unobtainable from adults.** In their interaction with each other, individuals imitate each other's behavior and identify with friends possessing admired competencies. Through providing models, reinforcement, and direct learning, peers shape a wide variety of social behaviors, attitudes, and perspectives.

2. **Interaction with peers provides support, opportunities, and models for prosocial behavior.** It is within interactions with peers that one helps, comforts, shares with, takes care of, assists, and gives to others. Without peers with whom to engage in such behaviors, many forms of prosocial values and commitments could not be developed. Conversely, whether individuals engage in problem or transition behavior, such as the use of illegal drugs and delinquency, is related to the perceptions of their friends' attitudes toward such behaviors. Being rejected by one's peers tends to result in antisocial behavioral patterns characterized by aggressiveness, disruptiveness, and other negatively perceived behaviors.

3. Individuals frequently lack the time perspective needed to tolerate delays in gratification. As they develop and are socialized, the focus on their own immediate impulses and needs is replaced with the ability to take longer time perspectives. **Peers provide models of, expectations of, directions for, and reinforcements of learning to control impulses.** Aggressive impulses provide an example. Peer interaction involving such activities as rough-and-tumble play promotes the acquisition of a repertoire of effective aggressive behaviors and helps establish the necessary regulatory mechanisms for modulating aggressive affect.

4. **Students learn to view situations and problems from perspectives other than their own through their interaction with peers.** Such perspective taking is one of the most critical competencies for cognitive and social development. All psychological development may be described as a progressive loss of egocentrism and an increase in ability to take wider and more complex perspectives. It is primarily in interaction with peers that egocentrism is lost and increased perspective taking is gained.

5. **Autonomy** is the ability to understand what others expect in any given situation and to be free to choose whether to meet their expectations. Autonomous people are independent of both extreme inner- or outer-directness. When making decisions concerning appropriate social behavior, autonomous people tend to consider both their internal values and the situational requirements and then respond in flexible and appropriate ways. Autonomy is the result of (1) the internalization of values (including appropriate self-approval) derived from caring and supportive relationships, and (2) the acquisition of social skills and sensitivity. **Relationships with peers are powerful influences on the development of the values and the social sensitivity required for autonomy.** Individuals with a history of isolation from or rejection by peers often are inappropriately other-directed. They conform to group pressures even when they believe the recommended actions are wrong or inappropriate.

6. While adults can provide certain forms of companionship, **students need close and intimate relationships with peers with whom they can share their thoughts and feelings, aspirations and hopes, dreams and fantasies, and joys and pains.** They need constructive peer relationships to avoid the pain of loneliness.

7. Throughout infancy, childhood, adolescence, and early adulthood, a person moves though several successive and overlapping identities. The physical changes involved in growth, the increasing number of experiences with other people, increasing responsibilities, and general cognitive and social development all cause changes in self-definition. The final result should be a coherent and integrated identity. In peer

relationships children and adolescents become aware of the similarities and differences between themselves and others. They experiment with a variety of social roles that help them integrate their own sense of self. In peer relationships values and attitudes are clarified and integrated into an individual's self-definition. **It is through peer relationships that a frame of reference for perceiving oneself is developed.** Gender typing and its impact on one's identity is an example.

8. **Coalitions formed during childhood and adolescence provide help and assistance throughout adulthood.**

9. The ability to maintain independent, cooperative relationships is a prime manifestation of psychological health. Poor peer relationships in elementary school predict psychological disturbance and delinquency in high school, and poor peer relationships in high school predict adult pathology. **The absence of any friendships during childhood and adolescence seems to increase the risk of mental disorder.**

10. **In both educational and work settings, peers have a strong influence on productivity.** Greater achievement is typically found in collaborative situations where peers work together than in situations where individuals work alone.

11. **Student educational aspirations may be more influenced by peers than by any other social influence.** Similarly, ambition in career settings is greatly influenced by peers. Within instructional settings, peer relationships can be structured to create meaningful interdependence through learning cooperatively with peers. Within cooperative learning situations students experience feelings of belonging, acceptance, support, and caring, and the social skills and social roles required for maintaining interdependent relationships can be taught and practiced.

Through repeated cooperative experiences students can develop the social sensitivity of what behavior is expected from others and the actual skills and autonomy to meet such expectations if they so desire. Through holding each other accountable for appropriate social behavior, students can greatly influence the values they internalize and the self-control they develop. It is through belonging to a series of interdependent relationships that values are learned and internalized. It is through prolonged cooperative interaction with other people that healthy social development with the overall balance of trust rather than distrust of other people, the ability to view situations and problems from a variety of perspectives, a meaningful sense of direction and purpose in life, an awareness of mutual interdependence with others, and an integrated and coherent sense of personal identity, takes place (Johnson, 1979; Johnson & Matross, 1977).

In order for peer relationships to be constructive influences, they must promote feelings of belonging, acceptance, support and caring, rather than feelings of hostility and rejection (Johnson, 1980). Being accepted by peers is related to willingness to engage in social interaction, utilizing abilities in achievement situations, and providing positive social rewards for peers. Isolation from peers is associated with high anxiety, low self-esteem, poor interpersonal skills, emotional handicaps, and psychological pathology. Rejection by peers is related to disruptive classroom behavior, hostile behavior and negative affect, and negative attitudes toward other students and school. In order to promote constructive peer influences, therefore, teachers must first ensure that students interact with each other and, second, must ensure that the interaction takes place within a cooperative context.

Psychological Health

Psychological Adjustment

When students leave college, they need the psychological health and stability required to build and maintain career, family, and community relationships, to establish a basic and meaningful interdependence with other people, and to participate effectively in society. We have conducted a series of studies on the relationship between cooperation and psychological health. Our studies (see Johnson & Johnson, 1989a) indicate that **cooperativeness** is

positively related to a number of indices of psychological health, namely: emotional maturity, well-adjusted social relations, strong personal identity, and basic trust in and optimism about people. **Competitiveness** seems also to be related to a number of indices of psychological health, while **individualistic attitudes** tend to be related to a number of indices of psychological pathology, such as emotional immaturity, social maladjustment, delinquency, self-alienation, and self-rejection. Colleges and college classes should be organized cooperatively to reinforce those traits and tendencies that promote students' psychological well-being.

Accuracy of Perspective Taking

Social perspective taking is the ability to understand how a situation appears to another person and how that person is reacting cognitively and emotionally to the situation. The opposite of perspective taking is **egocentrism**, the embeddedness in one's own viewpoint to the extent that one is unaware of other points of view and of the limitation of one's perspective. Cooperative learning experiences tend to promote greater cognitive and affective perspective taking than do competitive or individualistic learning experiences (Johnson & Johnson, 1989a). Bovard (1951a, 1951b) and McKeachie (1954) found that students participating in class discussions (as opposed to listening to lectures) showed greater insight (as rated by clinical psychologists) into problems of the young women depicted in the film "The Feeling of Rejection."

Self-Esteem

From Table 2.5 it may be seen that cooperation tended to promote higher levels of self-esteem than did competitive and individualistic efforts (effect sizes = 0.58 and 0.44, respectively). When only the college and adult samples were included in the analyses, the results were similar for the cooperation and competition comparison (effect size = 0.67) but the effect size of 0.19 for the cooperative and individualistic comparison is lower. There was only one study that compared competitive and individualistic efforts on self-esteem at the college level. High self-esteem seems desirable as individuals with low self-esteem tend to (Johnson & Johnson, 1989):

1. Have low productivity due to setting low goals for themselves, lacking confidence in their ability, and assuming that they will fail no matter how hard they try.

2. Be critical of others as well as themselves by looking for flaws in others and trying to "tear them down."

3. Withdraw socially due to feeling awkward, self- conscious, and vulnerable to rejection.

4. Be conforming, agreeable, highly persuasible, and high influenced by criticism.

5. Develop more psychological problems such as anxiety, nervousness, insomnia, depression, and psychosomatic symptoms.

Table 2.5 Social Interdependence and Self-Esteem

	mean	s.d.	n
Total Studies			
Cooperative vs. Competitive	0.58	0.56	56
Cooperative vs. Individualistic	0.44	0.40	38
Competitive vs. Individualistic	-0.23	0.42	19
High Quality Studies			
Cooperative vs. Competitive	0.67	0.31	24
Cooperative vs. Individualistic	0.45	0.44	29
Competitive vs. Individualistic	-0.25	0.46	13
Mixed Operationalizations			
Cooperative vs. Competitive	0.33	0.39	17
Cooperative vs. Individualistic	0.22	0.38	9
Pure Operationalizations			
Cooperative vs. Competitive	0.74	0.59	36
Cooperative vs. Individualistic	0.51	0.40	27
College And Adult			
Cooperative vs. Competitive	0.67	0.93	18
Cooperative vs. Individualistic	0.19	0.47	5
Competitive vs. Individualistic	-0.46	0.00	1

Our studies have not only examined the level of students' self- esteem, but also the cognitive processes they use to determine whether they are worthwhile or not (see Johnson & Johnson, 1989a). Within **competitive** situations self-esteem tends to be based on the contingent view of one's competence that, "If I win, then I have worth as a person, but if I lose, then I have no worth." Winners attribute their success to superior ability and attribute the failure of others to lack of ability, both of which contribute to self-aggrandizement. Losers, who are the vast majority, defensively tend to be self-disparaging, apprehensive about evaluation, and tend to withdraw psychologically and physically. Within **individualistic** situations, students are isolated from one another, receive little direct comparison with or feedback from peers, and perceive evaluations as inaccurate and unrealistic. A defensive avoidance, evaluation apprehension, and distrust of peers results. Within **cooperative** situations, individuals tend to interact, promote each other's success, form multi-dimensional and realistic impressions of each other's competencies, and give accurate feedback. Such interaction tends to promote a basic self-acceptance of oneself as a competent person.

Reciprocal Relationships Among The Three Outcomes

> *"The reason we were so good, and continued to be so good, was because he (Joe Paterno) forces you to develop an inner love among the players. It is much harder to give up on your buddy, than it is to give up on your coach. I really believe that over the years the teams I played on were almost unbeatable in tight situations. When we needed to get that six inches we got it because of our love for each other. Our camaraderie existed because of the kind of coach and kind of person Joe was."*
>
> Dr. David Joyner

Efforts to achieve, positive interpersonal relationships, and psychological health are reciprocally related (see Figure 2.1). Within cooperative situations, the causal arrows connecting the three outcomes are all bidirectional. Each induces the others.

Joint efforts to achieve mutual goals create caring and committed relationships; caring and committed relationships among group members increase their effort to achieve (Johnson & Johnson, 1989a). From working together to accomplish academic tasks students develop camaraderie and friendships. As students strive together, helping each other, sharing materials, exchanging ideas and information, and encouraging each other's efforts they get to know each other, become committed to each other, and develop friendships. Caring relationships come from mutual accomplishment, mutual pride in joint work, and the bonding that results from joint efforts. **At the same time**, caring and committed relationships promote joint efforts to achieve mutual goals. Individuals seek out opportunities to work with those they care about. As caring increases, so does regular attendance, commitment to learning and achievement, personal responsibility to do one's share of the work, willingness to take on difficult tasks, motivation and persistence in working toward goal achievement, willingness to listen to and be influenced by groupmates, and willingness to endure pain and frustration on behalf of the group (Johnson & F. Johnson, 1991; Johnson & R. Johnson, 1989; Watson & Johnson, 1972). All these contribute to group productivity. The most successful leaders in business and industry are ones that build teams with such personal closeness that team members feel like a family (Kouses & Posner, 1987).

Joint efforts to achieve mutual goals promote psychological health and social competence; the more healthy psychologically group members are, the more able they are to contribute to the joint effort (Johnson & Johnson, 1989b). Cooperating involves contributing to other's success and well-being, knowing there are others who contribute to your success and well-being, and being involved in a joint effort greater than oneself. Working together to complete academic tasks increases a person's social competencies, success, sense of meaning and purpose, ability to cope with failure and anxiety, self-esteem, and self-efficacy. Contributing to others' success has been found to cure the blues (i.e., decrease depression). Knowing that one's efforts contribute to the success of others as well as oneself gives added meaning and value to academic work. **At the same time**, the healthier psychologically individuals are, the better able they are to work with others to achieve mutual goals. States of depression, anxiety, guilt, shame, and fear interfere with ability to cooperate and decrease the energy a person has to devote to a cooperative effort. Joint efforts require coordination, effective communication, leadership, and conflict management which, in turn, require social competencies.

The more caring and committed the relationships among group members, the greater their psychological health and social competencies tend to be; the healthier members are psychologically, the more able they are to build and maintain caring and committed relationships (Johnson & Johnson, 1989a). Psychological health is built on the internalization of the caring and respect received from loved- ones. Through the internalization of positive relationships, direct social support, shared intimacy, and expressions of caring, psychological health and the ability to cope with stress are built. Friendships are developmental advantages that promote self-esteem, self-efficacy, and general psychological adjustment. Destructive relationships, and even the absence of caring and committed relationships, tend to increase psychological pathology. **At the same time**, the healthier people are psychologically (i.e., free of psychological pathology such as depression, paranoia, anxiety, fear of failure, repressed anger, hopelessness, and meaninglessness), the more able they are to initiate, build, and maintain caring and committed relationships.

Reducing The Discrepancy

The research results consistently indicate that cooperative learning will promote higher achievement, more positive interpersonal relationships, and higher self-esteem than will competitive or individualistic efforts. While there may be a place for competitive and individualistic efforts in college classrooms (see Johnson & R. Johnson, 1991), there are those who believe that competition is inherently destructive (Kohn, 1986). From his review of the research, Alfie Kohn concludes that making others fail is not only an unproductive way to work and learn but also devastating to individuals and society, as competition (a) causes anxiety, selfishness, self-doubt, and poor communication, (b) poisons relationships among individuals thereby making life more unpleasant than it needs to be, and (c) often results in outright aggression. Kohn (1990) also notes that competitive structures create a negative view of human nature as solitary individuals striving to maximize personal gain. He presents evidence that there is a brighter side to human nature based on our relationships with others characterized by altruism, empathy, caring, and commitment. Kohn would replace all competition in higher education with cooperative efforts.

With the amount of research evidence available, it is surprising that college classroom practice is so oriented toward competitive and individualistic learning and colleges are so dominated by competitive and individualistic organizational structures. **It is time for the discrepancy to be reduced between what the research indicates is effective in teaching and what college faculty actually do.** In order to do so, faculty must understand the role of the instructor in implementing cooperative learning experiences. In the next three chapters we focus on the instructor's role in using formal cooperative learning groups, informal cooperative learning groups, and cooperative base groups.

Final Note

During one very difficult trek across an ice field in Don Bennett's hop to the summit of Mount Rainier, his daughter stayed by his side for four hours and with each new hop told him, "You can do it, Dad. You're the best dad in the world. You can do it, Dad." There was no way Bennett would quit climbing with his daughter yelling words of love and encouragement in his ear. Her encouragement strengthened his commitment to make it to the top and kept him moving forward. College life is similar. With members of their cooperative group cheering them on, students amaze themselves and their instructors with what they can achieve.

Learning Outcomes Promoted By Cooperative Learning

1. Higher achievement and increased retention.

2. More frequent higher-level reasoning, deeper- level understanding, and critical thinking.

3. More ontask and less disruptive behavior.

4. Greater achievement motivation and intrinsic motivation to learn.

5. Greater ability to view situations from others' perspectives.

6. More positive, accepting, and supportive relationships with peers regardless of ethnic, sex, ability, social class, or handicap differences.

7. Greater social support.

8. More positive attitudes toward teachers, principals, and other school personnel.

9. More positive attitudes toward subject areas, learning, and school.

10. Greater psychological health, adjustment, and well-being.

11. More positive self-esteem based on basic self- acceptance.

12. Greater social competencies.

Johnson, D. W., & Johnson, R. (1989). **Cooperation and competition**. Edina, MN: Interaction Book Company.

Research Rationale Statement

Task: Write an explanation why you are using cooperative learning. The written rationale statement should include:

1. An introduction that includes these two statements:
   a. *"Cooperative learning is not new, it is an American tradition."*
   b. *"In my classroom students learn in three ways: cooperatively, competitively, and individualistically."*
2. A definition of cooperative learning that includes an example.
3. A summary of the more important consequences of cooperative learning. State that, *"There is a great deal of research validating the use of cooperative learning."* Then include information about:
   a. The importance of peer relationships.
   b. The interaction process promoted by cooperation.
   c. The outcomes resulting from cooperative efforts.
   Also include the research outcomes most important to you and to the person asking, *"Why."*
4. At least one classroom incident that illustrates the power of cooperative learning.
5. A summary or conclusion.

Cooperative: All members must sign each other's rationale statements indicating that they agree with the statement and verify its quality. The signature also means that they have followed the peer editing procedure.

Criteria For Success: A well-written research rationale statement by each participant that they can deliver orally.

Individual Accountability:
1. Each participant understands the breath and depth of the research on cooperative learning. This knowledge is reflected in his or her composition.
2. Each participant is able to explain why he or she is using cooperative learning to a member of another group.

Expected Behaviors: Explaining and listening.

Intergroup Cooperation: Whenever it is helpful to do so, check procedures and information with another group.

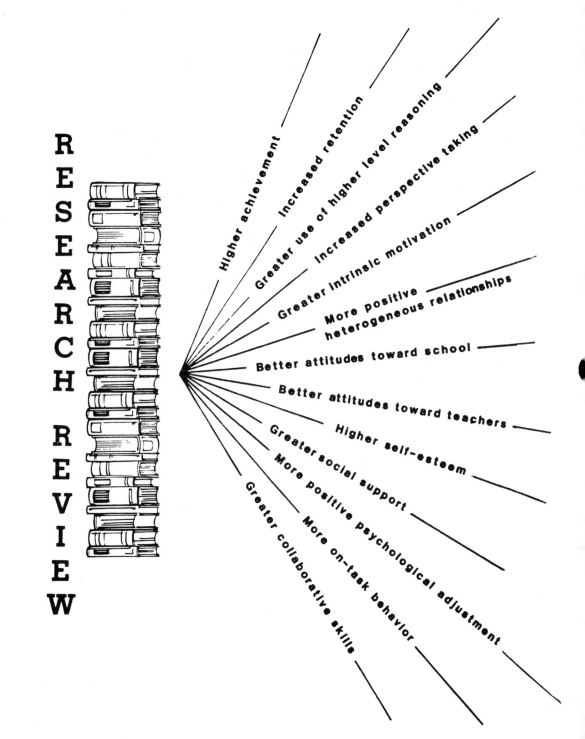

RESEARCH REVIEW

Higher achievement

Increased retention

Greater use of higher level reasoning

Increased perspective taking

Greater intrinsic motivation

More positive heterogeneous relationships

Better attitudes toward school

Better attitudes toward teachers

Higher self-esteem

Greater social support

More positive psychological adjustment

More on-task behavior

Greater collaborative skills

Basic Elements
of Cooperative Learning

Leaving The Ivy Tower And Facing The Real World

> *Coming together is a beginning; Keeping together is progress; Working together is success.*
>
> Henry Ford

Self-managing teams in business and industry are teams of 5 to 15 employees who produce an entire product or provide an entire service. Team members learn all tasks and rotate from job to job. The teams take over managerial duties, including work and vacation scheduling, the ordering of supplies and materials, and the hiring of new members. Self-managing teams can increase productivity 30 percent or more and substantially raise quality. They fundamentally change the way work is organized, giving employees control over their jobs, wiping out tiers of managers, and tearing down bureaucratic barriers between departments. A flatter organization results. Self-managing teams were used by a few companies in the 1960s and 1970s and have rapidly spread in the mid-to-late 1980s. They appear to be the wave of the future.

This new organizational structure of self-managing teams stands in opposition to the principles developed by Frederick W. Taylor. Taylor advocated divisions of labor in which simple, repetitive tasks were performed by low skilled workers under close supervisory control. In the new organizational model work is handed over to small teams of highly skilled employees who make incremental improvements in products and services. Products must continually change, as current products can become obsolete quickly. **Where before companies sold a "product," now they sell a team "process."**

The keys to today's and tomorrow's workplace are the team and the employee. To flourish, companies will need involved and committed employees, who are self-directed and creative thinkers, who continuously seek to upgrade their knowledge and skills, who rapidly and continuously improve products and services, and who are willing to move from job to job. Teamwork makes this possible because the employees usually are "cross-trained" to perform all tasks. They can fill in for absent coworkers and respond quickly to changes. They can teach knowledge and skills to each other. They can monitor coworkers' actions and ensure high quality of work and products.

It is time for faculty to leave the ivy tower of placing students in rows to see who is best and enter the modern world of team- based cooperative organizational structures. Life in classrooms should match more closely the real world of work for which students are supposedly being trained. In many modern corporations, a college graduate can only be employed if he or she can work as part of a team. As can be seen from Chapter 2, student achievement **and** team skills are both maximized through the use of cooperative learning. It takes far more to create a team, however, than placing a number of people in physical proximity and telling them to work together. This is as true in the college classroom as it is in work situations. There are many ways in which group efforts may be ineffective. Less able members sometimes "leave it to George" to complete the group's tasks thus creating a **free rider** effect (Kerr & Bruun, 1983) whereby group members expend decreasing amounts of effort and just go through the team-work motions. At the same time, the more able group member may expend less effort to avoid the **sucker effect** of doing all the work (Kerr, 1983). High ability group members may be deferred to and may take over the important leadership roles in ways that benefit them at the expense of the other group members (**rich-get-richer** effect). In a learning group, for example, the more able group member may give all the explanations of what is being learned. Since the amount of time spent explaining correlates highly with the amount learned, the more able member learns a great deal while the less able members flounder as a captive audience. The time spent listening in group brainstorming can reduce the amount of time any individual can state his or her ideas (Hill, 1982; Lamm & Trommsdorff, 1973). Group efforts can be characterized by self-induced helplessness (Langer & Benevento, 1978), diffusion of responsibility and social loafing (Latane, Williams, & Harkin, 1979), ganging up against a task, reactance (Salomon, 1981), dysfunctional divisions of labor ("I'm the thinkist and you're the typist") (Sheingold, Hawkins, & Char, 1984), inappropriate dependence on authority (Webb, Ender, & Lewis, 1986), destructive conflict (Collins, 1970; Johnson & Johnson, 1979), and other patterns of behavior that debilitate group performance. Cooperation often goes wrong due to a lack of understanding of the critical elements that mediate its effectiveness.

It is only under certain conditions that cooperative efforts may be expected to be more productive than competitive and individualistic efforts. Those conditions are:

1. Clearly perceived positive interdependence.

2. Considerable promotive (face-to-face) interaction.

Table 3.1 What Is The Difference?

Cooperative Learning Groups	Traditional Learning Groups
Positive Interdependence	No Interdependence
Individual Accountability	No Individual Accountability
Heterogeneous Membership Encouraged	Homogeneous Membership
Shared Leadership	One Appointed Leader
Task And Relationships Emphasized	Only Task Emphasized
Social Skills Directly Taught	Social Skills Assumed Or Ignored
Teacher Monitors Groups And Intervenes	Teacher Ignores Groups
Group Processing	No Group Processing

3. Clearly perceived individual accountability and personal responsibility to achieve the group's goals.

4. Frequent use of the relevant interpersonal and small group skills.

5. Frequent and regular group processing of current functioning to improve the group's future effectiveness.

Using Cooperative Learning

The best answer to the question, "What is the most effective method of teaching?" is that it depends on the goal, the students, the content, and the teacher. But the next best answer is, "Students teaching other students." There is a wealth of evidence that peer teaching is extremely effective for a wide range of goals, content, and students of different levels and personalities.

McKeachie, et al. (1986, p. 63)

A professor at the University of Minnesota, in his Introductory Astronomy classes of from 300 to 500 students, randomly assigns students to groups of four. He provides explicit directions concerning students' group work and maintains an extensive file system to pass information between the students and the instructor. After students become accustomed to working in groups, he often differentiates the role assignments. Each group member is assigned one of these roles. The **recorder** records the group's work by writing out the steps for solving each astronomy problem assigned. The **checker** makes sure that all members can explain how to solve each problem correctly (or can give appropriate rationale for the group's answer). The **encourager** in a friendly way encourages all members of the group to participate in the discussion, sharing their ideas and feelings. The **elaborator** relates present to past learning.

Within this lesson **positive interdependence** is structured by the group agreeing on (1) the answer and (2) the process for solving each problem. Since the group certifies that each member has the correct answer written on their answer sheet and can correctly explain how to solve each problem, **individual accountability** is structured by having the professor randomly ask one group member to explain how to solve one of the problems. The **cooperative skills** emphasized in the lesson are checking, encouraging, and elaborating. Finally, at the end of the period the groups **process** how well they are functioning by answering two questions: (a) What is something each member did that was helpful for the group? and (b) What is something each member could do to make the group even better tomorrow?

What differentiates cooperative learning from traditional grouping is the careful implementation of the five elements largely mediating the effectiveness of cooperative efforts. Those five elements are discussed below.

Positive Interdependence

All for one and one for all.

Alexandre Dumas

Within a football game, the quarterback who throws the pass and the receiver who catches the pass are positively interdependent. The success of one depends on the success of the other. It takes two to complete a pass. One player cannot succeed without the other. Both have to perform competently if their mutual success is to be assured. They sink or swim together.

The first requirement for an effectively structured cooperative lesson is that students believe that they "sink or swim together." Within cooperative learning situations students have two responsibilities: learn the assigned material and ensure that all members of their group learn the assigned material. The technical term for that dual responsibility is positive interdependence. **Positive interdependence** exists when students perceive that they are linked with groupmates in a way so that they cannot succeed unless their groupmates do (and vice versa) and/or that they must coordinate their efforts with the efforts of their groupmates to complete a task. Positive interdependence promotes a situation in which students (a) see that their work benefits groupmates and their groupmates' work benefits them and (b) work together in small groups to maximize the learning of all members by sharing their resources, providing mutual support and encouragement, and celebrating their joint success. When positive interdependence is clearly understood, it highlights:

1. Each group member's efforts are required and indispensable for group success (i.e., there can be no "free- riders").

2. Each group member has a unique contribution to make to the joint effort because of his or her resources and/or role and task responsibilities.

There are a number of ways of structuring positive interdependence within a learning group:

1. **Positive Goal Interdependence:** Students perceive that they can achieve their learning goals if and only if all the members of their group also attain their goals. The group is united around a common goal--a concrete reason for being. To ensure that students believe "they sink or swim together" and care about how much each other learns, you (the instructor) have to structure a clear group or mutual goal such as "learn the assigned material and make sure that all members of your group learn the assigned material." The group goal always has to be a part of the lesson.

2. **Positive Reward/Celebration Interdependence:** Each group member receives the same reward when the group achieves its goals. To supplement goal interdependence, you may wish to add joint rewards (if all members of the group score 90 percent correct or better on the test, each will receive 5 bonus points). Sometimes instructors give students a group grade for the overall production of their group, individual grades resulting from tests, and bonus points if all members of the group achieve up to the criterion on the tests. Regular celebrations of group efforts and success enhances the quality of cooperation.

3. **Positive Resource Interdependence**: Each group member has only a portion of the resources, information, or materials necessary for the task to be completed and the members' resources have to be combined in order for the group to achieve its goals. You may wish to highlight the cooperative relationships by giving students limited resources that must be shared (one copy of the problem or task per group) or giving

each student part of the required resources that the group must then fit together (the jigsaw procedure).

4. **Positive Role Interdependence:** Each member is assigned complementary and interconnected roles that specify responsibilities that the group needs in order to complete the joint task. You create role interdependence among students when you assign them complementary roles such as reader, recorder, checker of understanding, encourager of participation, and elaborator of knowledge. Such roles are vital to high-quality learning. The role of checker, for example, focuses on periodically asking each groupmate to explain what is being learned. Rosenshine and Stevens (1986) reviewed a large body of well-controlled research on teaching effectiveness at the pre-collegiate level and found "checking for comprehension" to be one specific teaching behavior that was significantly associated with higher levels of student learning and achievement. While the instructor cannot continually check the under-standing of every student (especially if there are 300 students in the class), the instructor can engineer such checking by having students work in cooperative groups and assigning one member the role of checker.

There are other types of positive interdependence. **Positive task interdependence** exists when a division of labor is created so that the actions of one group member have to be completed if the next member is to complete his or her responsibility. **Positive identity interdependence** exists when a mutual identity is established through a name or motto. **Outside enemy interdependence** exists when groups are placed in competition with each other. **Fantasy interdependence** exists when a task is given that requires group members to imagine that they are in a hypothetical situation.

The authors have conducted a series of studies investigating the nature of positive interdependence and the relative power of the different types of positive interdependence (Hwong, Caswell, Johnson, & Johnson, 1990; Johnson, Johnson, Stanne, & Garibaldi, 1990; Johnson, Johnson, Ortez, & Stanne, in press; Lew, Mesch, Johnson, & Johnson, 1986a, 1986b; Mesch, Johnson, & Johnson, 1988; Mesch, Lew, Johnson, & Johnson, 1986). Our research indicates that positive interdependence provides the context within which promotive interaction takes place, group membership and interpersonal interaction among students do not produce higher achievement unless positive interdependence is clearly structured, the combination of goal and reward interdependence increases achievement over goal interdependence alone, and resource interdependence does not increase achievement unless goal interdependence is present also.

Face-To-Face Promotive Interaction

In an industrial organization it's the group effort that counts. There's really no room for stars in an industrial organization. You need talented people, but they can't do it alone. They have to have help.

John F. Donnelly, President, Donnelly Mirrors

Positive interdependence results in promotive interaction. **Promotive interaction** may be defined as individuals encouraging and facilitating each other's efforts to achieve, complete tasks, and produce in order to reach the group's goals. While positive interdependence in and of itself may have some effect on outcomes, it is the face-to-face promotive interaction among individuals fostered by the positive interdependence that most powerfully influences efforts to achieve, caring and committed relationships, and psychological adjustment and social competence. Promotive interaction is characterized by individuals providing each other with efficient and effective help and assistance, exchanging needed resources such as information and materials and processing information more efficiently and effectively, providing each other with feedback in order to improve their subsequent performance, challenging each other's conclusions and reasoning in order to promote higher quality decision making and greater insight into the problems being considered, advocating the exertion of effort to achieve mutual goals, influencing each other's efforts to achieve the group's goals, acting in trusting and trustworthy ways, being motivated to strive for mutual benefit, and a moderate level of arousal characterized by low anxiety and stress.

Individual Accountability/Personal Responsibility

What children can do together today, they can do alone tomorrow.

Vygotsky

Among the early settlers of Massachusetts there was a saying "If you do not work, you do not eat." Everyone had to do their fair share of the work. The third essential element of cooperative learning is **individual accountability**, which exists when the performance of each individual student is assessed, the results given back to the individual and the group, and the student is held responsible by groupmates for contributing his or her fair share to the group's success. It is important that the group knows who needs more assistance, support, and encouragement in completing the assignment. It is also important that group members know they cannot "hitch-hike" on the work of others. When it is difficult to identify members' contributions, when members' contributions are redundant, and when members are not responsible for the final group outcome, members sometimes seek a free ride (Harkins & Petty, 1982; Ingham, Levinger, Graves, & Peckham, 1974; Kerr & Bruun, 1981; Latane, Williams & Harkins, 1979; Moede, 1927; Petty, Harkins, Williams, & Lantane, 1977; Williams, 1981; Williams, Harkins, & Latane, 1981). This is called social loafing.

The purpose of cooperative learning groups is to make each member a stronger individual in his or her own right. Individual accountability is the key to ensuring that all group members are in fact strengthened by learning cooperatively. After participating in a cooperative lesson, group members should be better prepared to complete similar tasks by themselves.

To ensure that each student is individually accountable to do his or her fair share of the group's work you need to assess how much effort each member is contributing to the group's work, provide feedback to groups and individual students, help groups avoid redundant efforts by members, and ensure that every member is responsible for the final outcome. Common ways to structure individual accountability include:

1. Keeping the size of the group small. The smaller the size of the group, the greater the individual accountability may be.

2. Giving an individual test to each student.

3. Randomly examining students orally by randomly calling on one student to present his or her group's work to you (in the presence of the group) or to the entire class.

4. Observing each group and recording the frequency with which each member contributes to the group's work.

5. Assigning one student in each group the role of checker. The **checker** asks other group members to explain the reasoning and rationale underlying group answers.

6. Having students teach what they learned to someone else. When all students do this, it is called simultaneous explaining (see Chapter 5).

There is a pattern to classroom learning. **First**, students learn knowledge, skills, strategies, or procedures in a cooperative group. **Second**, students apply the knowledge or perform the skill, strategy, or procedure alone to demonstrate their personal mastery of the material. Students learn it together and then perform it alone.

Interpersonal and Small Group Skills

I will pay more for the ability to deal with people than any other ability under the sun.

John D. Rockefeller

The fourth essential element of cooperative learning is the appropriate use of **interpersonal and small group skills.** In order to coordinate efforts to achieve mutual goals, students must (1) get to know and trust each other, (2) communicate accurately and unambiguously, (3) accept and support each other, and (4) resolve conflicts constructively (Johnson, 1990, 1991; Johnson & F. Johnson, 1991). Placing socially unskilled students in a group and telling them to cooperate does not guarantee that they are able to do so effectively. We are not born instinctively knowing how to interact effectively with others. Interpersonal and small group skills do not magically appear when they are needed. Students must be taught the social skills required for high quality collaboration and be motivated to use them if cooperative groups are to be productive. The whole field of group dynamics is based on the premise that social skills are the key to group productivity (Johnson & F. Johnson, 1991).

The more socially skillful students are, and the more attention instructors pay to teaching and rewarding the use of social skills, the higher the achievement that can be expected within cooperative learning groups. In their studies on the long-term implementation of cooperative learning, Lew and Mesch (Lew, Mesch, Johnson & Johnson, 1986a, 1986b; Mesch, Johnson, & Johnson, 1988; Mesch, Lew, Johnson, & Johnson, 1986) investigated the impact of a reward contingency for using social skills as well as positive interdependence and a contingency for academic achievement on performance within cooperative learning groups. In the cooperative skills conditions students were trained weekly in four social skills and each member of a cooperative group was given two bonus points toward the quiz grade if all group members were observed by the teacher to demonstrate three out of four cooperative skills. The results indicated that the combination of positive interdependence, an academic

Constructing a T-Chart

1. *Write the name of the skill to be learned and practiced at the top of the chart and draw a large T below it.*

2. *Label the left side of the T "Looks Like" and the right side "Sounds Like."*

3. *Think of an example for each of the columns and write that below the crossbar.*

4. *Ask students for other behaviors that operationalize the skill and list those on the left side.*

5. *Ask students for further phrases that operationalize the skill and list those on the right side.*

6. *Have group members practice both Looks Like and Sounds Like.*

7. *Observe the groups working on a lesson and record the frequency with which the skill is used in each group.*

contingency for high performance by all group members, and a social skills contingency promoted the highest achievement. One way to define a social skill for students is through the use of a **T-Chart**.

Group Processing

Take care of each other. Share your energies with the group. No one must feel alone, cut off, for that is when you do not make it.

Willi
Unsoeld, Renowned Mountain Climber

The fifth essential component of cooperative learning is group processing. Effective group work is influenced by whether or not groups reflect on (i.e., process) how well they are functioning. A **process** is an identifiable sequence of events taking place over time, and **process goals** refer to the sequence of events instrumental in achieving outcome goals (Johnson & F. Johnson, 1991). **Group processing** may be defined as reflecting on a group session to (a) describe what member actions were helpful and unhelpful and (b) make decisions about what actions to continue or change. The purpose of group processing is to clarify and improve the effectiveness of the members in contributing to the collaborative efforts to achieve the group's goals.

Stuart Yager examined the impact on achievement of (a) cooperative learning in which members discussed how well their group was functioning and how they could improve its effectiveness, (b) cooperative learning without any group processing, and (c) individualistic learning (Yager, Johnson, & Johnson, 1985). The results indicate that the high-, medium-, and low-achieving students in the cooperation- with-group-processing condition achieved higher on daily achievement, post-instructional achievement, and retention measures than did the students in the other two conditions. Students in the cooperation-without-group-processing condition, furthermore, achieved higher on all three measures than did the students in the individualistic condition. Johnson, Johnson, Stanne, and Garibaldi (1990) conducted a follow-up study comparing

Figure 3.1 Group Processing And Achievement

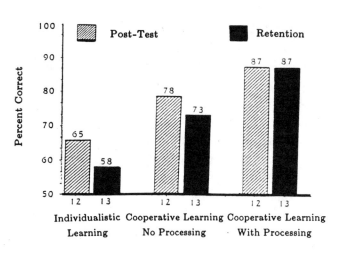

Source: Yager, Johnson, & Johnson (1985). Data summarized by Ted Graves.

cooperative learning with no-processing, cooperative learning-with-instructor processing (instructor specified cooperative skills to use, observed, and gave whole-class feedback as to how well students were using the skills), cooperative learning with instructor and student processing (instructor specified cooperative skills to use, observed, gave whole-class feedback as to how well students were using the skills, and had learning groups discuss how well they interacted as a group), and individualistic learning. Forty-nine high ability Black American high school seniors and entering college freshmen at Xavier University participated in the study. A complex computer-assisted problem-solving assignment was given to the students. All three cooperative conditions performed higher than did the individualistic condition. The combination of teacher and student processing resulted in greater problem-solving success than did the other cooperative conditions.

While the instructor systematically observes the cooperative learning groups he or she attains a "window" into what students do and do not understand as they explain to each other how to complete the assignment. Listening in on the students' explanations provides valuable information about how well the students understand the instructions, the major concepts and strategies being learned, and the basic elements of cooperative learning. Wilson (1987, p.18) conducted a three-year, teaching- improvement study as part of a college faculty development program. Both faculty and students agreed that faculty needed help on knowing if the class understood the material or not. Listening to students explain how to complete the assignment to groupmates provides better information about what students do and do not know than do correct answers on a test or homework assignments handed in.

There are two levels of processing--small group and whole class. In order to ensure that **small group processing** takes place, instructors allocate some time at the end of each class session for each cooperative group to process how effectively members worked together. Groups need to describe what member actions were helpful and unhelpful in completing the group's work and make decisions about what behaviors to continue or change. Such processing (1) enables learning groups to focus on maintaining good working relationships among members, (2) facilitates the learning of cooperative skills, (3) ensures that members receive feedback on their participation, (4) ensures that students think on the meta-cognitive as well as the cognitive level, and (5) provides the means to celebrate the success of the group and reinforce the positive behaviors of group members. Some of the keys to successful small group processing are allowing sufficient time for it to take place, providing a structure for processing (such as "List three things your group is doing well today and one thing you could improve"), emphasizing positive feedback, making the processing specific rather than general, maintaining student involvement in processing, reminding students to use their cooperative skills while they process, and communicating clear expectations as to the purpose of processing.

In addition to small group processing, the instructor should periodically engage in **whole-class processing**. When cooperative learning groups are used, the teacher observes the groups, analyzes the problems they have working together, and gives feedback to each group on how well they are working together. The instructor systematically moves from group to group and observes them at work. A formal observation sheet may be used to gather specific data on each group. At the end of the class period the instructor can then conduct a whole-class processing session by sharing with the class the results of his or her observations. If each group has a peer observer, the results of his or her observations may be added together to get overall class data.

An important aspect of both small-group and whole-class processing is group and class celebrations. It is feeling successful, appreciated, and respected that builds commitment to learning, enthusiasm about working in cooperative groups, and a sense of self-efficacy in terms of subject-matter mastery and working cooperatively with classmates.

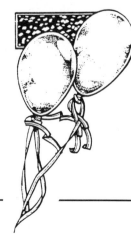

Structuring the Five Basic Elements
Is Like Using Pulleys to Lift Weights

Using the five basic elements of cooperation skillfully increases an instructor's power to increase student achievement, build a more caring and supportive learning community, and enhance students' psychological adjustment and social competencies. The power that each of the five elements adds is like using ropes and pulleys to lift weights. Putting students in groups and having them interact face to face gives little advantage over having each student work alone. Adding each of the five essential elements, however, doubles the amount of weight a person can lift with the same amount of effort. Thus, with two pulleys 100 pounds of effort lifts 200 pounds of weight, with three pulleys 100 pounds of effort lifts 300 pounds, and with five pulleys 100 pounds of effort lifts 500 pounds. Whenever instructors want learning groups to be more powerful, they only needs to operationalize the five basic elements in more precise and refined ways.

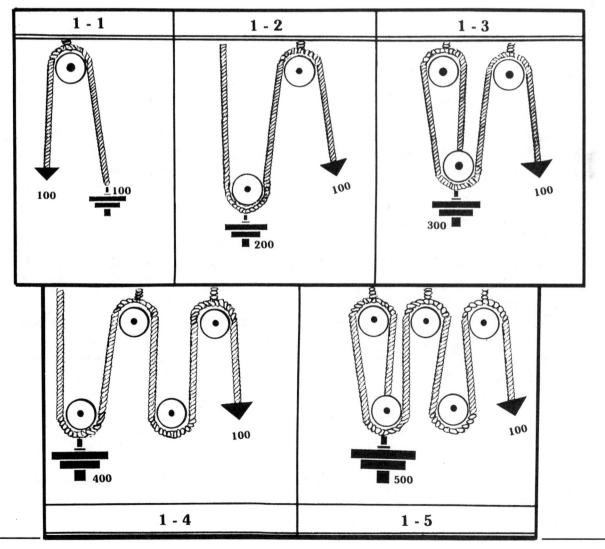

Positive Interdependence And Intellectual Conflict

The greater the positive interdependence within a learning group, the greater the likelihood of intellectual disagreement and conflict among group members. When members of a cooperative learning group become involved in a lesson, their different information, perceptions, opinions, reasoning processes, theories, and conclusions will result in intellectual disagreement and conflict. When such controversies arise, they may be dealt with constructively or destructively, depending on how they are managed and the level of interpersonal and small group skills of the participants. When managed constructively, controversy promotes uncertainty about the correctness of one's conclusions, an active search for more information, a reconceptualization of one's knowledge and conclusions and, consequently, greater mastery and retention of the material being discussed and the more frequent use of higher-level reasoning strategies (Johnson & Johnson, 1987, 1989a). Individuals working alone in competitive and individualistic situations do not have the opportunity for such intellectual challenge and, therefore, their achievement and quality of reasoning suffer.

Seeing The Beauty In The Beast

There is a fairy tale about the beautiful daughter of a wealthy merchant who, to rescue her father, agreed to live with a beast. When seeing the beast for the first time she let out a cry of horror and fainted. When she awoke she heard the beast sobbing as if its heart would break. Ashamed and sorry she said, "Do not weep, my friend, your ugly shape is not your doing. True beauty lies within, not in what is without." When at last she embraced the beast in love and commitment, the beast was transformed to a handsome price. And she lived in love and luxury forever after.

The inner beauty of cooperative efforts lies in seeing beyond students talking to each other to the five essential components described in this chapter. The inner beauty of cooperation comes from feeling bonded to others through a mutual interdependence, providing help and encouragement out of a true commitment to each other's success and well-being, striving to do one's personal best to help the team, providing leadership and enhancing communication, and reflecting jointly on how members may work together even more effectively.

Many educators who believe that they are using cooperative learning are, in fact, missing its essence. There is a crucial difference between simply putting students in groups to learn and in structuring cooperation among students. Cooperation is **not** having students sit side-by-side at the same table to talk with each other as they do their individual assignments. Cooperation is **not** assigning a report to a group of students where one student does all the work and the others put their names on the product as well. Cooperation is **not** having students do a task individually with instructions that the ones who finish first are to help the slower students. Cooperation is much more than being physically near other students, discussing material with other students, helping other students, or sharing material among students, although each of these is important in cooperative learning.

To be cooperative a group must have clear positive interdependence, members must promote each other's learning and success face-to-face, hold each other personally and individually accountable to do his or her fair share of the work, appropriately use the interpersonal and small group skills needed for cooperative efforts to be successful, and process as a group how effectively members are working together (see Table 2.1). These five essential components must be present for small group learning to be truly cooperative. There are three types of cooperative learning groups within which these five essential elements must be structured: formal, informal, and base groups. They are discussed in depth in the following chapters.

 asic Elements Of Cooperative Learning

Positive Interdependence

Students perceive that they need each other in order to complete the group's task ("sink or swim together"). Teachers may structure positive interdependence by establishing **mutual goals** (learn and make sure all other group members learn), **joint rewards** (if all group members achieve above the criteria, each will receive bonus points), **shared resources** (one paper for each group or each member receives part of the required information), and **assigned roles** (summarizer, encourager of participation, elaborator).

Face-to-Face Promotive Interaction

Students promote each other's learning by helping, sharing, and encouraging efforts to learn. Students explain, discuss, and teach what they know to classmates. Teachers structure the groups so that students sit knee-to-knee and talk through each aspect of the assignment.

Individual Accountability

Each student's performance is frequently assessed and the results are given to the group and the individual. Teachers may structure individual accountability by giving an individual test to each student or randomly selecting one group member to give the answer.

Interpersonal And Small Group Skills

Groups cannot function effectively if students do not have and use the needed social skills. Teachers teach these skills as purposefully and precisely as academic skills. Collaborative skills include leadership, decision-making, trust-building, communication, and conflict-management skills.

Group Processing

Groups need specific time to discuss how well they are achieving their goals and maintaining effective working relationships among members. Teachers structure group processing by assigning such tasks as (a) list at least three member actions that helped the group be successful and (b) list one action that could be added to make the group even more successful tomorrow. Teachers also monitor the groups and give feedback on how well the groups are working together to the groups and the class as a whole.

4 Formal Cooperative Learning

Sisyphus And The Old Paradigm

And I saw Sisyphus at his endless task, raising his prodigious stone, with both his hands. With hands and feet he tried to roll it up to the top of the hill, but always, just before he could roll it over onto the other side, its weight would be too much for him, and the pitiless stone would come thundering down again onto the plain. Then he would begin trying to push it uphill again, as the sweat ran off him and steam rose after him.

Homer (Oddyessy, Book 11)

Repetitive but futile efforts were personified by the ancient Greeks in the person of Sisyphus. Sisyphus was the legendary king of Corinth who was punished in Hades by having to roll a stone uphill eternally. As he neared the top of the hill, the stone always slipped from his grasp, and he had to start again. It is easy to feel that way while teaching in the old paradigm. The old paradigm of teaching assumes that the way you impart knowledge is to pour it into students' heads. What we have found is that telling students what we know feels like rolling a boulder up a hill with the students bored and uninterested. In essence we felt like Sisyphus.

Our next step was to break their knowledge up into small parts and take it up the hill a few parts at a time. This did not seem to increase the intellectual interest or involvement of students. If anything, it may have made the class even more boring. At that point we had to ask ourselves, **Who is doing the hard intellectual work in the course?** Who is doing the conceptualizing, the organizing, the elaborating, the presenting, the summarizing, the synthesizing, and the reconceptualizing? If the answer is, "The instructor," you know that everything is backwards. It is the students who are supposed to be doing the hard intellectual work in their courses. At that point we had to ask, **Who is having the most fun?** The answer may be, "No one." But if the answer is, "The Instructor," you know that everything is backwards. It is the students who are supposed to be enjoying the class.

We did not obtain the results we wanted with our teaching until we directly involved students in the learning process through cooperative learning groups. Instead of our rolling

the rock up the hill only to have it slip from our grasp when we analyzed the results of midterms and finals, we structured our courses so that all students helped to roll the boulder up the hill. When everyone, students as well as faculty, works together to roll it up the hill, then it does not slip from our grasp--it stays. As was reviewed in Chapter 2, structuring lessons cooperatively results in a number of advantages for achievement, interpersonal relationships, and psychological well-being. In addition, cooperative learning makes the classroom more realistic by making learning situations more similar to the real world of work.

Formal Cooperative Learning Groups

Howard Eaton, an English professor at Douglas College in Vancouver, British Columbia introduces his course, **Argumentative Writing for College Students,** by stating to the students, "You have bought an opportunity to learn something, not a service. This is not a prison and it is not social entertainment of the useless and unemployable. This is work. Your tuition, furthermore, only pays for 15 percent of the cost for this course. The taxpayers fund the other 85 percent. You have, therefore, a social obligation that translates into two responsibilities:

1. You are responsible for your own learning. It is up to you to get something useful and interesting from this course.

2. You are **equally** responsible for the learning of your groupmates. It is up to you to ensure that they get something useful and interesting from this course."

This introduction prepares students to do much of their work in formal cooperative learning groups. **Formal cooperative learning groups** have fixed membership, usually last from a few days to a few weeks, and have a well-defined task to accomplish. There is a wide variety of ways to structure formal cooperative learning groups. They may be structured specifically for learning of information, concept learning, problem solving, or composition. Before exploring each of these structures, the aspects of the instructor's role common to all are described.

The Instructor's Role: Being "A Guide On The Side"

Each class session instructors must make the choice of being "a sage on the stage" or "a guide on the side." In doing so they might remember that the challenge in college teaching is not **covering** the material **for** the students, it's **uncovering** the material **with** the students.

One of Roger's favorite demonstration science lessons is to ask students to determine how long a candle burns in a quart jar. He assigns students to groups of two, making the pairs as heterogeneous as possible. Each pair is given one candle and one quart jar (resource interdependence). He gives the instructional task of timing how long the candle will burn and the cooperative goal of deciding on one answer that both pair members can explain. Students are to encourage each other's participation and elaborate what they are learning to previous lessons (social skills). Students light their candle, place the quart jar over it, and time how long the candle burns. The answers from the pairs are announced. Roger then gives the pairs the task of generating a number of answers to the question, "How many factors make a difference in how long the candle burns in the jar?" The answers from the pairs are written on the board. The pairs then repeat the experiment in ways that test which of the suggested factors do in fact make a difference in how long the candle burns. The next day students individually take a quiz on the factors affecting the time a candle burns in a quart jar (individual accountability) and their scores are totaled to determine a joint score that, if high enough, earns them bonus points (reward interdependence). They spend some time discussing the helpful actions of each member and what they could do to be even more effective in the future (group processing).

Science experiments are only one of the many places cooperative learning may be used. Cooperative learning is appropriate for any instructional task. Whenever the learning goals are highly important, the task is complex or conceptual, problem solving is required, divergent thinking or creativity is desired, quality of performance is expected, higher level reasoning strategies and critical thinking are needed, long-term retention is desired, or when the social development of students is one of the major instructional goals--cooperative learning should be used (Johnson & Johnson, 1989a).

Within cooperative learning situations, the instructor forms the learning groups, teaches the basic concepts and strategies, monitors the functioning of the learning groups, intervenes to teach small group skills, provides task assistance when it is needed, evaluates students' learning using a criterion-referenced system, and ensures that the cooperative groups process how effectively members worked together. Students look to their peers for assistance, feedback, reinforcement, and support.

The instructor's role in using formal cooperative learning groups includes five parts (Johnson & Johnson, 1991; Johnson, Johnson, & Holubec, 1990):

1. Specifying the objectives for the lesson.

2. Making decisions about placing students in learning groups before the lesson is taught.

3. Explaining the task and goal structure to the students.

4. Monitoring the effectiveness of the cooperative learning groups and intervening to provide task assistance (such as answering questions and teaching task skills) or to increase students' interpersonal and group skills.

5. Evaluating the students' achievement and helping students discuss how well they collaborated with each other.

Specifying the Instructional Objectives

There are two types of objectives that an instructor needs to specify before the lesson begins. The **academic objective** needs to be specified at the correct level for the students and matched to the right level of instruction according to a conceptual or task analysis. The **social skills objective** details what interpersonal and small group skills are going to be emphasized during the lesson. A common error many instructors make is to specify only

Handy Hints for Better Learning Groups

I. Before the group begins:

Expect to learn, to enjoy, and to discover.
Team up with people you don't know.
Make your group heterogeneous.

II. As the group begins:

Make a good first impression.
Build the team.
- Have a sociable, relaxed dinner together, without spouses or dates.
- Do something that requires self-disclosure.
- Take interpersonal risks that build trust.
- Establish team goals.

Plan ahead the data on group process that you need.
- Harness computer skills for data analysis.
- Examine and discuss the data for what it means about the group.

III. While the group is in existence:

Work at increasing self-disclosure.
Work at giving good feedback.
Get the silent members involved.
Confront the problems squarely and immediately.
- Apply lessons from class work that address the problem.
- Work on issues in the group even if they appear to be just between two members.
- Don't assume you can't work with someone just because you don't like or respect them.
- If the group can't solve a problem, consult the instructor as a group.

Regularly review your data.
Vary the leadership style needed.

IV. Wrapping up the group:

Summarize and review your learning from group experience.
- Analyze the data to discover why the group was more effective or less so.
- Provide final feedback to members on their behavior or contribution.

Celebrate the group's accomplishments.
- Have a dinner party with spouses/dates to help you celebrate.
- Hold a final feedback meeting.
- If it is hard to say "goodby," do so nonverbally.

Source: Bowen & Jackson (1985-86)

academic objectives and to ignore the social skills objectives needed to train students to cooperate effectively with each other.

Preinstructional Decisions

Deciding on the Size of the Group

Once the objectives of the lesson are clear, the instructor must decide which size of learning group is optimal. Cooperative learning groups typically range in size from 2 to 4. In selecting the size of a cooperative learning group remember that the shorter the amount of time available, the smaller the group should be; the larger the group, the more resources available for the group's work but the more skills required to ensure that the group works productively. Sometimes the materials or equipment available or the specific nature of the task may dictate a group size.

Assigning Students to Groups

Teachers often ask four basic questions about assigning students to groups:

1. **Should students be placed in learning groups homogeneous or heterogeneous in member ability?** There are times when cooperative learning groups homogeneous in ability may be used to master specific skills or to achieve certain instructional objectives. Generally, however, we recommend that instructors maximize the heterogeneity of students, placing high-, medium-, and low-achieving students within the same learning group. More elaborative thinking, more frequent giving and receiving of explanations, and greater perspective taking in discussing material seems to occur in heterogeneous groups, all of which increase the depth of understanding, the quality of reasoning, and the accuracy of long-term retention.

2. **Should nontask-oriented students be placed in learning groups with task-oriented peers or be separated?** To keep nonacademically-oriented students on task it often helps to place them in a cooperative learning group with task-oriented peers.

3. **Should students select whom they want to work with or should the instructor assign students to groups?** Teacher-made groups often have the best mix since instructors can put together optimal combinations of students. Random assignment, such as having students "count off" is another possibility for getting a good mix of

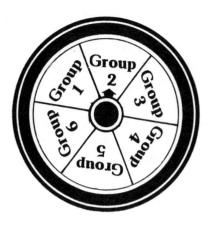

students in each group. Having students select their own groups is often not very successful. Student-selected groups often are homogeneous with high-achieving students working with other high-achieving students, white students working with other white students, minority students working with other minority students, and males working with other males. Often there is less on-task behavior in student-selected than in instructor-selected groups. A useful modification of the "select your own group" method is to have students list whom they would like to work with and then place them in a learning group with one person they choose and one or two or more students that the instructor selects.

4. **How long should the groups stay together?** Actually, there is no formula or simple answer to this question. Some instructors keep cooperative learning groups together for an entire year or semester. Other instructors like to keep a learning group together only long enough to complete a task, unit, or chapter. Sooner or later, however, every student should work with every other classmate. Our best advice is to allow groups to remain stable long enough for them to be successful. Breaking up groups that are having trouble functioning effectively is often counterproductive as the students do not learn the skills they need to resolve problems in collaborating with each other.

Arranging the Room

How the instructor arranges the room is a symbolic message of what is appropriate behavior and it can facilitate the learning groups within the classroom. Members of a learning group should sit close enough to each other that they can share materials, maintain eye contact with all group members, and talk to each other quietly without disrupting the other learning groups. The instructor should have a clear access lane to every group. Within each learning group students need to be able to see all relevant task materials, see each other, converse with each other without raising their voices, and exchange ideas and materials in a comfortable atmosphere. The groups need to be far enough apart so that they do not interfere with each other's learning.

Planning the Instructional Materials to Promote Interdependence

Materials need to be distributed among group members so that all members participate and achieve. When a group is mature and experienced and group members have a high level of interpersonal and small group skills, the instructor may not have to arrange materials in any specific way. When a group is new or when members are not very skilled, however, instructors may wish to distribute materials in carefully planned ways to communicate that the assignment is to be a joint (not an individual) effort and that the students are in a "sink or swim together" learning situation. Three of the ways of doing so are:

1. **Materials Interdependence**: Give only one copy of the materials to the group. The students will then have to work together in order to be successful. This is especially effective the first few times the group meets. After students are accustomed to working cooperatively, instructors can give a copy of the materials to each student.

2. **Information Interdependence**: Group members may each be given different books or resource materials to be synthesized. Or the materials may be arranged like a jigsaw puzzle so that each student has part of the materials needed to complete the task. Such procedures require that every member participate in order for the group to be successful.

3. **Interdependence from Outside Enemies**: Materials may be structured into a tournament format with intergroup competition as the basis to promote a perception of interdependence among group members. Such a procedure was introduced by DeVries and Edwards (1973). In the teams-games-tournament format students are divided into heterogeneous cooperative learning teams to prepare members for a tournament in which they compete with the other teams. During the intergroup competition the students individually compete against members of about the same ability level from other teams. The team whose members do the best in the competition is pronounced the winner by the instructor.

All of these procedures may not be needed simultaneously. They are alternative methods of ensuring that students perceive that they are involved in a "sink or swim together" learning situation and behave collaboratively.

Assigning Roles to Ensure Interdependence

Positive interdependence may also be structured through the assignment of complementary and interconnected roles to group members. In addition to their responsibility to learn, each group member can be assigned a responsibility to help groupmates work together effectively. Such roles include a **summarizer** (who restates the group's major conclusions or answers), a **checker of understanding** (who ensures that all group members can explicitly explain how to arrive at an answer or conclusion), an **accuracy coach** (who corrects any mistakes in another member's explanations or summaries), an **elaborator** (who relates current concepts and strategies to material studied previously), a **researcher-runner** (who gets needed materials for the group and communicates with the other learning groups and the instructor), a **recorder** to write down the group's decisions and edit the group's report, an **encourager of participation** who ensures that all members are contributing, and an **observer** who keeps track of how well the group is cooperating. Assigning such roles is an effective method of teaching students social skills and fostering positive interdependence.

Roles such as checking for understanding and elaborating are vital to high-quality learning but are often absent in college classrooms. The role of checker, for example, focuses on periodically asking each groupmate to explain what is being learned. From their research review, Rosenshine and Stevens (1986) concluded that "checking for comprehension" was significantly associated with higher levels of student learning and achievement. Wilson (1987) conducted a three-year, teaching-improvement study as part of a college faculty development program and found that the teaching behavior faculty and students perceived faculty needing the most help on was "knows if the class is understanding the material or not." Wilson found that checking for understanding was highly correlated with overall effectiveness as an instructor. While the instructor cannot continually check the understanding of every student in the class (especially if there are 300 students in the class), the instructor can engineer such checking by having students work in cooperative groups and assigning one member the role of checker.

Structuring The Task And Positive Interdependence

Explaining the Academic Task

Instructors explain the academic task so that students are clear about the assignment and understand the objectives of the lesson. Direct teaching of concepts, principles, and strategies may take place at this point. Instructors may wish to answer any questions students have about the concepts or facts they are to learn or apply in the lesson. Instructors need to consider several aspects of explaining an academic assignment to students:

1. **Set the task so that students are clear about the assignment.** Most instructors have considerable practice with this already. Instructions that are clear and specific are crucial in warding off student frustration. One advantage of cooperative learning groups is that they can handle more ambiguous tasks (when they are appropriate) than can students working alone. In cooperative learning groups students who do not understand what they are to do will ask their group for clarification before asking the instructor.

2. **Explain the objectives of the lesson and relate the concepts and information to be studied to students' past experience and learning to ensure maximum transfer and retention.** Explaining the intended outcomes of the lesson increases the likelihood that students will focus on the relevant concepts and information throughout the lesson.

3. **Define relevant concepts, explain procedures students should follow, and give examples to help students understand what they are to learn and do in completing the assignment.** To promote positive transfer of learning, point out the critical elements that separate this lesson from past learnings.

4. **Ask the class specific questions to check the students' understanding of the assignment.** Such questioning ensures thorough two-way communication, that the assignment has been given effectively, and that the students are ready to begin completing it.

Explaining Criteria for Success

Evaluation within cooperatively structured lessons needs to be criterion-referenced. Criteria must be established for acceptable work (rather than grading on a curve). Instructors may structure a second level of cooperation by not only keeping track of how well each group and its members are performing, but also by setting criteria for the whole class to reach. Improvement (doing better this week than one did last week) may be set as a criterion of excellence.

Structuring Positive Interdependence

Communicate to students that they have a group goal and must work cooperatively. We cannot overemphasize the importance of communicating to students that they are in a "sink or swim together" learning situation. In a cooperative learning group students are responsible for learning the assigned material, making sure that all other group members learn the assigned material, and making sure that all other class members successfully learn the assigned material, in that order. Instructors can do this in several ways.

1. **Structure positive goal interdependence by giving the group the responsibility of ensuring that all members achieve a prescribed mastery level on the assigned materials.** Teachers may wish to say, "One answer from the group, everyone has to agree, and everyone has to be able to explain how to solve the problem or complete the assignment." Teachers may establish the prescribed mastery level as (a) individual levels of performance that each group member must achieve in order for the group as a whole to be successful (the group goal is for each member to demonstrate 90 percent mastery on a curriculum unit) or (b) improvement scores (the group goal is to ensure that all members do better this week than they did last week).

2. **Structure positive reward interdependence by providing group rewards.** Bonus points may be added to all members' academic scores when everyone in the group achieves up to criterion. Or bonus points may be given to each member when the total of all group members' scores is above a preset criterion of excellence.

Positive interdependence creates peer encouragement and support for learning. Such positive peer pressure influences underachieving students to become academically involved. Members of cooperative learning groups should give two interrelated messages, "Do your work--we're counting on you!" and "How can I help you to do better?"

Structuring Individual Accountability

One of the purposes of a cooperative group is to make each member a stronger individual in his or her own right. This is usually accomplished by maximizing the learning of each member. A group is not truly cooperative if members are "slackers" who let others do all the work. To ensure that all members learn, and that groups know which members to provide with encouragement and help, instructors need to assess frequently the level of performance of each group member. Observing the participation patterns of each group member, giving practice tests, randomly selecting members to explain answers, having members edit each other's work, having students teach what they know to someone else, and having students use what they have learned on a different problem are ways to structure individual accountability.

Structuring Intergroup Cooperation

The positive outcomes found within a cooperative learning group can be extended throughout a whole class by structuring intergroup cooperation. Bonus points may be given if all members of a class reach a preset criteria of excellence. When a group finishes its work, the instructor should encourage the members to find other groups who are finished and compare and explain answers and strategies.

Specifying Desired Behaviors

The word **cooperation** has many different connotations and uses. Instructors will need to define cooperation operationally by specifying the behaviors that are appropriate and desirable within the learning groups. There are beginning behaviors, such as "stay with your group and do not wander around the room," "use quiet voices," "take turns," and "use each other's names." When groups begin to function effectively, expected behaviors may include:

1. Having each member explain how to get the answer.

2. Asking each member to relate what is being learned to previous learnings.

3. Checking to make sure everyone in the group understands the material and agrees with the answers.

4. Encouraging everyone to participate.

5. Listening accurately to what other group members are saying.

6. Not changing your mind unless you are logically persuaded (majority rule does not promote learning).

7. Criticizing ideas, not people.

Instructors should not make the list of expected behaviors too long. One or two behaviors to emphasize for a few lessons is enough. Students need to know what behavior is appropriate and desirable within a cooperative learning group, but they should not be subjected to information overload.

Monitoring And Intervening

Monitoring Students' Behavior

The instructor's job begins in earnest when the cooperative learning groups start working. Resist that urge to go get a cup of coffee or grade some papers. Much of your time in cooperative learning situations should be spent observing group members in order to (a) obtain a "window" into students' minds to see what they do and do not understand and (b) see what problems they are having in working together cooperatively. Through working cooperatively students will make hidden thinking processes overt and subject to observation and commentary. You will be able to observe how students are constructing their understanding of the assigned material. A variety of observation instruments and procedures that can be used for these purposes can be found in Johnson and F. Johnson (1991) and in Johnson, Johnson, and Holubec (1991a, 1991b).

Providing Task Assistance

In monitoring the groups as they work, instructors will wish to clarify instructions, review important procedures and strategies for completing the assignment, answer questions, and teach task skills as necessary. In discussing the concepts and information to be learned, instructors will wish to use the language or terms relevant to the learning. Instead of saying, "Yes, that is right," instructors will wish to say something more specific to the assignment, such as, "Yes, that is one way to find the main idea of a paragraph." The use of the more specific statement reinforces the desired learning and promotes positive transfer by helping the students associate a term with their learning. One way to intervene is to interview a cooperative learning group by asking them (a) What are you doing?, (b) Why are you doing it?, and (c) How will it help you?

Intervening to Teach Social Skills

While monitoring the learning groups instructors will also find students who do not have the necessary social skills and groups where problems in cooperating have arisen. **In these cases the instructor will wish to intervene to suggest more effective procedures for working together and more effective behaviors for students to engage in.** Instructors may also wish to intervene and reinforce particularly effective and skillful behaviors that they notice. The social skills required for productive group work, along with activities that may be used in teaching them, are covered in Johnson and F. Johnson (1991) and Johnson (1990, 1991).

Instructors should not intervene any more than is absolutely necessary in the groups. Most of us as instructors are geared to jumping in and solving problems for students to get them back on track. With a little patience we would find that cooperative groups can often work their way through their own problems (task and maintenance) and acquire not only a solution, but also a method of solving similar problems in the future. Choosing when to intervene and when not to is part of the art of teaching. Even when intervening, instructors can turn the problem back to the group to solve. Many instructors intervene in a group by having members set aside their task, pointing out the problem, and asking the group to create three possible solutions and decide which solution they are going to try first.

Evaluating Learning And Processing Interaction

Providing Closure to the Lesson

At the end of the lesson students should be able to summarize what they have learned and to understand where they will use it in future lessons. Instructors may wish to summarize the major points in the lesson, ask students to recall ideas or give samples, and answer any final questions students have.

Evaluating the Quality and Quantity of Students' Learning

Tests should be given and papers and presentations should be graded. The learning of group members must be evaluated by a criterion-referenced system for cooperative learning to be successful.

Processing How Well the Group Functioned

An old observational rule is, **if you observe, you must process your observations with the group.** Even if class time is limited, some time should be spent in **small group processing** as members discuss how effectively they worked together and what could be improved. Instructors may also wish to spend some time in **whole-class processing** where they give the class feedback and have students share incidents that occurred in their groups.

Discussing group functioning is essential. A common teaching error is to provide too brief a time for students to process the quality of their cooperation. Students do not learn from experiences that they do not reflect on. If the learning groups are to function better tomorrow than they did today, members must receive feedback, reflect on how their actions may be more effective, and plan how to be even more skillful during the next group session.

Cooperative Learning Structures

Any assignment in any subject area may be structured cooperatively. The instructor decides on the objectives of the lesson, makes a number of preinstructional decisions about the size of the group and the materials required to conduct the lesson, explains to students the task and the cooperative goal structure, monitors the groups as they work, intervenes when it is necessary, and then evaluates student learning and ensures groups process how effectively they are functioning.

One of the things we have been told many times by instructors who have mastered the use of cooperative learning is, "Don't say it is easy!" We know it's not. It can take years to become an expert. There is a lot of pressure to teach like everyone else, to have students learn alone, and not let students look at each other's papers. Students will not be accustomed to working together and are likely to have a competitive orientation. You may wish to start small by taking one topic or one class and use cooperative learning until you feel comfortable, and then expand into other topics or classes. In order to implement cooperative learning successfully, you will need to teach students the interpersonal and small group skills required to collaborate, structure and orchestrate intellectual inquiry within learning groups, and form collaborative relations with others. **Implementing cooperative learning in your classroom is not easy, but it is worth the effort.** The following ways in which formal cooperative learning groups may be structured within college classrooms may prove helpful.

Problem Solving Lesson

TASK: Solve the problem(s) correctly.

COOPERATIVE: One set of answers from the group, everyone has to agree, everyone has to be able to explain the strategies used to solve each problem.

EXPECTED CRITERIA FOR SUCCESS: Everyone must be able to explain the strategies used to solve each problem.

INDIVIDUAL ACCOUNTABILITY: One member from your group will be randomly chosen to explain (a) the answer and (b) how to solve each problem. Alternatively, use the simultaneous responding procedure of having each group member explain the group's answers to a member of another group.

EXPECTED BEHAVIORS: Active participating, checking, encouraging, and elaborating by all members.

INTERGROUP COOPERATION: Whenever it is helpful, check procedures, answers, and strategies with another group.

Math 3310

Geology 3216

Jigsaw Procedure

When you have information you need to communicate to students, an alternative to lecturing is a procedure for structuring cooperative learning groups called **jigsaw** (Aronson, 1978).

Task: Think of a reading assignment you will give in the near future. Divide the assignment in three parts. Plan how you will use the jigsaw procedure. Script out exactly what you will say to your class in using each part of the jigsaw procedure.

Procedure: One way to structure positive interdependence among group members is to use the jigsaw method of creating resource interdependence. The steps for structuring a "jigsaw" lesson are:

1. **Cooperative Groups**: Distribute a set of materials to each group. The set needs to be divisible into the number of members of the group (2, 3, or 4 parts). Give each member one part of the set of materials.

2. **Preparation Pairs**: Assign students the cooperative task of meeting with someone else in the class who is a member of another learning group and who has the same section of the material and complete two tasks:

   a. Learning and becoming an expert on their material.

   b. Planning how to teach the material to the other members of their groups.

3. **Practice Pairs**: Assign students the cooperative task of meeting with someone else in the class who is a member of another learning group and who has learned the same material and share ideas as to how the material may best be taught. These "practice pairs" review what each plans to teach their group and how. The best ideas of both are incorporated into each's presentation.

4. **Cooperative Groups**: Assign students the cooperative tasks of:

   a. Teaching their area of expertise to the other group members.

   b. Learning the material being taught by the other members.

5. **Evaluation**: Assess students' degree of mastery of all the material. Reward the groups whose members all reach the preset criterion of excellence.

Peer Editing: Cooperative Learning In Composition

Whenever you assign a paper or composition to be written by students, cooperative learning groups should be used. Whenever we give an assignment that requires students to write a paper, for example, we ask them to hand in a paper revised on the basis of two reviews by members of their cooperative learning group. In other words, we use a process writing procedure requiring a cooperative group.

Task: Write a composition.

Cooperative: All group members must verify that each member's composition is perfect according to the criteria set by the teacher. One of their scores for the composition will be the total number of errors made by the pair (the number of errors in their composition plus the number of errors in their partner's composition). An individual score on the quality of the composition may also be given.

Procedure:

1. The teacher assigns students to pairs with at least one good reader in each pair. The task of writing individual compositions is given.

2. Student A describes to Student B what he or she is planning to write. Student B listens carefully, probes with a set of questions, and outlines Student A's composition. The written outline is given to Student A.

3. This procedure is reversed with Student B describing what he or she is going to write and Student A listening and completing an outline of Student B's composition, which is then given to Student B.

4. The students research individualistically the material they need to write their compositions, keeping an eye out for material useful to their partner.

5. The two students work together to write the first paragraph of each composition to ensure that they both have a clear start on their compositions.

6. The students write their compositions individualistically.

7. When completed, the students proofread each other's compositions, making corrections in capitalization, punctuation, spelling, language usage, topic sentence usage, and other aspects of writing specified by the teacher. Suggestions for revision are also encouraged.

8. The students revise their compositions, making all of the suggested revisions.

9. The two students then reread each other's compositions and sign their names (indicating that they guarantee that no errors exist in the composition).

While the students work, the teacher monitors the pairs, intervening where appropriate to help students master the needed writing and cooperative skills. When the composition is completed, the students discuss how effectively they worked together (listing the specific actions they engaged in to help each other), plan what behaviors they are going to emphasize in the next writing pair, and thank each other for the help and assistance received.

Criteria For Success: A well-written composition by each student. Depending on the instructional objectives, the compositions may be evaluated for grammar, punctuation, organization, content, or other criteria set by the teacher.

Individual Accountability: Each student writes his or her own composition.

Expected Behaviors: Explaining and listening.

Intergroup Cooperation: Whenever it is helpful to do so, check procedures with another group.

Drill-Review Pairs

This procedure was developed for math classes. Any class in which drill-review is required, however, may use this procedure.

Task: Correctly solve the assigned problems.

Cooperative: The mutual goal is to ensure that both pair members understand the strategies and procedures required to solve the problems correctly. Two roles are assigned: **explainer** (explains step-by-step how to solve the problem) and **accuracy checker** (verifies that the explanation is accurate, encourages, and provides coaching if needed). The two roles are rotated after each problem.

Procedure: Assign students to pairs. Assign each pair to a foursome. Implement the following procedure:

1. Person A reads the problem and explains step-by-step the procedures and strategies required to solve it. Person B checks the accuracy of the solution and provides encouragement and coaching if it is needed.

2. Person B solves the second problem, describing step-by-step the procedures and strategies required to solve it. Person A checks the accuracy of the solution and provides encouragement and coaching if it is needed.

3. When two problems are completed, the pair checks their answers with another pair. If they do not agree, they resolve the problem until there is consensus about the answer. If they do agree, they thank each other and continue work in their pairs.

4. The procedure continues until all problems are completed.

Individual Accountability: One member will be picked randomly to explain how to solve a randomly selected problem.

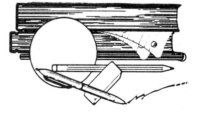

Checking Homework

One repetitive activity within math classes is checking students' homework. Such responsibilities may be turned over to cooperative learning groups through the use of the following procedure. Once planned, the procedure should be used daily until the students automatically perform the procedure in a quick and orderly way.

Subject Area: Any

Grade Level: Any

Instructional Objectives: The **academic** objective is to ensure that all class members have completed the homework and understand how to do it. The **social skills** objective is to increase students' ability to check the accuracy of the groupmate's explanation of how to solve the math problems.

Lesson Summary: Go through the answers one-by-one and ensure that everyone agrees. If there is disagreement, discuss until consensus is reached and all members understand how to answer the question correctly. The group should concentrate on parts of the assignments where members were confused and did not understand. Ensure that all members understand how to do each problem assigned. For any problem on which the group members do not agree on the answer, the page number and paragraph of the textbook where the procedure for solving the problem is explained must be identified.

Procedure: Quickly discuss each problem. One member (the explainer) explains how to solve the problem and the other members (accuracy checkers) check the explanation for accuracy. The roles are rotated so that each member does an equal amount of explaining.

If there is disagreement as to how part of the assignment is completed correctly, discuss until consensus is reached. The group should concentrate on parts of the assignments where members were confused and did not understand. For any part of the assignment on which the group members do not agree, the page number and paragraph of the textbook where the procedure for completing the assignment is explained must be identified.

When the homework has been verified, the group places members' homework in the group folder and places it on the teacher's desk.

Materials: A group folder, current homework from each student, and textbook (one per student).

Time Required: 10 minutes when students learn and master the procedure.

Preinstructional Decisions

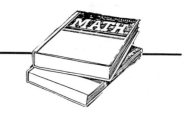

Group Size: Four

Assignment To Groups: Stratified Random. One high achieving student and one low achieving student in each group.

Roles:

Runner: Goes to the teacher's desk, picks up the group's folder, and hands out any materials in the folder to the appropriate members. The runner also records how much of the assignment each member completed.

Explainer: Explains step-by-step how to solve the problem. The role of explainer is rotated around the group. The other three members are accuracy checkers while one explains.

Accuracy checker: Verifies that the explanation is accurate.

Encourager of participation: Recognizes the hard work and the quality of the explanations of each group member.

Explaining Task and Cooperation

Students enter the classroom and meet in their cooperative learning groups. The groups should be heterogeneous in terms of math and reading ability. One member (the **runner**) goes to the teacher's desk, picks up the group's folder, and hands out any materials in the folder to the appropriate members. Once the homework is all checked, the runner puts the members' homework in the group folder and replaces it on the teacher's desk.

The **tasks** are to (a) check to see that each member has completed the homework and (b) go through the answers one-by-one and ensure that everyone agrees (if there is disagreement, discuss until consensus is reached and all members understand how to answer the question correctly). The group should concentrate on parts of the assignments where members were confused and did not understand. Ensure that all members understand how to do each problem assigned. For any problem on which the group members do not agree on the answer, the page number and paragraph of the textbook where the procedure for solving the problem is explained must be identified.

The **cooperative goal** is for all members to have completed the homework correctly and understand how to do the assignment. The runner records how much of the assignment each member completed. Then each problem is quickly discussed. One member explains how to solve the problem and the other members check the explanation for accuracy. The roles are rotated so that each member does an equal amount of explaining.

Individual accountability is implemented through regular examinations and daily randomly selecting group members to explain how to solve randomly selected problems from the homework.

The **criteria for success** are for all group members to complete correctly the homework and understand how to solve each assigned problem.
The **expected behaviors** are the participation of all members, encouragement of each other's participation, and checking to ensure that all members understand the homework.

Intergroup cooperation is encouraged. When your group finishes, find another group to help until all class members understand how to do the homework.

Monitoring and Intervening

Monitoring: While the students are working, watch to see how easily they are solving the problems and how well they are working together. Occasionally, ask a student to explain one of the answers already agreed on and recorded to emphasize the fact that all group members need to be able to explain the answers. Often, turn students' questions back to the group to solve, or ask students to check with a neighboring group.

Intervening: When a group is obviously struggling, watch for a moment, then intervene. Point out the problem and ask the group what can be done about it. This establishes the teacher's role as one of consultant rather than answer giver.

Evaluating and Processing

Evaluating: Randomly pick homework papers from each group and evaluate to ensure that the work has been done correctly.

Processing: Have students turn to their partner and list three things they did to help each other learn and one thing they could do to be even better tomorrow.

Closure: Inform students that the time is up. The runner should return the group's folder to the teacher's desk. The teacher then begins today's lesson.

Preparing For A Test

Whenever a test is given, cooperative learning groups can serve as bookends by preparing members to take the test and providing a setting in which students review the test. Two of the purposes of testing are to evaluate how much each student knows and assess what he or she needs to review. Using the following procedure will result in achieving both purposes **and** students learning the material they did not understand before the test. It also prevents post-test arguments with students over which answer is correct.

Instructors give students (a) study questions on which the examination will be based and (b) class time to prepare for the examination. Students meet in a cooperative group of four and work to understand how to answer correctly each study question.

Subject Area: Any

Grade Level: Any

Instructional Objectives: Prepare students to take a test.

Time Required: 10 - 20 minutes

Lesson Summary: Students meet in their cooperative groups. Teacher gives each group (a) study questions on which the examination will be based and (b) class time to prepare for the examination. Students discuss each study question and come to consensus about its answer. They ensure that all group members understand how to answer the question correctly. For any question for which there is disagreement among group members about how to derive the answer, the page number and paragraph on which the procedures required to attain the answer must be found. After the review time is over, the teacher gives the exam. Each student takes it individually.

Pre-Instructional Decisions

Group Size: Three

Assignment to Groups: Random to ensure heterogeneity in terms of math and reading ability.

Roles: Explainer and accuracy checker. While one group member explains how to answer a question, the other two listen carefully and check for accuracy. The roles are rotated after each question.

Materials: Copy of study questions for each group.

Explaining Task And Cooperation

Instructional Task: Understand how to answer correctly each study question.

Positive Interdependence: One answer from the group, everyone must agree, and everyone must be able to explain how to answer each question correctly. All group members must know and understand the material on which they will be tested.

If all group members score over 90 percent correct on the test, each will receive five bonus points.

Criteria For Success: Each group member understands the material on which they are to be tested.

Expected Behaviors: Roles of explainer and accuracy checker. The roles are rotated after each question.

Monitoring And Processing

Monitoring: While the students are working, watch to see how easily they are solving the problems and how well they are working together. Occasionally, ask a student to explain one of the answers already agreed on and recorded to emphasize the fact that all group members need to be able to explain the answers. Often, turn students' questions back to the group to solve, or ask students to check with a neighboring group.

Intervening: When a group is obviously struggling, watch for a moment, then intervene. Point out the problem and ask the group what can be done about it. This establishes the teacher's role as one of consultant rather than answer giver.

Processing: At the end of the lesson, have groups list three things they did to help each other learn and one thing they could do to be even better tomorrow.

Individual Test Followed By Group Test

Subject Area: Any

Grade Level: Any

Materials: Two answer sheets and one copy of the test for each student.

Instructional Objectives: To evaluate how much each student knows and to assess what students need to review.

Time Required: 50 minutes

Lesson Summary: Cooperative groups work together to complete their assignments all week. On Friday, an examination is given. The test is given first individually for a grade. Students make two copies of their answers. One answer sheet they hand in to the teacher (who then scores the answers). One answer sheet they keep. After all members have finished the test, the group meets to take the test again. The test is then regiven to a cooperative group for understanding.

Preinstructional Decisions

Group Size: Four

Assignment To Groups: Random to ensure heterogeneity in terms of reading and math ability.

Explaining Task And Goal Structures

Individual Test: An examination is given individually for a grade. The **individual goal** is to answer each question correctly. Students make two copies of their answers. One answer sheet they hand in to the teacher (who then scores the answers). One answer sheet they keep. After all members have finished the test, it is given again in cooperative groups.

Group Test: The test is regiven in cooperative groups to ensure that all students understand how to answer each question correctly.

The next class period, the teacher randomly assigns students to groups of four. Each group is divided into two pairs. Each pair takes the test, conferring on the answer to each question. The **task** is to correctly answer each question. The **cooperative goal** is to have one answer for each question that both agree upon and both can explain. Group members cannot proceed until they agree on the answer.

The groups of four meet. Their **task** is to answer each question correctly. Their **cooperative goal** is for all group members to understand the material covered by the test. Group members confer on each question. On any question to which the two pairs have different answers, they find the page number and paragraph in the textbook where the procedures required to solve the problem are explained. Each group is responsible for ensuring that all members understand the material they missed on the test. If necessary, group members assign review homework to each other.

Individual Accountability: Teacher observes the groups to ensure that they are following the procedure.

Criteria for Success: All students understand the material covered by the test. If all members of a group score 90 percent or better on the individual test, each receives 5 bonus points. These bonus points are added to their individual scores to determine their individual grade for the test.

Expected Behaviors: The expected behaviors include active participation by all members, helping, and explaining. A variety of roles may be used, including problem restater, strategy suggester, approximator, checker, and accuracy coach.

Intergroup Cooperation: If there is any question that the group cannot answer and cannot find the page and paragraph in the text where the answer is explained, the group should ask other groups for help.

Monitoring And Processing

Monitoring: While the students are working, watch to see how easily they are solving the problems and how well they are working together. Occasionally, ask a student to explain one of the answers already agreed on and recorded to emphasize the fact that all group members need to be able to explain the answers. Often, turn students' questions back to the group to solve, or ask students to check with a neighboring group.

Intervening: When a group is obviously struggling, watch for a moment, then intervene. Point out the problem and ask the group what can be done about it. This establishes the teacher's role as one of consultant rather than answer giver.

Processing: At the end of the lesson, have groups list three things they did to help each other learn and one thing they could do to be even better tomorrow.

Classroom Presentations

When students are required to give class presentations assign them to cooperative groups and require each group to prepare and conduct a group presentation.

Task: Prepare and present an informative and interesting presentation.

Cooperation: The **cooperative goal** is for all members to learn the material being presented and gain experience in making presentations. The **reward interdependence** may be either a group grade for the presentation **or** each student may be graded on their part of the presentation and bonus points given if all members participate in an integrated (rather than sequential) way.

Procedure:

1. Assign students to groups of four, give each group a topic, require them to prepare one presentation that all will participate in. The presentation should be given within a certain time frame and should be supported with visuals and/or active participation by students.

2. Give students time to prepare and to rehearse. All group members should be able to give the presentation.

3. Divide the class into four groups and place them in separate corners of the classroom. Have each group member make the presentation to one-fourth of the class simultaneously. In this way, all group members demonstrate their mastery of the topic and are individually accountable for learning the assigned material.

4. Systematically observe all presentations. Evaluate the presentations on the basis of whether or not it was (a) scholarly and informative, (b) interesting, concise, easy to follow, (c) involving (audience active, not passive), and (d) intriguing (audience interested in finding out more on their own). In addition, add points if all members contributed, and if their contributions were integrated not sequential.

5. Have presentation groups process how well they worked together as a group.

Individual Accountability: All members must make a presentation to a subgroup of the class.

Criteria for Success: All students make a presentation that meets the criteria listed above.

Expected Behaviors: The expected behaviors include presenting and explaining.

Intergroup Cooperation: If there are any questions about the assignment or procedures ask other groups for help.

Johnson, Johnson, & Smith

Laboratory Groups

One of the most common ways to involve students actively in the learning situation is the use of laboratory or experimental groups where students use the scientific method to conduct an inquiry. Instructors direct and supervise students working in pairs, triads, or fours to investigate, prove, and formulate hypotheses. In the **old paradigm**, labs were demonstrations of a theory or concept that followed lectures. The rule was, "Teach them the basic science, teach them the applied science, then give a practicum." Students were often told what to do and what their findings should be.

In the **new paradigm**, labs are introductory activities that build direct experiences in which to understand the procedures, concepts, and theories being studied. The rule is, "Give them a problem, coach their problem solving, have them present their solutions, and give the relevant theory."

Task: To conduct an inquiry using the scientific method.

Cooperation: The **cooperative goal** is for each group to complete the project. Members sign the project to indicate that they have contributed their share of the work, agree with its content, and can present/explain it. When a variety of materials are used (such as microscopes, slides, samples), each group member may be given the responsibility for one of the materials. If appropriate, assign each student a specific role.

Procedure:

1. Students are assigned an initial problem to solve and are placed in cooperative learning groups to do so. The required materials such as microscopes are given to each group.

2. The group solves the problem and prepares a preliminary written report.

3. The instructor presents the relevant algorithm, procedure, concept, or theory required to solve the problem.

4. Students are given a more complex problem that requires them to apply the algorithm, procedure, theory, or concept they have just learned. The instructor systematically observes the groups and provides coaching where it is needed.

5. Students are given an even more complex problem in which they have to go beyond the algorithm, procedure, concept, or theory in order to solve it. The instructor systematically observes the groups and provides coaching where it is needed.

6. Each group writes a report on their solution and hands the report in to the instructor.

7. The instructor pairs each group member with a member of another group. Each presents their group's solution to the other.

8. The groups process how well they worked together.

Individual Accountability:

1. Have each group member present his or her group's report to a member of another group.

2. Observe the groups to verify that all members are actively participating.

3. Give an individual test on the content covered by the problems.

Criteria for Success: Defensible solution to each problem that all members can explain.

Expected Behaviors: All students participate actively in solving the problems and explain their group's solutions to a member of another group.

Intergroup Cooperation: If there are any questions about the assignment or procedures ask other groups for help.

Cooperative Reading Pairs

Donald Dansereau (1987) defines **cooperative reading** as an activity which "typically involves two or more students working together to improve their understanding and retention of text material." Dansereau (1985) calls his strategy for cooperative reading MURDER and states it is effective for college students learning procedural, technical, and narrative text while working in cooperative dyads. The roles of recaller and listener/facilitator are given to each student interacting as equal partners. The steps in MURDER are for the instructor to set the **mood** to study (creating a supportive environment) and for the students to read for **understanding** (marking important and difficult ideas); **recall** the material without referring to the text; correct recall and amplify and store it so as to **digest** the assigned material; **expand** knowledge by self-inquiry; and finally, **review** mistakes (learning from tests).

Conclusions

At this point you know what cooperative learning is and how it is different from competitive and individualistic learning. You know that there are three types of cooperative learning groups--formal cooperative learning groups, informal cooperative learning groups, and cooperative base groups. You know that **the essence of cooperative learning is positive interdependence** where students recognize that "we are in this together, sink or swim." Other essential components include individual accountability (where every student is accountable for both learning the assigned material and helping other group members learn), face-to-face interaction among students within which students promote each other's success, students appropriately using interpersonal and group skills, and students processing how effectively their learning group has functioned. These five essential components of cooperation form the conceptual basis for constructing cooperative procedures. You know that the research supports the propositions that cooperation results in greater effort to achieve, more positive interpersonal relationships, and greater psychological health and self-esteem than do competitive or individualistic efforts. You know the instructor's role in implementing formal cooperative learning. What is covered in the next chapter is the instructor's role in implementing informal cooperative learning groups.

The Teacher's Role in Cooperation

Make Decisions

Specify Academic and Collaborative Objectives. What academic and/or collaborative skills do you want students to learn or practice in their groups? Start with something easy.

Decide on Group Size. Students often lack collaborative skills, so start with groups of two or three students; later advance cautiously to fours.

Assign Students to Groups. Heterogeneous groups are the most powerful, so mix abilities, sexes, cultural backgrounds, and task orientations. Assign students to groups randomly or select groups yourself.

Arrange the Room. The closer the students are to each other, the better they can communicate. Group members should be "knee to knee and eye to eye."

Plan Materials. Materials can send a "sink or swim together" message to students if you give only one paper to the group or give each member part of the material to learn and then teach the group.

Assign Roles. Students are more likely to work together if each one has a job which contributes to the task. You can assign work roles such as Reader, Recorder, Calculator, Checker,Reporter, and Materials Handler or skill roles such as Encourager of Participation, Praiser, and Checker for Understanding.

Set the Lesson

Explain the Academic Task. Prepare students by teaching them any material they need to know, then make certain they clearly understand what they are to do in the groups. This might include explaining lesson objectives, defining concepts, explaining procedures, giving examples, and asking questions.

*Structure Positive Interdependence. Students must feel that they need each other to complete the group's task, that they "sink or swim together." Some ways to create this are by establishing mutual goals (students must learn the material and make certain group members learn the material), joint rewards (if all group members achieve above a certain percentage on the test, each will receive bonus points), shared materials and information, and assigned roles.

*Structure Individual Accountability. Each student must feel responsible for learning the material and helping the group. Some ways to ensure this feeling include frequent oral quizzing of group members picked at random, giving individual tests, having everyone in the group write (pick one paper at random to grade), or having students do work first to bring to the group.

Structure Intergroup Cooperation. Having groups check with and help other groups and giving rewards or praise when all class members do well can extend the benefits of cooperation to the whole class.

Explain the Criteria for Success. Student work should be evaluated on a criteria-referenced rather than a norm-referenced basis. Make clear your criteria for evaluating the groups' work.

Specify Expected Behaviors. The more specific you are about the behaviors you want to see in the groups, the more likely students will do them. Make it clear that you expect to see everyone contributing, helping, listening with care to others, encouraging others to participate, and asking for help or clarification. Younger students may need to be told to stay with their group, take turns, share, ask group members questions, and use quiet voices.

*Teach Collaborative Skills. After students are used to working in groups, pick one collaborative skill they need to learn, point out the need for it, define it carefully, have students give you phrases they can say when using the skill, post the phrases (praise, bonus points, stars), and observe for and encourage the use of the skill until students are doing it automatically. Then teach a second skill. Consider praising, summarizing, encouraging, checking for understanding, asking for help, or generating further answers.

Monitor and Intervene

*Arrange Face-to-Face Interaction. The beneficial educational outcomes of cooperative learning groups are due to the interaction patterns and verbal exchanges that take place among students. Make certain there is oral summarizing, giving and receiving explanations, and elaborating going on.

Monitor Students' Behavior. This is the fun part! While students are working, you circulate to see whether they understand the assignment and the material, give immediate feedback and reinforcement, and praise good use of group skills.

Provide Task Assistance. If students are having trouble with the task, you can clarify, reteach, or elaborate on what they need to know.

Intervene to Teach Collaborative Skills. If students are having trouble with group interactions, you can suggest more effective procedures for working together or more effective behaviors for them to engage in. You can ask students to figure out how to work more effectively together. If students are learning or practicing a skill, record on an observation sheet how often you hear that skill, then share your observations with the groups.

Evaluate and Process

Evaluate Student Learning. Assess how well students completed the task and give them feedback.

*Process Group Functioning. In order to improve, students need time and procedures for analyzing how well their group is functioning and how well they are using collaborative skills. Processing can be done by individuals, small groups, or the whole class. To start, have groups routinely list three things they did well in working together today and one thing they will do better tomorrow. Then summarize as a whole class.

Provide Closure. To reinforce student learning you may wish to have groups share answers or paper, summarize major points in the lesson, or review important facts.

COOPERATIVE LESSON WORKSHEET

Grade Level: _____   Subject Area: _____

Step 1.   Select a lesson: _____

_____

Step 2.   Make Decisions.

    a. Group size: _____

    b. Assignment to groups: _____

_____

    c. Room arrangement: _____

_____

    d. Materials needed for each group:

_____

_____

    e. Assigning roles: _____

_____

_____

Step 3.   Set the Lesson. State, in language your students understand:

    a. Task: _____

_____

    b. Positive interdependence: _____

_____

_____

    c. Individual accountability: _____

_____

    d. Criteria for success: _____

_____

    e. Specific behaviors expected: _____

_____

Step 4. Monitor and Process

    a. Evidence of expected behaviors (appropriate actions):

    _____

    _____

    b. Observation form: _____

       Observer(s): _____

    c. Plans for processing (feedback): _____

    _____

Step 5. Evaluate Outcomes

    a. Task achievement: _____

    _____

    b. Group functioning: _____

    _____

    c. Notes on individuals: _____

    _____

    d. Suggestions for next time: _____

    _____

    _____

    _____

    _____

    _____

Informal Cooperative Learning

The Lure Of Lecturing

Our survey of teaching methods suggests that...if we want students to become more effective in meaningful learning and thinking, they need to spend more time in active, meaningful learning and thinking--not just sitting and passively receiving information.

McKeachie (1986)

No logic or wisdom or will-power could prevail to stop the sailors. Buffeted by the hardships of life at sea, the voices came out of the mist to the ancient Greek sailors like a mystical, ethereal love song with tempting and seductive promises of ecstasy and delight. The voices and the song were irresistible. The mariners helplessly turned their ships to follow the Sirens' call with scarcely a second thought. Lured to their destruction, the sailors crashed their ships on the waiting rocks and drowned in the tossing waves, struggling with their last breath to reach the source of that beckoning song.

Centuries later, the Sirens still call. Professors seem drawn to lecturing, crashing their teaching on the rocks due to the seductive and tempting attractions of explicating knowledge to an adoring audience and teaching as they were taught. The old paradigm has an irresistible call to many faculty. The new paradigm may seem idealistic but undoable. Cooperative learning provides an alternative to the "empty vessel" model of the teaching and learning process and encourages the development of student talent by proving a very carefully structured approach to getting students actively involved in constructing their own knowledge. Getting students cognitively, physically, emotionally, and psychologically involved in learning is an important step in turning around the passive and impersonal character of many college classrooms.

What Is Lecturing?

Introduction

The obstacles to learning from a lecture were (again) made painfully aware to us recently. This was during a workshop for students and faculty in Norway. While conducting a workshop on cooperative learning for faculty and students at the Norwegian Institute of Technology, Karl was convinced that a short lecture (given in the informal cooperative learning format) on the latest research on learning would be very useful and effective. He asked a focus question at the start, lectured for about 12 minutes, and asked the participants to prepare a summary of the main points and to formulate at least one question. When he finished the short lecture, and asked for a summary, people didn't know what to write. One student jokingly said, "Karl, what did you say between 'Here's the research' and 'Your task is to create a summary?'" He got a big laugh, but when we took a break, several of the faculty came to him and said, "I didn't know what you were talking about. The concepts were somewhat new to me, you were enthusiastic and spoke slowly and clearly, but I really didn't understand what you were talking about."

After the break, Karl apologized to the workshop participants for wasting their time. It was painful since he thought he had given an excellent lecture. A couple of faculty came to his defense. They said, "Well, you know, it was a pretty good lecture. It was just kind of new to us." But then a student in the back said, "I understood a little at the beginning, but a lot of lectures are like this for me." And a student in the front said (with emphasis), "This is what it's like for me every day."

The look on the faces of those faculty! If only a photograph could have been taken. For the first time in a long time, we think they understood what it's like to be a student out there, trying to make sense out of these lectures, and not understanding, and being frustrated with not understanding. Perhaps Karl should have followed Wilbert McKeachie's advice on lecturing: "I lecture only when I'm convinced it will do more good than harm."

In this chapter we shall discuss the lure of lecturing and define what it is. The problems and enemies of lecturing will be detailed. The use of informal cooperative learning groups to make students cognitively active during lectures will then be described.

Definition

A **lecture** is an extended presentation in which the instructor presents factual information in an organized and logically sequenced way. It typically results in long periods of uninterrupted teacher-centered, expository discourse that relegates students to the role of passive "spectators" in the college classroom. Normally, lecturing includes the use of reference notes, an occasional use of visuals to enhance the information being presented, and responding to students' questions as the lecture progresses or at its end. Occasionally, students are provided with handouts to help them follow the lecture. The lecturer presents the material to be learned in more or less final form, gives answers, presents principles, and elaborates the entire content of what is to be learned.

Lecturing is currently the most common teacher behavior in colleges and universities, as well as secondary and elementary schools. Lecturing is particularly popular in the teaching of large introductory sections of courses in a wide variety of disciplines (e.g., psychology, chemistry, mathematics). Even in training programs within business and industry, lecturing dominates. Some of the reasons why lecturing is so popular are that it can be adapted to different audiences and time frames and it keeps the professor at the center of all communication and attention in the classroom.

The rationale for and the pedagogy of lecturing are based on (a) theories of the structure and organization of knowledge, (b) the psychology of meaningful verbal learning, and (c) ideas from cognitive psychology associated with the representation and acquisition of knowledge. Jerome Bruner (1960) emphasized that knowledge structures exist and become a means for organizing information about topics, dividing information into various categories, and showing relationships among various categories of information. David Ausubel (1963) emphasized that meaning emerges from new information only if it is tied into existing cognitive structures and, therefore, instructors should organize information for students, present it in clear and precise ways, and anchor it into cognitive structures formed from prior learning. Ellen Gagne (1985) emphasized that (a) declarative knowledge is represented in interrelated propositions or unifying ideas, (b) existing cognitive structures must be cued so that students bring them from long-term memory into working memory, and (c) students must process new knowledge by coding it and then storing it in their long-term memory.

Appropriate Use

The correct question is not, "Is lecturing better or worse than other alternative teaching methods?" but "For what purposes is the lecture method appropriate?" There has been considerable research on lecturing. From the research directly evaluating lecturing (see reviews by Bligh, 1972; Costin, 1972; Eble, 1983; McKeachie, 1967; Verner & Dickinson, 1967) it may be concluded that lecturing is appropriate when the purpose is to:

1. **Disseminate information:** Lecturing is appropriate when faculty wish to communicate a large amount of material to many students in a short period of time, when faculty may wish to supplement curriculum materials that need updating or elaborating, the material has to be organized and presented in a particular way, or when faculty want to provide an introduction to an area.

2. **Present material that is not available elsewhere:** Lecturing is appropriate when information is not available in a readily accessible source, the information is original, or the information might be too complex and difficult for students to learn on their own.

3. **Expose students to content in a brief time that might take them much longer to locate on their own.** Lecturing is appropriate when faculty need to teach information that must be integrated from many sources and students do not have the time, resources, or skills to do so.

4. **Arouse students' interest in the subject.** When a lecture is presented by a highly authoritative person and/or in a skillful way with lots of humor and examples, students may be intrigued and want to find out more about the subject. Skillful delivery of a lecture includes maintaining eye contact, avoiding distracting behaviors, modulating voice pitch and volume, and using appropriate gestures. Achievement is higher when presentations are clear (Good & Grouws, 1977; Smith & Land, 1981), delivered with enthusiasm (Armento, 1977), and delivered with appropriate gestures and movements (Rosenshine, 1968).

5. **Teach students who are primarily auditory learners.**

Parts Of A Lecture

A lecture has three parts: the introduction, the body, and the conclusion. Proponents of lecturing advise instructors, "Tell them what you are going to tell them; then tell them; then tell them what you told them." First you describe the learning objectives in a way that alerts students to what is to be covered in the lecture. You then present the material to be learned in small steps organized logically and sequenced in ways that are easy to follow. You end with an integrative review of the main points. More specifically, during the **introduction** you will want to:

1. Arouse students' interest by indicating the relevance of the lecture to their goals.

2. Provide motivational cues, such as telling students that the material to be covered is important, useful, difficult, and will be included on a test.

3. Make the objectives of the lecture clear and explicit and set expectations as to what will be included.

4. Use advance organizers by telling students in advance how the lecture is organized. **Advance organizers** are concepts given to the student prior to the material actually to be learned that provide a stable cognitive structure in which the new knowledge can be subsumed (Ausubel, 1963). The use of advance organizers may be helpful when (1) the students have no relevant information to which they can relate the new learning and (2) when relevant cognitive structures are present but are not likely to be recognized as relevant by the learner. Advance organizers provide students with general learning sets that help cue them to key ideas and organize these ideas in relationship to one another. Announce the topic as a title, summarize the major points to be made in the lecture, and define the terms they might not know. Give them a cognitive structure to fit the material being presented into. This will improve their comprehension of the material, make it meaningful to them, and improve their ability to recall and apply what they hear.

5. Prompt awareness of students' relevant knowledge by asking questions about knowledge or experience related to the topic. Give and ask for examples. Ask questions to show how the students' prior knowledge relates to the material covered in the lecture. Explicitly relate students' prior knowledge to the topic of the lecture.

During the **body** of the lecture, you will want to cover the content while providing a logical organization for the material being presented. There are a variety of ways of organizing the body of a lecture (see Bligh, 1972 for examples). What is important is that the body have a logical organization that is explicitly communicated to students.

Conclude by summarizing the major points, asking students to recall ideas or give examples, and answering any questions.

Despite the popularity of lecturing, there are (a) obstacles to and (b) problems associated with its use.

Problems With Lecturing

Much of the research on lecturing has compared lecturing with group discussion. While the conditions under which lecturing is more successful than group discussion have **not** been identified, a number of problems with lecturing have been found.

The first problem with lectures is that students' attention to what the instructor is saying decreases as the lecture proceeds. Research in the 1960s by D. H. Lloyd, at the University of Reading in Berkshire, England found that student attending during lectures followed the pattern of five minutes of settling in, five minutes of readily assimilating material, confusion and boredom with assimilation falling off rapidly and remaining low for the bulk of the lecture, and some revival of attention at the end of the lecture (Penner, 1984). The concentration during lectures of medical students, who presumably are highly motivated, rose sharply and peaked 10 to 15 minutes after the lecture began, and then fell steadily thereafter (Stuart & Rutherford, 1978). J. McLeish in a research study in the 1960s analyzed the percentage of content contained in student notes at different time intervals through the lecture (reported in Penner, 1984). He found that students wrote notes on 41 percent of the content presented during the first fifteen minutes, 25 percent presented in a thirty-minute time period, and only 20 percent of what had been presented during forty-five minutes.

The second problem with lecturing is that it takes an educated, intelligent person oriented toward auditory learning to benefit from listening to lectures. Verner and Cooley (1967) found that in general, very little of a lecture can be recalled except in the case of listeners with above average education and intelligence. Even under optimal conditions, when intelligent, motivated people listen to a brilliant scholar talk about an interesting topic there can be serious problems with a lecture. Verner and Dickinson (1967, p. 90) give this example:

...ten percent of the audience displayed signs of inattention within fifteen minutes. After eighteen minutes one-third of the audience and ten percent of the platform guests were fidgeting. At thirty-five minutes everyone was inattentive; at forty-five minutes, trance was more noticeable than fidgeting; and at forty-seven minutes some were asleep and at least one was reading. A causal check twenty-four hours later revealed that the audience recalled only insignificant details, and these were generally wrong.

The third problem with lecturing is that it tends to promote only lower-level learning of factual information. Bligh (1972), after an extensive series of studies, concluded that while lecturing was as (but not more) effective as reading or other methods in transmitting information, lecturing was clearly less effective in promoting thinking or in changing attitudes. A survey of 58 studies conducted between the years of 1928 and 1967 comparing various characteristics of lectures versus discussions, found that lectures and discussions did not differ significantly on lower-level learning (such as learning facts and principles), but discussion appeared superior in developing higher-level problem- solving capabilities and positive attitudes toward the course (Costin, 1972). McKeachie and Kulik (1975) separated studies on lecturing according to whether they focused on factual learning, higher-level reasoning, attitudes, or motivation. They found lecture to be superior to discussion for promoting factual learning, but discussion was found to be superior to lecture for promoting higher-level reasoning, positive attitudes, and motivation to learn. Lecturing at best tends to focus on the lower-level of cognition and learning. When the material is complex, detailed, or abstract; when students need to analyze, synthesize, or integrate the knowledge being studied; or when long-term retention is desired, lecturing is not such a good idea. Formal cooperative learning groups should be used to accomplish goals such as these.

Fourth, there are problems with lecturing as it is based on the assumptions that all students need the same information, presented orally, presented at the same pace, without dialogue with the presenter, and in an impersonal way. While students have different levels of knowledge about the subject being presented, the same information is presented to all. The material covered in a lecture may often be communicated just as well in a text assignment or a handout. Lectures can waste student time by telling them things that they could read for themselves. While students learn and comprehend at different paces, a lecture proceeds at the lecturer's pace. While students who listen carefully and cognitively process the information presented will have questions that need to be answered, lectures typically are one-way communication situations and the large number of classmates inhibit questioning asking. If students cannot ask questions, misconceptions, incorrect under-standing, and gaps in understanding cannot be identified and corrected. Stones (1970), for example, surveyed over 1,000 college students and found that 60 percent stated that the presence of a large number of classmates would deter them from asking questions, even if the instructor encouraged them to do so. Lecturing by its very nature impersonalizes learning. There is research indicating that personalized learning experiences have more impact on achievement and motivation.

The fifth problem with lecturing is that students tend not to like it. Costin's (1972) review of literature indicates that students like the course and subject area better when they learn in discussion groups than when they learn by listening to lectures. This is important in introductory courses where disciplines often attempt to attract majors.

Finally, there are problems with lecturing as it is based on a series of assumptions about the cognitive capabilities and strategies of students. When you lecture you assume that all students learn auditorially, have high working memory capacity, have all the required prior knowledge, have good notetaking strategies and skills, and are not susceptible to information processing overload.

Besides the identified problems of lecturing, there are obstacles to making lectures effective.

Enemies Of The Lecture

There are a number of obstacles that interfere with the effectiveness of a lecture. We call these obstacles the enemies of the lecture. They are as follows.

1. **Preoccupation with what happened during the previous hour or with what happened on the way to class.** In order for lectures to succeed faculty must take students' attention away from events in the hallway or campus and focus student attention on the subject area and topic being dealt with in class.

2. **Emotional moods that block learning and cognitive processing of information.** Students who are angry or frustrated about something are **not** open to new learning. In order for lectures to work, faculty must set a constructive learning mood. Humor helps.

3. **Disinterest by students who go to sleep or who turn on a tape recorder while they write letters or read comic books.** In order for lectures to work, faculty must focus student attention on the material being presented and ensure that they cognitively process the information and integrate it into what they already know.

4. Failure to understand the material being presented in the lecture. Students can learn material incorrectly and incompletely because of lack of understanding. In order to make lectures work there has to be some means of checking the accuracy and completeness of students' understanding of the material being presented.

5. Feelings of isolation and alienation and beliefs that no one cares about them as persons or about their academic progress. In order to make lectures work students have to believe that there are other people in the class who will provide help and assistance because they care about the students as people and about the quality of their learning.

6. Entertaining and clear lectures that misrepresent the complexity of the material being presented. While entertaining and impressing students is nice, it often does not help students understand and think critically about complex material. To make lectures work students must think critically and use higher-level reasoning in cognitively processing course content. One of our colleagues is a magnificent lecturer. His explanation of the simplex algorithm for solving linear programming problems is so clear and straightforward that the students go away with the view that it is very simple. Later when they try to solve a problem on their own, they find that they don't have a clue as to how to begin. Our colleague used to blame himself for not explaining well enough. Sometimes he blamed the students. Now he puts small cooperative groups to work on a simple linear programming problem, circulates and checks the progress of each student, provides help where he feels it is appropriate, and only gives his brilliant lectures when the students understand the problem and are ready to hear his proposed solution. Both he and the students are much happier with their increased understanding.

After considering these problems and barriers, it may be concluded that alternative teaching strategies have to be interwoven with lecturing if the lecture method is to be effective. While lecturing and direct teaching have traditionally been conducted within competitive and individualistic structures, lectures can be made cooperative. Perhaps the major procedure to interweave with lecturing is informal cooperative learning groups.

Informal Cooperative Learning Groups

In order for lecturing to be successful, and to overcome the obstacles to effective lecturing, students must become active cognitively. In what traditionally has been a passive learning environment for students created by lecturing, instructors must activate the learner through cooperative interaction with peers.

Informal cooperative learning groups are temporary, ad hoc groups that last for only one discussion or one class period. Their **purposes** are to focus student attention on the material to be learned, set a mood conducive to learning, help organize in advance the material to be covered in a class session, ensure that students cognitively process the material being taught, and provide closure to an instructional session. Informal cooperative learning groups also ensure that misconceptions, incorrect understanding, and gaps in understanding are identified and corrected, and learning experiences are personalized. They may be used at any time, but are especially useful during a lecture or direct teaching.

During lecturing and direct teaching the instructional challenge for the teacher is to ensure that students do the intellectual work of organizing material, explaining it, summarizing it, and integrating it into existing conceptual networks. This may be achieved by having students do the advance organizing, cognitively process what they are learning, and provide closure to the lesson. Breaking up lectures with short cooperative processing times will give you slightly less lecture time, but will help counter what is proclaimed as the main problem of lectures: "The information passes from the notes of the professor to the notes of the student without passing through the mind of either one."

Lecturing With Informal Cooperative Learning Groups

The following procedure will help you plan a lecture that keeps students more actively engaged intellectually. It entails having **focused discussions** before and after the lecture (i.e., bookends) and interspersing **pair discussions** throughout the lecture. Two important aspects of using informal cooperative learning groups are to (a) make the task and the instructions explicit and precise and (b) require the groups to produce a specific product (such as a written answer). The procedure is as follows.

1. **Introductory Focused Discussion**: Assign students to pairs. The person nearest them will do. You may wish to require different seating arrangements each class period so that students will meet and interact with a number of other students in the class. Then give the pairs the cooperative assignment of completing the initial (advance organizer) task. Give them only four or five minutes to do so. The discussion task is aimed at promoting **advance organizing** of what the students know about the topic to be presented and **establishing expectations** about what the lecture will cover.

2. **Lecture Segment One:** Deliver the first segment of the lecture. This segment should last from 10 to 15 minutes. This is about the length of time an adult can concentrate on a lecture.

3. **Pair Discussion 1**: Give the students a discussion task focused on the material you have just presented that may be completed within three or four minutes. Its purpose is to ensure that students are actively thinking about the material being presented. The discussion task may be to (a) give an answer to a question posed by the instructor, (b) give a reaction to the theory, concepts, or information being presented, or (c) elaborate (relate material to past learning so that it gets integrated into existing conceptual frameworks) the material being presented. Discussion pairs respond to the task in the following way:

   a. Each student **formulates** his or her answer.

   b. Students **share** their answer with their partner.

   c. Students **listen** carefully to partner's answer.

   d. Pairs **create** a new answer that is superior to each member's initial formulation through the process of association, building on each other's thoughts, and synthesizing.

   Randomly choose two or three students to give 30 second summaries of their discussions. **It is important that students are randomly called on to share their answers after each discussion task.** Such **individual accountability** ensures that the pairs take the tasks seriously and check each other to ensure that both are prepared to answer.

4. **Lecture Segment 2:** Deliver the second segment of the lecture.

5. **Pair Discussion 2:** Give a discussion task focused on the second part of the lecture.

6. Repeat this sequence of lecture segment and pair discussion until the lecture is completed.

7. **Closure Focused Discussion**: Give an ending discussion task to summarize what students have learned from the lecture. Students should have four or five minutes to summarize and discuss the material covered in the lecture. The discussion should result in students integrating what they have just learned into existing conceptual frameworks. The task may also point students toward what the homework will cover or what will be presented in the next class session. This provides closure to the lecture.

Process the procedure with students regularly to help them increase their skill and speed in completing short discussion tasks. Processing questions may include (a) how well prepared were you to complete the discussion tasks and (b) how could you come even better prepared tomorrow?

The informal cooperative learning group is not only effective for getting students actively involved in understanding what they are learning, it also provides time for you to gather your wits, reorganize your notes, take a deep breath, and move around the class listening to what students are saying. Listening to student discussions can give you direction and insight into how well the concepts you are teaching are being grasped by your students (who, unfortunately, may not have graduate degrees in the topic you are presenting).

In the following sections more specific procedures for the initial focused discussion, the intermittent pair discussions, and the closure focused discussion will be given.

Introductory Focused Discussion

At the beginning of a class session students may be required to meet in a permanent base group or in ad-hoc informal cooperative discussion pairs or triads to (a) review their homework and (b) establish expectations about what the class session will focus on. Three ways of structuring such informal cooperative learning groups are discussion pairs, peer critiques of advanced preparation papers and question-and-answer pairs.

Introductory
Focussed Discussion Pairs

To prepare for the class session students may be required to complete a short initial focused discussion task. Plan your lecture around a series of questions that the lecture answers. Prepare the questions on an overhead transparency or write them on the board so that students can see them.

Task: Answer the questions.

Cooperative: Create a joint answer to each question within a pair through the following sequence:

1. Each student **formulates** his or her answer.

2. Students **share** their answer with their partner.

3. Students **listen** carefully to partner's answer.

4. Pairs **create** a new answer that is superior to each member's initial formulation through the process of association, building on each other's thoughts, and synthesizing.

The discussion is aimed at promoting advance organizing of what the students know about the topic to be presented and to set expectations as to what the lecture will cover.

Expected Criteria For Success: Each student must be able to explain the answer.

Individual Accountability: One member from the pair will be randomly chosen to explain the answer. Periodically use the simultaneous explaining procedure of having each group member explain the group's answers to a member of another group.

Expected Behaviors: Explaining, listening, synthesizing by all members.

Intergroup Cooperation: Whenever it is helpful, check procedures, answers, and strategies with another group.

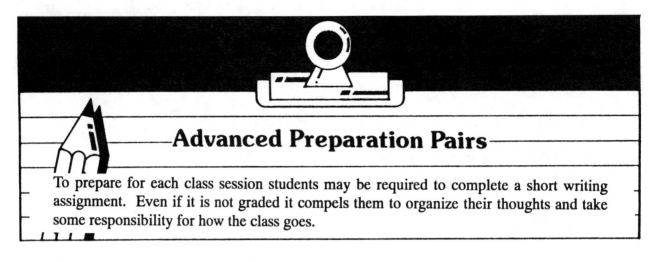

Advanced Preparation Pairs

To prepare for each class session students may be required to complete a short writing assignment. Even if it is not graded it compels them to organize their thoughts and take some responsibility for how the class goes.

Task: Write a short paper on an aspect of the assigned readings to prepare for class. Before each class session students:

1. Choose a major theory, concept, research study, or theorist/researcher discussed in the assigned reading.

2. Students write a two-page analysis of it:

   a. Summarizing the relevant assigned reading.

   b. Adding material from another source (research article or book) to enrich their analysis of the theory, concept, research study, or theorist/researcher.

Cooperative: Students bring four copies of the paper to the class. The members of their base group or discussion pair will read, edit, and criticize the paper. The criteria they will use to do so include the following. Does each paper have a(n):

1. Introductory paragraph that outlines the content of the paper.

2. Clear conceptual definition of concepts and terms.

3. Summary of and judgment about what is known empirically. (R = Substantial Research Support, r = some research support).

4. Description of and judgment about theoretical significance. (T = Substantial Theoretical Significant, t = some theoretical significance)

5. Description of and judgment about practical significance. (P = Substantial Practical Significance, p = some practical significance)

6. Brief description of relevant research study that should be conducted.

7. New information beyond what is contained in the assigned readings.

Expected Criteria For Success: Each student writes a paper and edits groupmates' papers.

Individual Accountability: Each student writes a paper and signs each paper he or she edits. If each group member uses a different color ink pen the quality of their editing is easily apparent. Periodically use the simultaneous explaining procedure of having each group member explain their papers to a member of another group.

Expected Behaviors: Critically evaluating the papers of groupmates.

Intergroup Cooperation: Whenever it is helpful, check editing procedures and strategies with another group.

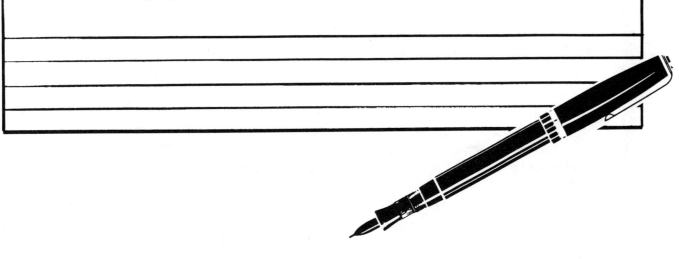

Question-and-Answer Pairs

Task: Answer questions on the homework.

Cooperative: Question-and-answer pairs alternate asking and answering questions on the assigned reading:

1. To prepare for the discussion, students read an assignment and write questions dealing with the major points raised in the assigned reading or other related materials.

2. At the beginning of each class, students are randomly assigned to pairs, and one person (Student A) is chosen randomly to ask their first question.

3. Their partner (Student B) gives an answer. Student A can correct B's answer or give additional information.

4. Student B now asks the first member a question and the process is repeated.

5. During this time, the instructor goes from dyad to dyad, giving feedback and asking and answering questions.

A similar procedure was promoted by Marcel Goldschmid of the Swiss Federal Institute of Technology in Lausanne (Goldschmid, 1971). A variation on this procedure is the **jigsaw**, in which each student reads or prepares different materials. Each member of the group then teaches the material to the other member and vice versa.

Expected Criteria For Success: Each student writes a paper and edits groupmates papers.

Individual Accountability: Each student writes out a set of questions on the assignment and must answer his or her partner's questions. The instructor observes to ensure that each student arrived with a set of questions and gives reasonable answers to his or her partner's questions.

Expected Behaviors: Ask and answer questions, giving good explanations.

Intergroup Cooperation: Whenever it is helpful, check answers, procedures, and strategies with another group.

Progress Checks

Students can be given a progress check (similar to a quiz but not graded). **A progress check** consists of questions (multiple choice, short answer, essay) testing students' knowledge of the assigned reading. Similar to the test procedures described in Chapter 4, students (a) individually complete the progress check (b) retake the progress check and compare answers with a partner from their base group and, if time permits, (c) retake the progress check in the whole base group to broaden the discussion of each question. On any question that the students do not agree on, students should identify the page number and paragraph in the text where the correct answer may be found.

Intermittent Discussion Pairs

Whole-class discussions rarely involve many students. Barnes (1980) found in an observational study of instructor-student interaction that when instructors attempted to solicit student participation through whole-class questioning, students responded only 50 percent of the time. When faculty do manage to obtain student participation, a very small minority of students tends to dominate. Karp and Yoels (1987) documented that in classes of less than 40 students, four to five students accounted for 75 percent of all interactions and, in classes with more than 40 students, two to three students accounted for over half of the exchanges. In his survey of over 1,000 college students, Stones (1970) found that 60 percent stated that the presence of a large number of classmates would deter them from asking questions, even if the instructor encouraged them to do so.

Students often say, "I understood it at the time, but I do not remember it now." Experimental research on human memory (Kappel & Underwood, 1962; Waugh & Norman, 1965) indicates that two types of memory interference build up to cause forgetting during long periods of uninterrupted information processing such as an hour-long lecture. The two types are **retroactive interference** which occurs when the information processed toward the end of the lecture interferes with the retention of the information processed at the beginning of the lecture and **proactive interference** when the information processed at the beginning of the lecture interferes with retention of information processes at the end of the lecture. The rehearsal of information soon after it has been received or processed results in greater retention of that information (Atkinson & Shiffrin, 1971; Broadbent, 1970). This is due to the fact that the rate of human forgetting is sharpest immediately after the information is received. If the information is rehearsed orally soon after its reception, however, the brain has an opportunity to consolidate or lock in the memory trace and offset the rapid rate of forgetting that normally follows just- processed information. By interspersing pair discussions throughout the lecture such long periods of uninterrupted listening and information-processing can be avoided thus minimizing retroactive and proactive interference. Students' retention of lecture information would thereby be enhanced. In addition, pair discussions provide the opportunity for students to receive from classmates frequent and immediate feedback regarding their performance. Such frequent and immediate feedback serves to increase students' motivation to learn (Mackworth, 1970).

There is evidence that college students do their best in courses that include frequent checkpoints of what they know, especially when the checkpoints occur in small cooperative groups. Ruhl, Hughes, and Schloss (1987) conducted a study on the use of cooperative discussion pairs in combination with lecturing. The study was conducted in separate courses over two semesters. In the two experimental classes the instructor paused for two minutes three times during each of five lectures. The intervals of lecturing between the two-minute pauses ranged from 12 to 18 minutes. During the pauses there was no instructor-student interaction. The students worked in pairs to discuss and rework the notes they took during the lecture. Two types of tests were given--immediate free-recall tests given at the end of each lecture (students were given three minutes to write down everything they could remember from the lecture) and a sixty-five item multiple-choice test measuring long-term retention (administered twelve days after the final lecture). A control group received the same lectures without the pauses and were tested in the same manner. In both courses, students who engaged in the pair discussions achieved significantly higher on the free-recall quizzes and the comprehensive retention test than did the students who did not engage in the pair discussions. The eight-point difference in the means between the experimental and control groups was large enough to make a difference of up to two letter grades, depending on the cutoff points.

During the lecture the instructor stops every ten to fifteen minutes and gives students a short discussion task that students can complete in three or four minutes. Such a use of informal cooperative learning groups ensures that students are actively thinking about the material being presented. The discussion task may be to (a) give an answer to a question posed by the instructor, (b) give a reaction to the theory, concepts, or information being presented, or (c) elaborate (relate material to past learning so that it gets integrated into existing conceptual frameworks) on the material being presented. This can be done through a variety of types of pairing.

Requesting Active Responses

There are a number of other active-response strategies that may be used as part of lectures. They include asking students to indicate their answer or opinion by "raise your hand," "thumbs up or thumbs down" or "clap once if you agree."

Simultaneous Explanation Pairs

When a teacher asks a class "Who knows the answer?" and one student is chosen to respond, that student has an opportunity to clarify and extend what he or she knows through explaining. In this situation only one student is involved and active. The rest of the class is passive. A teacher may ensure that all students are active by using a procedure that requires all students to explain their answers simultaneously. When each student has to explain his or her answer and reasoning to a classmate, all students are active and involved. No one is allowed to be passive. There are two basic ways of structuring simultaneous explaining: (a) the individual student formulates an answer and then explains to a classmate or (b) a small group formulates an answer and each member explains their group's answer and reasoning to a member of another group.

Task: Each student is to explain his or her answers and reasoning to a classmate.

Cooperative: Create a joint answer within a pair through the following sequence:
1. Each student **formulates** his or her answer.
2. Students **share** their answer with their partner.
3. Students **listen** carefully to partner's answer.
4. Pairs **create** a new answer that is superior to each member's initial formulation through the process of association, building on each other's thoughts, and synthesizing.

Expected Criteria For Success: Each student must be able to explain the answer.

Individual Accountability: One member from the pair will be randomly chosen to explain the answer. Periodically use the simultaneous explaining procedure of having each group member explain the group's answers to a member of another group.

Expected Behaviors: Explaining, listening, synthesizing by all members.

Intergroup Cooperation: Whenever it is helpful, check procedures, answers, and strategies with another group.

There needs to be a quick turnaround of what is being learned. Knowledge must be communicated to another person as soon as possible after it is learned.

Cooperative Note-Taking Pairs

The notes students take during a lecture are of great importance in understanding what a student learns. In fact, most of the research on lecturing has focused on the value of notetaking, distinguishing between the encoding function of notes and the storage function of notes (Anderson & Armbruster, 1986). There is support for both the encoding (i.e., notetaking assists learning from lectures) and storage (i.e., review of notes is helpful) functions of notetaking. Taking notes during lectures has been shown to be more effective than listening (Kiewra, 1989), but using the notes for review is more important than the mere fact of taking notes (Kiewra, 1985b).

Students often take notes very incompletely (Hartley & Marshall, 1974; Kiewra, 1985a). There are several reasons why notes may be incomplete:

1. Students with low working memory capacity have difficulty taking notes during lectures, possibly because of difficulties in keeping information available in memory while writing it down (Kiewra & Benton, 1988).

2. The information processing load of a student in a lecture is increased when the student has little prior knowledge of the information (White & Tisher, 1986). When the lecturer uses visual aids frequently a student may become overloaded from the pressure to take notes from visual presentations in addition to the verbal statements.

3. Students who are unskilled in notetaking may take incomplete notes.

4. Students may have a false sense of familiarity with the material presented and, therefore, not bother taking notes.

To improve learning from lectures, students may focus on increasing the quantity and quality of the notes they take and/or improving their methods of reviewing the notes they have taken. Research on improving the quantity and quality of notes taken by students during lectures has often focused on the stimulus characteristics of the lecture itself (e.g, pace of the lecture, use of advance organizers) or on the characteristics of the lecturer (White & Tisher, 1986).

Task: For students to focus on increasing the quantity and quality of the notes they take and/or improving their methods of reviewing the notes they have taken.

Cooperative: Two students work together with the common goal of mastering the information being presented.

Procedure: After exposure to a lecture segment, one partner summarizes his or her notes to the other, who in turn adds and corrects. Students may ask each other, "What have you got in your notes so far?" "What are the three key points made by the instructor?" "What was the most surprising thing the instructor said?" The **rule** is that each member must take something from the other's notes to improve his or her own.

Individual Accountability: The notes of a student may be randomly chosen to be examined by the instructor.

Criteria For Success: Complete and accurate notes that have been orally reviewed by each student.

Expected Behaviors: Explaining, listening, synthesizing by all group members.

Intergroup Cooperation: Whenever it is helpful, check procedures, answers, and strategies with another group.

Cooperative notetaking pairs are a tool for structuring active cognitive processing by students during lectures and reducing the information processing load of students. Among other things, it allows for a quick turnaround of what is being learned. Knowledge must be communicated to another person as soon as possible after it is learned if it is to be retained and fully understood. The cooperative note-taking pair procedure results in:

1. The students immediately rehearsing and more deeply processing the information. Appropriate encoding of information in long-term memory requires rehearsal, reorganization, or elaboration of the information. A typical student rarely has the opportunity to rehearse the information from a lecture while that information is still fresh in his or her mind.

2. Students making multiple passes through the material, cognitively processing the information they are learning, and explicitly using metacognitive strategies.

When students are provided with the instructor's lecture notes for review, performance is improved (e.g., Masqud, 1980).

Read-and-Explain Pairs

Whenever reading material is given to students, it may be read in cooperative pairs more effectively than by individuals.

Task: Establish the meaning of each paragraph and then integrate the meaning of the paragraphs into the meaning of the assigned material as a whole.

Cooperative: Both members become experts on the assigned material. Students are to agree on the meaning of each paragraph, formulate one summary, and be able to explain the meaning of their answer.

Procedure:
1. Both persons silently read the first paragraph. Person A summarizes the content to Person B.
2. They identify the question being asked in the paragraph.
3. They agree on a summary of the paragraph that answers the question.
4. They relate the meaning of the paragraph to previous learning.
5. They move on to the next paragraph and repeat the procedure.

Expected Criteria For Success: Everyone must be able to explain the meaning of the assigned material correctly.

Individual Accountability: One group member will be randomly chosen to explain the meaning of a paragraph.

Expected Behaviors: Active participating, checking, encouraging, and elaborating by all members.

Intergroup Cooperation: Whenever it is helpful, check procedures, answers, and strategies with another group. When you are finished, compare your answers with those of another group and discuss.

Concept Induction

Concepts may be taught inductively as well as deductively. Concept formation may be done inductively by instructing students to figure out why the examples have been placed in the different boxes.

Tasks: Analyze the examples the teacher places in each box. Identify the concept represented by each box. Then create new examples that may be placed in the boxes.

Cooperative: Students turn to the person next to them and create an answer they can agree on.

Procedure:
1. Draw two (or three) boxes on the chalkboard. Label them Box 1, Box 2, or Box 3.
2. Place one item in each box.
3. Instruct students to use the **formulate, explain, listen, create** procedure to discuss how the items are different.
4. Place another item in each box and repeat. Tell students not to say outloud to another group or the class how the items are different. Each pair must discover it.
5. Once a pair "has it," the members are to make a definition for each box. They then create new examples that may be placed in the boxes.

The procedure for students is:
1. **Formulate** an individual answer.
2. **Share** their answer with their partner.
3. **Listen** carefully to their partner's answer.
4. **Create** a new answer that is superior to their initial formulations through the processes of association, building on each other's thoughts, and synthesizing.

Expected Criteria For Success: Each student must be able to identify the concept represented by each box.

Individual Accountability: One member from the pair will be randomly chosen to explain the answer.

Expected Behaviors: Explaining, listening, synthesizing by all members.

Closure Focussed Discussion

After the lecture has ended, students should work in small discussion groups to reconstruct the lecture conceptually. Menges (1988) states that a number of research studies conducted in the 1920's document students' forgetting curve for lecture material. The average student had immediate recall of 62 percent of the material presented in the lecture, but that recall declined to 45 percent after three to four days, and fell to 24 percent after 8 weeks. If students were asked to take an examination immediately after the lecture (systematically reviewing what they had just learned), however, they retained almost twice as much information after 8 weeks, both in terms of factual information and conceptual material. There is every reason to believe that other types of systematic reviews, such as focused discussions and writing assignments, will have similar effects on the retention of the material being lectured on. At the end of the lecture have students discuss the content presented.

Task: Summarize what has been learned from the lecture and answer questions posed by the instructor that point towards the homework and future class topics.

Cooperative: One set of answers from the pair, both members have to agree, and both members have to be able to explain their answers.

Procedure: The instructor gives an ending discussion task to summarize what students have learned from the lecture. Students should have four or five minutes to summarize and discuss the material covered in the lecture. The discussion should result in students integrating what they have just learned into existing conceptual frameworks. The task may also point students toward what the homework will cover or what will be presented in the next class session. This provides closure to the lecture. The pairs of students may be asked to list:

1. What are the five most important things you learned?

2. What are two questions you wish to ask?

The instructor collects the answers and records them to support the importance of the procedure and to see what students have learned. Handing the papers back periodically with brief comments from the instructor on them helps reinforce this procedure for students.

Individual Accountability: One group member will be randomly selected to explain the group's answers.

Expected Behaviors: Explaining, listening, synthesizing by all members.

Intergroup Cooperation: Whenever it is helpful, check procedures, answers, and strategies with another group. When you are finished, compare your answers with those of another group and discuss.

Closure Cooperative Writing Pairs

Faculty benefit from asking students to write a "one-minute paper" at the end of each teaching session describing the "major point you learned today" and "the main unanswered question you still have" (Light, 1990). This helps students to focus on the central themes of the course. In writing their papers, students should first write an introductory paragraph that outlines the content of the lecture, clear conceptual definitions of concepts and terms presented, a summary of and judgment about the information presented, a description of and judgment about theoretical significance of the information presented, a description of and judgment about practical significance, and anything the student knows beyond what was covered in the lecture.

Closure Note-Taking Pairs

Closure note-taking pairs are similar to the cooperative note- taking pairs used intermittently during the lecture. Students review and complete their lecture notes, reflecting on the lecture, and writing the major concepts and pertinent information presented. More specifically, two students work together with the common goal of mastering the information being presented. After the lecture, one partner summarizes his or her notes to the other, who in turn adds and corrects. Students may ask each other, "What have you got in your notes?" "What are the three key points made by the instructor?" "What was the most surprising thing the instructor said today?"

Implementation Assignment

Task: For students to make a specific contract with their base group as to how they will apply what they have learned.

Cooperative: Each group member must commit him- or herself to the group to apply what they have learned. The group becomes the keeper of the contract.

Procedure: At the end of the class session each member plans how to apply what they have learned. This implementation assignment functions as a learning contract with the base group. Each member discusses with the group and then writes down three specific answers to the questions:

1. What have I learned?

2. How will I use it?

In planning how to implement what they have learned, it is important for students to be as specific as possible about implementation plans and to keep a careful record of their implementation efforts.

Individual Accountability: Each group member may be randomly selected by the instructor to explain his or her implementation plans and results.

Expected Behaviors: Explaining, listening, summarizing by all members.

Other Informal Cooperative Learning Groups

Book-Ends For Films Or Demonstrations

A **demonstration** is the modeling of skills or procedures. Use informal cooperative learning groups whenever you are giving a demonstration, showing a film, or having a guest speaker. Informal cooperative learning groups are very useful in setting an anticipatory set for the demonstration before it begins and processing what was learned from the demonstration afterwards.

Peer Feedback Groups

Students like courses that offer frequent opportunities to revise and improve their work as they go along. They learn best when they have a chance to submit an early version of their work, get detailed feedback and criticism, and then hand in a final version for a grade. While this can most easily be done with writing assignments, quizzes, tests, brief papers, and oral examinations will also work.

Cooperative Study Groups

The Harvard Assessment Seminars (Light, 1990) compared the grades of students who studied alone with those of students who studied in groups of four to six. Invariably, the students who studied in small groups did better than students who studied alone. The students in small study groups spoke more often, asked more questions, and were generally more engaged than those in the larger groups. Some class time may be allocated to form and organize study groups.

Conclusions

Do you want to be a sage on the stage or a guide on the side? The sage talks without interruption. The guide has students do the talking. When direct teaching procedures such as lecturing are being used, **informal cooperative learning groups** can be used to focus student attention on the material to be learned, set a mood conducive to learning, help set expectations as to what will be covered in a class session, ensure that students cognitively process the material being taught, keep students' attention focused on the content, ensure that misconceptions, incorrect understanding, and gaps in understanding are corrected, provide an opportunity for discussion and elaboration which promote retention and transfer, make learning experiences personal and immediate, and provide closure to an instructional session. Students can summarize in three-to-five minute discussions what they know about a topic before and after a lecture. Short five minute discussions in cooperative pairs can be interspersed throughout a lecture. In this way the main problem of lectures can be countered: "The information passes from the notes of the professor to the notes of the student without passing through the mind of either one."

Besides the use of formal and informal cooperative learning groups, there is a need for a permanent base group that provides relatively long-term relationships among students. It is to this use of cooperative learning that we now turn.

Informal Cooperative Learning Planning Form

Description of the Lecture

1. **Lecture Topic:**_____

2. **Objectives** (Major Understandings Students Need To Have At The End Of The Lecture):

   a._____

   b._____

3. **Time Needed:**_____

4. **Method For Assigning Students To Pairs Or Triads:**_____

5. **Method Of Changing Partners Quickly:**_____

6. **Materials** (such as transparencies listing the questions to be discussed and describing the **formulate, share, listen, create** procedure):_____
   _____

Advanced Organizer Question(s)

Questions should be aimed at promoting **advance organizing** of what the students about the topic to be presented and **establishing expectations** as to what the lecture will cover.

1.

2.

3.

4.

Cognitive Rehearsal Questions

List the specific questions to be asked every 10 or 15 minutes to ensure that participants understand and process the information being presented. Instruct students to use the **formulate, share, listen, and create** procedure.

1.

2.

3.

4.

Monitor by systmatically observing each pair. Intervene when it is necessary. Collect data for whole class processing. Students' explanations to each other provide a window into their minds that allows you to see what they do and do not understand. Monitoring also provides an opportunity for you to get the know your students better.

Summary Question(s)

Give an ending discussion task and require students to come to consensus, write down the pair or triad's answer(s), sign the paper, and hand it in. Signatures indicate that students agree with the answer, can explain it, and guarantee that their partner(s) can explain it. The questions could ask for a summary of the lecture, an elaboration or extension of the material presented, or precue a lab assignment or the next lecture.

1.

2.

Celebrate Students' Hard Work

1.

2.

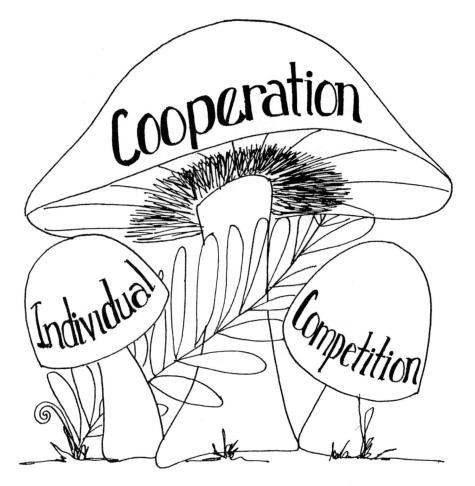

Cooperative Base Groups

Introduction

The biggest disease today is not leprosy or tuberculosis, but rather the feeling of being unwanted, uncared for, and deserted by everybody.

Mother Teresa, Nobel Peace Prize 1979

Author William Manchester wrote several years ago in Life Magazine about revisiting Sugar Loaf Hill in Okinawa, where 34 years before he had fought as a Marine. He describes how he had been wounded, sent to a hospital and, in violation of orders, escaped from the hospital to rejoin his Army unit at the front. Doing so meant almost certain death. "Why did I do it?" he wondered. The answer lies in long-term relationships in which group members depend upon and support each other.

The more social support a student has, the higher the student's achievement will tend to be, the more the student will persist on challenging tasks, the more likely students will be graduated, the healthier psychologically and physically the students will tend to be, the better able students will be to manage stress, and the more likely students will be to challenge their competencies to grow and develop (Johnson & Johnson, 1989a). The success of a college depends largely on the social support students have while they are in attendance.

Cooperative Learning And Social Support

To state quite simply what we learn in time of pestilence:...There are more things to admire in men than to despise.

Albert Camus (1947)

Like anyone else, college students can feel isolated, lonely, and depressed. Their achievements can be seen as meaningless when parents get divorced, their peers reject them, or they are victims of crime. Anyone, no matter how intelligent or creative, can have such feelings. Recently in a Minnesota school district, a popular star athlete committed suicide. Even though he was widely liked, the note he left indicated feelings of loneliness, depression, and isolation. He is not unusual. A recent national survey reported that growing feelings of worthlessness and isolation led 30 percent of America's brightest teenagers to consider suicide, and 4 percent have tried it.

We are in an epidemic of depression and anxiety among our adolescents and young adults (Seligman, 1988). And it seems to be spreading downward as more and more elementary school students are becoming depressed. The stark emptiness of the self and the vacuousness of "me" is revealed when students are faced with a personal crisis. What is denied is that personal well-being cannot exist without commitment to and responsibility for joint well-being.

A number of years ago, a speeding car carrying five teenagers slammed into a tree, killing three of them. It was not long before small, spontaneous memorials appeared at the tree. A yellow ribbon encircled its trunk. Flowers were placed nearby on the ground. There were a few goodbye signs. Such quiet testimonies send an important message: When it really matters, we are part of a community, not isolated individuals. We define ourselves in such moments as something larger than our individual selves--as friends, classmates, teammates, and neighbors.

Many students have the delusion that each person is separate and apart from all other individuals. It is easy to be concerned only with yourself. But when classmates commit suicide and when cars slam into trees killing classmates, the shock waves force us out of the shallowness of self into the comforting depth of community. An important advantage of placing students in cooperative learning groups and having them work together with a wide variety of peers to complete assignments is the sense of belonging, acceptance, and caring that results. In times of crisis, such community may mean the difference between isolated misery and deep personal talks with caring friends.

Being part of a community does not "just happen" when a student enters college. Being known, being liked and respected, and being involved in relationships that provide help and support do not magically happen when the freshman year begins. College and university life can be lonely. Many students arrive on campus without a clear support group. Students can attend class without ever talking to other students. While many students are able to develop the relationships with classmates and fellow students to provide themselves with support systems, other students are unable to do so. Colleges have to carefully structure student experiences to build a learning community. A **learning community** is characterized by two types of social support. The **first** is an academic support group that provides any needed assistance and helps students succeed academically in college. The **second** is a personal support group made up of people who care about and are personally committed to the student. Working in formal and informal cooperative groups provides an opportunity to begin long-term relationships, but for some students it is not enough. Base groups may be needed. Two years ago, for example, a student in the Social Psychology of Education gave David the following feedback. "This is my last quarter of course work for my doctorate. I have taken 120 quarter hours of courses. This is the first class in which I really got to know other students on a personal level. I got to know the members of my base group. Why didn't this happen in all my classes?"

It is important that some of the relationships built within cooperative learning groups are permanent. College has to be more than a series of temporary encounters that last for only a semester. College students should be assigned to permanent base groups to create permanent caring and committed relationships with classmates who will provide the support, help, encouragement, and assistance students need to make academic progress and develop cognitively and socially in healthy ways. In this chapter we will first define base groups and then detail how they may be used to provide a permanent support system for each student.

Base Groups: What Are They?

United we stand, divided we fall.

Watchword of the American Revolution

Aesop tells a story of a man who had four sons. The father loved them very much, but they troubled him greatly, for they were always fighting with each other. Nothing the father said stopped their quarreling. "What can I do to show my sons how wrong it is to act this way?" the father thought. One day he called his sons to him and showed them a bundle of sticks. "Which of you, my sons, can break this bundle of sticks?" he asked them. All the boys tried in turn, but not one of them could do it. Then the father untied the bundle and gave each son a single stick. "See if you can break that," he said. Of course, they could easily do it. "My sons," the father said, "each of you alone is weak. He is as easy to injure as one of these sticks. But if you will be friends and stick together, you will be as strong as the bundle of sticks."

Base groups:

1. Are heterogeneous in membership so that they represent a cross-section of the school population in terms of gender, ability, ethnic and cultural backgrounds.

2. Last for the duration of the class (a semester or year) and preferably from the freshman through the senior year. When students know that the cooperative base group will stay together until each member is graduated, they become committed to find ways to motivate and encourage their groupmates. Problems in working with each other cannot be ignored or waited out.

3. Meet regularly.

4. Personalize the work required and the learning experiences.

The two purposes of the base groups are for members to:

1. Provide each other with the support, encouragement, and assistance needed to complete assignments and make good academic progress. This includes letting absent group members know what went on in class and interacting informally every day within and between classes, discussing assignments and helping each other with homework.

2. Hold each other accountable for striving to make academic progress.

In other words, **base groups** are long-term, heterogeneous cooperative learning groups with stable membership whose primary responsibilities are to provide support, encouragement, and assistance in completing assignments and hold each other accountable for striving to learn.

There are several key ingredients in using base groups effectively. **First**, frequently use formal cooperative learning groups for instructional purposes until the five essential elements (see Chapter 2) are understood and some expertise in using cooperative learning groups is gained. **Second**, make base groups slightly larger than formal cooperative learning groups (base groups may have four or five members rather than two or three). **Third**, do not assign students to base groups the first day of class. Wait for a few days until you get to know the students somewhat and the class membership stabilizes. **Fourth**, schedule frequent meetings of base groups. **Fifth**, plan an important agenda for each meeting. The agendas for base groups can include:

1. **Academic support tasks,** such as checking to see what assignments each member has and what help they need to complete them. Members can give each other advice on how to take tests and "survive" in school. Members can prepare each other to take tests and go over the questions missed afterwards. Members can share their areas of expertise (such as art or computers) with each other. Above all, members monitor each other's academic progress and make sure all members are achieving.

2. **Routine tasks** such as taking roll or collecting homework.

3. **Personal support tasks,** such as listening sympathetically when a member has problems with parents or friends, having general discussions about life, giving each other advice about relationships, and helping each other solve nonacademic problems. Teachers may increase the likelihood of personal support by conducting trust-building exercises with the base groups, such as sharing their favorite movie, a childhood experience, a memory from high school, and so forth.

Finally, expect some base groups to have relationship problems. Not all base groups cohere right away. Be ready to help unskillful members integrate themselves into their groups. You may wish to periodically structure a base group meeting to process the relationships among members or give the group hypothetical problems to solve (such as, "What if one member of your group did 90 percent of the talking? What are three strategies to help them listen as well as contribute?"). Persistence and patience are good instructor qualities with poorly functioning base groups.

Base Group Procedures

There are two ways base groups may be used in the college level. The **first** is to have a base group in each college course. Class base groups stay together only for the duration of the course. The **second** is to organize all students within the college into base groups and have the groups function as an essential component of college life. College base groups stay together for at least a year and preferably for four years or until all members are graduated.

Class Base Groups

The larger or more impersonal the class, and the more complex the subject matter, the more important it is to have base groups. The members of base groups should exchange

Johnson, Johnson, & Smith

phone numbers and information about schedules as they may wish to meet outside of class. **The class base group functions as a support group for members that:**

1. Gives assistance, support, and encouragement for mastering the course content and skills and provides feedback on how well the content and skills are being learned.

2. Gives assistance, support, and encouragement for thinking critically about the course content, explaining precisely what one learns, engaging in intellectual controversy, getting the work done on time, and applying what is learned to one's own life.

3. Provides a set of interpersonal relationships to personalize the course and an arena for trying out the cooperative learning procedures and skills emphasized within the course.

4. Provides a structure for managing course procedures, such as homework, attendance, and evaluation.

Members of class base groups are responsible for mastering and implementing the theories, concepts, and skills emphasized in the course, to ensure that all members of their base group do likewise and, finally, to ensure that all members of the class master and appropriately implement the theories, concepts, and skills emphasized in the course. In other words, if the group is successful, members should find another group to help until all members of the class are successful. There is intergroup cooperation, not intergroup competition.

At the beginning of each session class members meet in their base groups to:

1. Congratulate each other for living through the time since the last class session and check to see that none of their group is under undue stress. The two questions to discuss are: "Are we all prepared for this class period?" and "How are you today?"

2. Check to see if members have completed their homework or need help and assistance in doing so. The questions to discuss are: "Did you do your homework?" "Is there anything you did not understand?" If there is not time to help each other during the base group meeting, an appointment is made to meet again during free time or lunch.

Periodically, the base groups may be given a checklist of academic skills and assess which ones each member needs to practice more.

3. Review what members have read and done since the last class session. Members should be able to give a brief, terse, succinct summary of what they have read, thought about, and done. They may come to class with resources they have found and want to share, or copies of work they have completed and wish to distribute to their base group members.

4. Get to know each other better and provide positive feedback by discussing such questions as: "What do you like about each other?" "What do you like about yourself?" and "What is the best thing that has happened to you this week?"

Class base groups are available to support individual group members. If a group member arrives late, or must leave early on an occasion, the group can provide information about what that student missed. Additionally, group members may assist one another in writing required papers. Assignments may be discussed in the base groups, papers may be planned, reviewed, and edited in base groups, and any questions regarding the course assignments and class sessions may be first addressed in the base group. If the group is not able to resolve the issue, it should be brought to the attention of the instructor or the teaching assistant.

All members are expected to contribute actively to the class discussion, work to maintain effective working relationships with other participants, complete all assignments, assist classmates in completing their assignments, express their ideas, not change their minds unless they are persuaded by logic or information to do so, and indicate agreement with base group's work by signing the weekly contract.

There is no way to overemphasize how important class base groups can be. In the early 1970's, for example, a graduate student in the Social Psychology of Education course suffered a psychological breakdown and was hospitalized for most of the quarter in a locked psychiatric ward of a local hospital. Two years later, she came to visit David and thank him for the course. She stated that it was the only course she had completed that very difficult year. The other members of her base group had obtained permission from her psychiatrist to visit her weekly in the hospital. They spent two hours a week with her, going over her assignments, helping her write her papers, giving her the tests, and ensuring that she completed the course. She got a "B."

College Base Groups

At the beginning of the academic year, students should be assigned to base groups. Class schedules should be arranged so that members of base groups are assigned to as many of the same classes as possible. Members will then spend much of the day together. In essence, the computer is programmed to assign base groups to classes (whenever possible) rather than individuals. Base groups should stay together for at least a year and ideally, for four years.

Some attention should be paid to building a group identity and group cohesion. The first week the base groups meet, for example, base groups can pick a name, design a flag, or choose a motto. If an instructor in the school has the proper expertise, the groups will benefit from participating in a "challenge course" involving ropes and obstacles. This type of physical challenge that the groups complete together builds cohesion quickly.

During the year, base groups meet either (a) twice each day or (b) twice a week, or some variation in between. When base groups meet twice each day, they meet first thing in the morning and last thing in the afternoon. **At the beginning of each day students meet in their base groups to:**

1. Congratulate each other for showing up with all their books and materials and check to see that none of their group is under undue stress. The two questions to discuss are: "Are we all prepared for the day?" and "How are you today?"

2. Check to see if members are keeping up with their work in their classes or need help and assistance in doing so. The questions to discuss are: "Tell us how you are doing in each of your classes?" "Is there anything you did not understand?" If there is not enough time to help each other during the base group meeting, an appointment is made to meet again during free time or lunch. Periodically, the base groups may be given a checklist of academic skills and assess which ones each member needs to practice more.

3. Review what members have read and done since the evening before. Members should be able to give a brief, terse, succinct summary of what they have read, thought about, and done. They may come to class with resources they have found and want to share, or copies of work they have completed and wish to distribute to their base group members.

4. Get to know each other better and provide positive feedback by discussing such questions as: "What do you like about each other?" "What do you like about yourself?" and "What is the best thing that has happened to you this week?"

At the end of the day members meet in their base groups to see that everyone is taking their homework home, understands the assignments to be completed, and has the help and assistance they need to do their work (during the evening students can confer on the telephone or even study together at one house). In addition, base groups may wish to discuss what members have learned during the day and check to see if all members have plans to do something fun and interesting that evening.

When base groups meet twice each week (perhaps first thing on Monday and last thing on Friday), they meet to discuss the academic progress of each member, provide help and assistance to each other, and hold each member accountable for completing assignments and progressing satisfactorily through the academic program. The **meeting on Monday morning** refocuses the students on school, provides any emotional support required after the weekend, reestablishes personal contact among base group members, and helps students set their academic goals for the week (what is still to be done on assignments that are due, and so forth). Members should carefully review each other's assignments and ensure that members have the help and assistance needed. In addition, they should hold each other accountable for committing serious effort to succeed in school. The **meeting on Friday afternoon** helps students review the week, set academic goals for the weekend (what homework has to be done before Monday), and share weekend plans and hopes.

The Advisee/Base Group

In many colleges it will seem difficult to implement base groups. One opportunity is advisor/advisee groups. Instructors may take their advisees and divide students into base groups and then plan an important agenda for them to follow during a daily or a weekly meeting.

In a college we work with all students are assigned an advisor. The instructor then meets once a week with all of his or her advisees. The meeting lasts for thirty minutes. The base groups are given four tasks:

1. A quick **self-disclosure task** such as, "What is the most exciting thing you doing over Christmas break? What is the worst thing that happened to you last weekend? What is your biggest fear? What is your favorite ice cream?"

2. An **administrative task** (such as registration for next semester) is conducted.

3. An **academic task** such as, "You have midterms coming up. As a group, write out three pieces of advice for taking tests. I will type up the suggestions from each group and hand them out next week."

4. A **closing task** such as wishing each other good luck for the day or week.

Why Use Cooperative Base Groups

Hold onto what is good
  Even if it is a handful of earth
Hold onto what you believe in
  Even if it is a tree which stands by itself
Hold onto what you must do
  Even if it is a long way from here
Hold onto life
  Even if it is easier to let go
Hold onto my hand
  Even when I have gone away from you

Pueblo Indian Poem

There are many reasons why cooperative base groups should be used in colleges. One of the major outcomes of cooperative learning is that students who "work together to get the job done" develop positive relationships with each other. The longer the group is together, the more positive and personal the relationships among members become. The caring and committed relationships built within base groups are essential for motivating long-term efforts to achieve, and for healthy social, cognitive, and physical development. The development of academically-oriented values depends on long-term caring relationships.

Need For Long-Term Permanent Relationships

Most relationships in colleges are, at best, ship-board romances. When most instructors face their classes, and when most classmates look at each other, they implicitly say, "I will know you for the duration of this course." Students know that next semester or year, they will have a different instructor and different classmates. Relationships are temporary because in most colleges it is assumed that "any classmate will do" and "any instructor will do." Classmates and instructors are perceived to be replaceable parts in the education machine. It is assumed that a student's instructors and classmates are basically irrelevant to the educational process.

It is important that some of the relationships built within college are permanent. College has to be more than a series of ship-board romances. **Receiving social support and being held accountable for appropriate behavior by peers who care about you and have a long-term commitment to your success and well-being is an important aspect of progressing through college.** It increases achievement and promotes psychological health. In permanent relationships there is increased opportunity to transmit achievement-oriented values. Learning for your caring and committed groupmates is a powerful motivator. Thus, permanent cooperative base groups may be formed to create the caring and committed relationships that improve attendance, personalize the school experience, increase achievement, and improve the quality of life within the classroom.

Meaning, Purpose, And Psychological Health

The feelings and commitment that drove William Manchester to risk his life to help protect his comrades do not automatically appear when students are placed in learning groups. There are barriers to positive interdependence. Among many current high school and college students, their own pleasures and pains, successes and failures, occupy center stage in their lives (Conger, 1988; Seligman, 1988). Each person tends to focus on gratifying his or her own ends without concern for others. Physical, psychological, and material self-indulgence has become a primary concern (Conger, 1988; National Association of Secondary School Principals, 1984). Over the past 20 years, self-interest has become more important than commitment to community, country, or God. Young adults have turned away from careers of public service to careers of self-service. Many young adults have a **delusion of individualism,** believing that (a) they are separate and apart from all other individuals and, therefore, (b) others' frustration, unhappiness, hunger, despair, and misery have no significant bearing on their own well-being. With the increase in the past two decades in adolescents' and youth's concern for personal well-being, there has been a corresponding

diminished concern for the welfare of others (particularly the less advantaged) and of society itself (Astin, Green, & Korn, 1987; Astin, Green, Korn, & Schalit, 1986). Self-orientation interferes with consideration of others' needs in that it actively prevents concern for others as equally deserving persons.

The self is a very poor site for finding meaning. Hope does not spring from competition. Meaning does not surface in individualistic efforts aimed at benefiting no one but yourself. Empowerment does not come from isolation. Purpose does not grow from egocentric focus on own material gain. Without involvement in interdependent efforts and the resulting concern for others, it is not possible to realize oneself except in the most superficial sense (Conger, 1981; Slater, 1971). Without a balance between concern for self and concern for others, concern for self leads to a banality of life and, even worse, to self- destructiveness, rootlessness, loneliness, and alienation (Conger, 1988). Individuals are empowered, are given hope and purpose, and experience meaning when they contribute to the well- being of others within an interdependent effort. Almost all people, when asked what makes their life meaningful, respond "friends, parents, siblings, spouses, lovers, children, and feeling loved and wanted by others (Klinger, 1977).

Accountability And Motivation

Education is not successful unless each student is working hard to do the best he or she can. Not everyone has a 130 IQ or complex talents. But every student can work hard to maximize his or her achievements, conceptual understanding of the material being studied, level of reasoning, and creativity. Numerous students, however, spend very little time studying, even those students who get good grades. Students often avoid hard subjects like math, science, and foreign languages and simply coast along, doing far less than they are capable of doing.

In order to increase the effort students commit to learning and achievement, they must be involved in caring and committed relationships within which they are (a) held accountable for exerting considerable effort to learn and (b) given the help, assistance, encouragement, and recognition they need to sustain their efforts to achieve. **Long-term, hard, persistent efforts to achieve come from the heart, not from the head.** When faced with the choice to watch television or do their homework, the decision may be based more on emotional than intellectual grounds. There may be no more powerful motivator than students realizing that they have to turn off the television and do their schoolwork because "their group is counting on them." Many a student who could care less what an instructor thinks will say, "I did my homework because I couldn't face my group and tell them I didn't do it. I couldn't let my group down."

Changing Students' Attitudes About Academic Work

There are many students who do not value schoolwork, do not aspire to do well in college, do not plan to take the more difficult courses, and plan to just get by. One of the responsibilities of the faculty is to change the attitudes of these students so that they value school, education, and hard work to learn. In doing so, there are several general principles, supported by research (see Johnson & F. Johnson, 1991), to guide your efforts:

1. Attitudes are changed in groups, not individual by individual. Focus your efforts on having students within small groups persuade each other to value education.

2. Attitudes are changed as a result of small group discussions that lead to public commitment to work harder in school and take education more seriously. Attitudes are rarely modified by information or preaching.

3. Messages from individuals who care about, and are committed to, the student are taken more seriously than messages from indifferent others. Build committed and caring relationships between academically-oriented and nonacademically- oriented students.

4. Personally tailor appeals to value education to the student. General messages are not nearly as effective as personal messages. The individuals best able to construct an effective personal appeal are peers who know the student well.

5. Plan for the long term, not sudden conversions. Internalization of academic values will take years of persuasion by caring and committed peers.

6. Support from caring and committed peers is essential to modifying attitudes and behaviors and maintaining the new attitudes and behaviors. Remember, "You can't do it alone. You need help from your friends."

Johnson, Johnson, & Smith

Students may be best encouraged to value education, work hard in school, take the valuable but difficult courses (such as math, science, and foreign languages), and aspire to go to graduate school, by placing them in permanent base groups that provide members with help and encouragement and hold members accountable for working hard in college. The base group provides a setting in which academic values may be encouraged and the necessary caring and committed relationships may be developed.

Base Groups And Dropping Out Of College

In many colleges large numbers of students drop out, especially during the freshman year. Base groups provide a means of both preventing and combating dropping out of school. Any student who believes that "in this college, no one knows me, no one cares about me, no one would miss me when I'm gone," is at risk of dropping out. Base groups provide a set of personal and supportive relationships that may prevent many students from dropping out of college. Dropping out often results from being alienated from the college and the other students. **Base groups also provide a means of fighting a student's inclination to drop out.** A faculty member may approach a base group and say, "Roger thinks he is dropping out of college. Go find and talk to him. We're not going to lose Roger without a fight."

The Necessities Of Life

There are certain basics in life that all students need to develop in healthy ways. One set of necessities involves good nutrition, adequate sleep, and appropriate clothing and shelter. Another set involves caring and committed relationships. All students need to know that there are people in the world who are committed to them and will provide them with help and assistance when it is needed. Colleges need to ensure that every student is involved in caring and committed relationships with peers. One way to do so is through cooperative base groups.

Staying In Love

Love is loyalty. Love is teamwork. Love respects the dignity of the individual. Heart-power is the strength of your corporation.

Vice Lombardi

In revisiting Sugar Loaf Hill in Okinawa William Manchester gained an important insight. "I understand at last, why I jumped hospital that long-ago Sunday and, in violation of orders, returned to the front and almost certain death. It was an act of love. Those men on the line were my family, my home. They were closer to me than I can say, closer than any friends had been or ever would be. They were comrades; three of them had saved my life. They had never let me down, and I couldn't do it to them. I had to be with them, rather than let them die and me live with the knowledge that I might have saved them. Men, I now knew, do not fight for flag or country, for the Marine Corps or glory or any other abstraction. They fight for their friends."

Long-term committed efforts to achieve come from the heart, not the head. It takes courage and hope to continue the quest. Striving for increased expertise is an arduous and long-term enterprise. Students can become exhausted, frustrated, and disenchanted. They can be tempted to exert minimal effort and just get by. They can be tempted to give up.

In the process of working to achieve shared goals students come to care about one another on more than just a professional level. Extraordinary accomplishments are not achieved without everyone getting personally involved with the task and each other. Genuine personal relationships are formed among members of cooperative groups, especially if the groups have stable membership for considerable period of time.

Base groups are long-term heterogeneous cooperative learning groups with stable membership whose primary responsibilities are to provide support, encouragement, and assistance in completing assignments and hold each other accountable for striving to learn. There are two ways base groups may be used. The first is to have a base group in each college course. The second is to organize all students within the college into base groups and have the groups function as an essential component of college life. College base groups stay together for at least a year and preferably for four years or until all members are graduated. Base groups focus the power of long-term relationships on supporting academic progress, motivating academic effort, creating positive attitudes toward learning, increase retention and graduation rates, and provide the caring and commitment necessary for a full and complete college experience.

The coordinated use of cooperative formal, informal, and base groups provides the basis for educating college students. As students spend more and more time in cooperative learning groups, however, the competitive/individualistic relationships among faculty become more apparent and less defensible. What is good for students is even better for faculty. Cooperation among faculty is discussed in Chapter Nine.

Base Group Meeting Worksheet

When: Base groups meet at the beginning and end of each class session.

Opening Tasks: Ask and answer two or more of the following questions:

1. How are you today? What is the best thing that has happened to you since the last class session?

2. Are you prepared for this class session?

3. Did you do your homework? Is there anything you do not understand?

4. What have you read, thought about, or done relevant to this course since the last class session?

5. May I read and edit your advanced preparation paper? Will you read and edit mine?

Closing Task: Answer the following questions.

1. Do you understand the assignment? What help do you need to complete it?

2. What are three things you learned in today's class session?

3. How will you use/apply what you have learned?

Celebrate the hard work and learning of group members.

Cooperative: One set of answers from the group, everyone must agree, and everyone must be able to explain.

Individual Accountability: One member of your group will be selected randomly to present your group's answers. The next class session group members will ask you if you have followed through on your assignments and plans.

Expected Behaviors: Active participating, encouraging, summarizing, and synthesizing.

Johnson, Johnson, & Smith

⟨ Cooperative Learning Contract ⟩

MAJOR LEARNINGS	IMPLEMENTATION PLANS

Date _____   Date of Progress Report Meeting _____

Participant's Signature _____

Signatures of Other Group Members _____ _____

_____ _____ _____

Johnson, Johnson, & Smith

𝕮𝖔𝖔𝖕𝖊𝖗𝖆𝖙𝖎𝖛𝖊 𝕷𝖊𝖆𝖗𝖓𝖎𝖓𝖌 𝕻𝖗𝖔𝖌𝖗𝖊𝖘𝖘 𝕽𝖊𝖕𝖔𝖗𝖙

NAME _____   SCHOOL _____

AGE LEVEL _____   SUBJECT _____

DAY and DATE	DESCRIPTION OF TASKS and ACTIVITIES PERFORMED	SUCCESSES EXPERIENCED	PROBLEMS ENCOUNTERED

Description of critical or interesting incidents:

Academic Controversy

Introduction

*Have you learned lessons only of
those who admired you, and were tender
with you, and stood aside for you?*

*Have you not learned great lessons
from those who braced themselves
against you, and disputed the passage
with you?*

Walt Whitman, 1860

In an English class students are considering the issue of civil disobedience. They learn that in the civil rights movement, individuals broke the law to gain equal rights for minorities. In numerous literary works, such as **Huckleberry Finn**, individuals wrestle with the issue of breaking the law to redress a social injustice. Huck wrestles with the issue of breaking the law in order to help Jim, the run-away slave. In the 1970s and 1980s, however, prominent public figures from Wall Street to the White House have felt justified in breaking laws for personal or political gain. In order to study the role of civil disobedience in a democracy, students are placed in a cooperative learning group of four members. The group is divided into two pairs. One pair is given the assignment of making the best case possible for the constructiveness of civil disobedience in a democracy. The other pair is given the assignment of making the best case possible for the destructiveness of civil disobedience in a democracy. In the resulting conflict students draw from such sources as the **Declaration of Independence** by Thomas Jefferson, **Civil Disobedience** by Henry David Thoreau, **Speech at Cooper Union, New York** by Abraham Lincoln, and **Letter from Birmingham Jail** by Martin Luther King, Jr. to challenge each other's reasoning and analyses concerning when civil disobedience is, and is not, constructive.

Such intellectual "disputed passages" create a high level of reasoning, thinking, and meta-cognition when they occur within cooperative learning groups and when they are carefully structured to ensure students manage them constructively. Cooperation, controversy, cognition, and metacognition are all intimately related. Cooperative learning provides the context within which cognition and metacognition best take place. The interpersonal exchange within cooperative learning groups, and especially the intellectual challenge resulting from conflict among ideas and conclusions (i.e., controversy), promotes critical thinking, higher-level reasoning, and metacognitive thought. Within this chapter cooperative learning is defined and its impact on cognition and metacognition is discussed. The nature of controversy and its effects on higher-level reasoning and critical thinking is then addressed.

Nature Of Controversy

The best way ever devised for seeking the truth in any given situation is advocacy: presenting the pros and cons from different, informed points of view and digging down deep into the facts.

Harold S. Geneen, Former CEO, ITT

A social studies teacher asks students to think about what problems the people described in a curriculum unit on the major problems facing hunting and gathering societies had to solve. Immediately, Jim jumps up and states that the major problem was how to hunt better so they could have more food. Jane disagrees. She says the major problem was how to store food so it would last longer. Jeremy stands up and tells both Jim and Jane that they are wrong; the major problem was how to domesticate the wild grains that grew in the area so that the people would be less dependent on hunting. Jim, Jane, and Jeremy begin to argue forcefully, bringing out the facts supporting why each thinks he or she is right.

Using academic conflicts for instructional purposes is one of the most dynamic and involving, yet **least-used** teaching strategies. Although creating a conflict is an accepted writer's tool for capturing an audience, teachers often suppress students' academic disagreements and consequently miss out on valuable opportunities to capture their own audiences and enhance learning.

Controversy exists when one student's ideas, information, conclusions, theories, and opinions are incompatible with those of another, and the two seek to reach an agreement. Structured academic controversies are most often contrasted with concurrence seeking, debate, and individualistic learning. For instance, students can inhibit discussion to avoid any disagreement and compromise quickly to reach a consensus while they discuss the issue (concurrence-seeking). Or students can appoint a judge and then debate the different positions with the expectation that the judge will determine who presented the better position (debate). Finally, students can work independently with their own set of materials at their own pace (individualistic learning).

Over the past 10 years, we have developed and tested a theory about how controversy promotes positive outcomes (Johnson, 1979, 1980; Johnson & Johnson, 1979, 1985, 1987). Based on our findings, we have developed a series of curriculum units on energy and environmental issues structured for academic controversies. We have also worked with schools and colleges through the United States and Canada to field-test and implement the units in the classroom. We will review these efforts by discussing the process of controversy, how teachers can organize and use it, and the advantages of using controversy to enhance learning and thinking.

How Students Benefit

Conflict is the gadfly of thought. It stirs us to observation and memory. It instigates invention. It shocks us out of sheep-like passivity, and sets us at noting and contriving...conflict is a 'sine qua non' of reflection and ingenuity.

John Dewey

When students interact, conflicts among their ideas, conclusions, theories, information, perspectives, opinions, and preferences are inevitable. Teachers who capitalize on these differences find that academic conflicts can yield highly constructive dividends. Over the past 15 years, we have conducted a systematic series of research studies to discover the consequences of structured controversy (Johnson & Johnson, 1979, 1985, 1987, 1989; Johnson, Johnson & Smith, 1986). Compared with concurrence-seeking, debate, and individualistic efforts, controversy tends to result in:

1. Greater student mastery and retention of the subject matter being studied as well as greater ability to generalize the principles learned to a wider variety of situations. In a meta- analysis of the available research, Johnson and Johnson (1989a) found that

Johnson, Johnson, & Smith

Table 7.1 Meta-Analysis Of Controversy Studies

	Voting			Effect-Size			Z-Score		
	Negative	NoDif	Positive	Mean	sd	n	Z	n	fsn
Controversy/Concurrence	13	54	94	0.42	0.57	49	8.55	55	1,421
Controversy/Debate	4	27	87	0.77	0.41	20	8.04	23	523
Controversy/Individualistic	1	34	89	0.65	0.32	20	8.89	24	672
Debate/Individualistic	0	8	0	0.36	1.03	3	1.76	6	1

controversy produced higher achievement that did debate (effect-size = 0.77), individualistic learning (effect- size = 0.65), and concurrence seeking (effect- size = 0.42).

2. Higher-quality decisions and solutions to complex problems for which different viewpoints can plausibly be developed. If students are to become citizens capable of making reasoned judgments about the complex problems facing society, they must learn to use the higher-level reasoning and critical thinking processes involved in effective problem solving, especially problems for which different viewpoints can plausibly be developed. Educating students to solve problems for which different points of view can plausibly be developed is an important aspect of schooling. To do so, students must enter empathically into the arguments of both sides of the issue and ensure that the strongest possible case is made for each side, and arrive at a synthesis based on rational, probabilistic thought. Participating in structured controversy teaches students of all ages how to find high-quality solutions to complex problems.

3. More frequent creative (a) insights into the issues being discussed and (b) synthesis combining both perspectives. Controversy increased the number of ideas, quality of ideas, creation of original ideas, the use of a wider range of ideas, originality of expression in problem solving, more creative solutions, more imaginative solutions, more novel solutions, and use of more varied strategies.

4. Greater exchange of expertise. Students often know different information and theories, make different assumptions, and have different opinions. Within any cooperative learning group, students with a wide variety of expertise and perspectives are told to work together to maximize each member's learning. Many times students study different parts of an assignment and are expected to share their expertise with the other members of their group. Conflict among their ideas, information, opinions, preferences, theories, conclusions, and perspectives is inevitable. Yet such controversies are typically avoided or managed destructively. Having the skills to manage the controversies constructively and knowing the procedures for exchanging information

and perspective among individuals with differing expertise are essential for maximal learning and growth.

5. Greater perspective-taking accuracy.

6. Greater task involvement reflected in greater emotional commitment to solving the problem, greater enjoyment of the process, more feelings of stimulation and enjoyment.

7. More positive relationships among participants and greater perceived peer academic support.

8. Higher academic self-esteem.

In addition to these outcomes, **there are a number of critical thinking skills required by the controversy structure.** Students must develop at least four sets of conceptual skills to prepare a "best case" presentation, based on evidence, of an assigned position (Johnson & Johnson, 1987). **First,** students must collect, analyze, and present evidence to support a position. This involves (a) researching, gathering, and collecting all facts, information, and experiences available and relevant to the issue being studied, (b) analyzing and organizing the information into a position statement or claim, a listing of all supporting evidence, and a coherent, reasoned, valid, and logical rationale (this requires conceptual analysis and the use of inductive and deductive reasoning), and (c) presenting that position with vigor, sincerity, and persuasiveness while keeping an open mind. Students must present and advocate that position in a way that takes into account who the audience is and how they may be persuaded. **Second,** students must evaluate and criticize the opposing positions. Students critically analyze the opposing position and challenge and attempt to refute it based on the rules of logic and evidence. At the same time, students rebut attacks on their position. This requires a continual reconceptualizing of both positions and determining when the opposing pair presents faulty information or uses faulty reasoning. **Third,** students are required to see the issue from both perspectives. **Fourth,** students make tentative conclusions based on a synthesis and/or integration of the best evidence from both sides. This requires probabilistic rather than dualistic or relativistic thinking. It also requires considerable divergent as well as convergent thinking. Such cognitive skills are valuable contributors to creative problem solving.

Process Through Which Controversy Affects Academic Outcomes

Since the general or prevailing opinion on any subject is rarely or never the whole truth, it is only by the collision of adverse opinion that the remainder of the truth has any chance of being supplied.

John Stuart Mill

Roger regularly conducts an academic controversy on whether or not the wolf should be a protected species. He gives students the cooperative assignment of writing a report on the wolf in which they summarize what they have learned about the wolf and recommend the procedures they think are best for regulating wolf populations and preserving wolves within the continental United States. Students are randomly assigned to groups of four, ensuring that both male and female and high-, medium-, and low- achieving students are all in the same group. The group is divided into two pairs; one pair is assigned the position of an environmental organization that believes wolves should be a protected species and the other pair is assigned the position of farmers and ranchers who believe that wolves should not be a protected species.

Each side is given a packet of articles, stories, and information that supports their position. During the **first** class period each pair develops their position and plans how to present the best case possible to the other pair. Near the end of the period pairs are encouraged to compare notes with pairs from other groups who represent the same position. During the **second** class period each pair makes their presentation. Each member of the pair has to participate in the presentation. Members of the opposing pair are encouraged to take notes and listen carefully. During the **third** class period the group members discuss the issue following a set of rules to help them criticize ideas without criticizing people, differentiate the two positions, and assess the degree of evidence and logic supporting each position. During the first half of the **fourth** hour the pairs reverse perspectives and present each other's positions. Students drop their advocacy positions, clarify their understanding of each other's information and rationale and begin work on their group report. The first half of the **fifth** period is spent finalizing their report. The report is evaluated on the basis of the quality of the writing, the evaluation of opinion and evidence, and the oral presentation of the report to the class. The students then each take an individual test on the wolf and, if every member of the group achieves up to criterion, they all receive bonus points. Finally, during the **sixth** class period each group makes a 10-minute presentation to the entire class summarizing their report. All four members of the group are required to participate orally in the presentation.

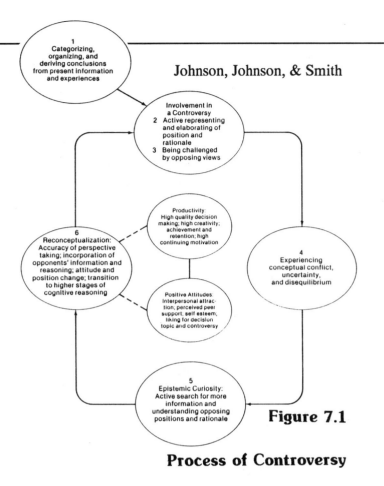

Johnson, Johnson, & Smith

Figure 7.1

Process of Controversy

Within this lesson **positive interdependence** is structured by having each group arrive at a consensus, submit one written report, and make one presentation; by jigsawing the materials to the pairs within the group; and by giving bonus points if all members learn the basic information contained in the two positions and score well on the test. **Individual accountability** is structured since each member of the pair orally participates in the presentation of the position and in the perspective reversal, each member of the group orally participates in the group presentation, and each member takes an individual test on the material. The **social skills** emphasized are those involved in systematically advocating an intellectual position and evaluating and criticizing the position advocated by others, as well as the skills involved in synthesis and consensual decision making.

The hypothesis that intellectual challenge promotes higher-level reasoning, critical thinking, and metacognitive thought is derived from a number of premises (see Figure 7.1):

1. When individuals are presented with a problem or decision, they have an initial conclusion based on categorizing and organizing incomplete information, their limited experiences, and their specific perspective.

2. When individuals present their conclusion and its rationale to others, they engage in cognitive rehearsal, deepen their understanding of their position, and discover higher-level reasoning strategies.

3. Individuals are confronted by other people with different conclusions based on other people's information, experiences, and perspectives.

4. Individuals become uncertain as to the correctness of their views. A state of conceptual conflict or disequilibrium is aroused.

5. Uncertainty, conceptual conflict, and disequilibrium motivate an active search for more information, new experiences, and a more adequate cognitive perspective and reasoning process in hopes of resolving the uncertainty. Berlyne (1965) calls this active search **epistemic curiosity**. Divergent attention and thought are stimulated.

6. By adapting their cognitive perspective and reasoning through understanding and accommodating the perspective and reasoning of others, a new, reconceptualized, and reorganized conclusion is derived. Novel solutions and decisions are detected that are, on balance, are qualitatively better.

When teachers structure controversies within cooperative learning groups, students are required to research and prepare a position (reasoning both deductively and inductively); advocate a position (thereby orally rehearsing the relevant information and teaching their knowledge to peers); analyze, critically evaluate, and rebut information; reason deductively and inductively; take the perspective of others; and synthesize and integrate information into factual and judgmental conclusions that are summarized into a joint position to which all sides can agree.

Controversies are resolved by engaging in the discussion of the advantages and disadvantages of proposed actions aimed at synthesizing novel solutions. In controversy there is advocacy and challenge of each other's positions in order to reach the highest possible quality decision based on the synthesis of both perspectives. There is a reliance on argumentative clash to develop, clarify, expand, and elaborate one's thinking about the issues being considered.

Structuring Academic Controversies

Difference of opinion leads to inquiry, and inquiry to truth.

Thomas Jefferson

Here is an example of a controversy on environmental education. The teacher assigns students to groups of four and asks them to prepare a report entitled, "The role of regulations in the management of hazardous waste." There is to be one report from the group representing the members' best analysis of the issue. The groups are divided into two-person advocacy teams with one team being given the position that "more regulations are needed" and the other team being given the "fewer regulations are needed" position. Both advocacy teams are given articles and technical materials supporting their assigned position. They are then given time to read and discuss the material with their partner and to plan how best to advocate their assigned position so that (a) they learn the information and perspective within the articles and technical reports, (b) the opposing team is convinced of the soundness of the team's position, and (c) the members of the opposing team learn the material contained within the articles and technical reports. To do so, students proceed through five steps.

First, students **research the issue, organize their information, and prepare their positions**. Learning begins with students gathering information. They then categorize and organize their present information and experiences so that a conclusion is derived. Second, the two advocacy teams actively **present and advocate their positions**. Each pair presents their position and reasoning to the opposition, thereby engaging in considerable cognitive rehearsal and elaboration of their position and its rationale. When the other team presents, students' reasoning and conclusions are **challenged by the opposing view** and they experience **conceptual conflict and uncertainty**. Third, students engage in a general discussion in which they advocate their position, rebut attacks on their position, refute the opposing position, and seek to learn both positions. The group discusses the issue, critically evaluates the opposing position and its rationale, defends positions, and compares the strengths and weaknesses of the two positions. When students are challenged by conclusions and information that are incompatible with and do not fit with their reasoning and conclusions, conceptual conflict, uncertainty, and disequilibrium result. As a result of their uncertainty, students experience **epistemic curiosity** and, therefore, students actively (a) search for more information and experiences to support their position and (b) seek to understand the opposing position and its supporting rationale. During this time students' uncertainty and information search are encouraged and promoted by the teacher. Fourth, students **reverse perspectives** and present the opposing position. Each advocacy pair presents the best case possible for the opposing position. Fifth, the group of four reach a consensus and prepare a group report. The emphasis during this instructional period is on students **reconceptualizing** their position and **synthesizing** the best information and reasoning from both sides. The group's report should reflect their best reasoned judgment. Each group member then individually takes an examination on the factual information contained in the reading materials.

For the past several years we have been training teachers and professors throughout North America in the use of structured academic controversies. Structured academic controversies are now being used at the University of Minnesota in engineering, psychology, and education courses. They are being used in elementary and secondary schools in the United States and Canada. The basic format for doing so follows. A more detailed description of conducting academic controversies may be found in Johnson, Johnson and Smith (1986) and Johnson and Johnson (1987).

Structure The Academic Task

The task must be structured (a) cooperatively and (b) so that there are at least two well-documented positions (e.g., pro and con). The choice of topic depends on the interests of the instructor and the purposes of the course. Topics on which we have developed curriculum units include the following and many others: "What caused the dinosaurs extinction? Should the wolf be a protected species? Should coal be used as an energy source? Should nuclear energy be used as an energy source? Should the regulation of hazardous wastes be increased? Should the Boundary Waters Canoe Area be a national park? How should acid precipitation be controlled?

Prepare Instructional Materials

Prepare the instructional materials so that group members know what position they have been assigned and where they can find supporting information. The following materials are needed for each position:

1. A clear description of the group's task.

2. A description of the phases of the controversy procedure and the interpersonal and small group skills to be used during each phase.

3. A definition of the position to be advocated with a summary of the key arguments supporting the position.

4. Resource materials (including a bibliography) to provide evidence for the elaboration of the arguments supporting the position to be advocated.

Structure The Controversy

The principal requirements for a successful structured controversy are a cooperative context, skillful group members, and heterogeneity of group membership. These are structured by:

1. Assigning students to groups of four. Divide each group into two pairs. A high reader and a low reader may be assigned to each pair. The responsibility of the pair is to get to know the information supporting its assigned position and prepare a presentation and a series of persuasive arguments to use in the discussion with the opposing pair.

2. Assigning pro and con positions to the pairs and giving students supporting materials to read and study. A bibliography of further sources of information may also be given. A section of resource materials may be set up in the library.

3. Highlighting the cooperative goals of (a) reaching a consensus on the issue, (b) mastering all the information relevant to both sides of the issue (measured by a test), and (c) writing a quality group report on which all members will be evaluated. Also highlight the group reward--each group member will receive five bonus points if all score 90 percent or better on the test.

Conduct The Controversy

1. Assign each pair the tasks of (a) learning its position and the supporting arguments and information, (b) researching all information relevant to its position, (c) giving the opposing pair any information found supporting the opposing position, (d) preparing a persuasive presentation to be given to the other pair, and (e) preparing a series of persuasive arguments to be used in the discussion with the opposing pair. They research and prepare their position, presentation, and arguments. Students are given the following instructions:

"Plan with your partner how to advocate your position effectively. Read the materials supporting your position. Find more information in the library reference books to support your position. Plan a persuasive presentation. Make sure you and your partner master the information supporting your assigned position and present it in a persuasive and complete way so that the other group members will comprehend and learn the information."

2. Have each pair present its position to the other. Presentations should involve more than one media and persuasively advocate the "best case" for the position. There is no arguing during this time. Students should listen carefully to the opposing position. Students are told:

"As a pair, present your position forcefully and persuasively. Listen carefully and learn the opposing position. Take notes, and clarify anything you do not understand."

3. Have students openly discuss the issue by freely exchanging their information and ideas. For higher-level reasoning and critical thinking to occur, it is necessary to probe and push each other's conclusions. Students ask for data to support each other's statements, clarify rationales, and show why their position is a rationale one. Students evaluate critically the opposing position and its rationale, defend their own positions, and compare the strengths and weaknesses of the two positions. Students refute the claims being made by the opposing pair, and rebut the attacks on their own position. Students are to follow the specific rules for constructive controversy. Students should also take careful notes on and thoroughly learn the opposing position. Sometimes a "time-out" period needs to be provided so that pairs can caucus and prepare new arguments. Teachers encourage more spirited arguing, take sides when a pair is in trouble, play devil's advocate, ask one group to observe another group engaging in a spirited argument, and generally stir up the discussions. Students are instructed to:

"Argue forcefully and persuasively for your position, presenting as many facts as you can to support your point of view. Listen critically to the opposing pair's position, asking them for the facts that support their viewpoint, and then present counter-arguments. Remember this is a complex issue, and you need to know both sides to write a good report."

4. Have the pairs reverse perspectives and positions by presenting the opposing position as sincerely and forcefully as they can. It helps to have the pairs change chairs. They can use their own notes, but may not see the materials developed by the opposing pair. Students' instructions are:

"Working as a pair, present the opposing pair's position as if you were they. Be as sincere and forceful as you can. Add any new facts you know. Elaborate their position by relating it to other information you have previously learned."

5. Have the group members drop their advocacy and reach a decision by consensus. Then they:

   a. Write a group report that includes their joint position and the supporting evidence and rationale. Often the resulting position is a third perspective or synthesis that is more rational than the two assigned. All group members sign the report indicating that they agree with it, can explain its content, and consider it ready to be evaluated.

b. Take a test on both positions. If all members score above the preset criteria of excellence, each receives five bonus points.

c. Process how well the group functioned and how members' performance may be improved during the next controversy. Teachers may wish to structure the group processing to highlight the specific conflict management skills students need to master.

Students are instructed to:

"Summarize and synthesize the best arguments for **both** points of view. Reach consensus on a position that is supported by the facts. Change your mind only when the facts and the rationale clearly indicate that you should do so. Write your report with the supporting evidence and rationale for your synthesis that your group has agreed on. When you are certain the report is as good as you can make it, sign it. Organize your report to present it to your entire class."

Teach Students Conflict Skills

...the noise could be heard all over the city. Our fights over words were furious, blasphemous, and frequent, but even in their hottest moments we both knew that we were arguing academically and not personally.

Richard Rodgers (recalling his work with lyricist Larry Hart)

No matter how carefully teachers structure controversies, if students do not have the interpersonal and small group skills to manage conflicts constructively the controversy does not produce its potential effects. Students should be taught the following skills.

1. Emphasize the mutuality of the situation and avoid win-lose dynamics. Focus on coming to the best decision possible, not on winning.

2. Confirm others' competence while disagreeing with their positions and challenging their reasoning. Be critical of ideas, not people. Challenge and refute the ideas of the opposing pair, but do not reject the students personally.

3. Separate your personal worth from criticism of your ideas.

4. Listen to everyone's ideas, even if you do not agree with them.

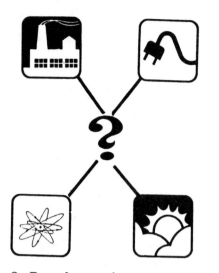

5. First bring out the all the ideas and facts supporting both sides and then try to put them together in a way that makes sense. Be able to differentiate the differences between positions before attempting to integrate ideas.

6. Be able to take the opposing perspective in order to understand the opposing position. Try to understand both sides of the issue.

7. Change your mind when the evidence clearly indicates that you should.

8. Paraphrase what someone has said if it is not clear.

9. Emphasize rationality in seeking the best possible answer, given the available data.

10. Follow the golden rule of conflict. The golden rule is, act towards your opponents as you would have them act toward you. If you want people to listen to you, then listen to them. If you want others to include your ideas in their thinking, then include their ideas in your thinking. If you want others to take your perspective, then take their perspective.

Controversy In Math

There are a number of ways to conduct controversies in mathematics courses. One **topic** is reaching a decision under risk while comparing the relative advantages of using expected value criterion and the minimax criterion. The **instructional task** is to determine the conditions under which each criterion is appropriate. Any problem may be given to students to solve. The students are organized into cooperative learning groups with four students in each group. Two students are assigned the position that the solution should be derived by using the expected-value criterion. The other two students are assigned the position that the solution should be derived by the minimax criterion. The controversy procedure is then conducted. Another topic is to compare the Newton-Raphson and Bisection ways of solving for roots of a polynominal.

Structured Controversies In Science

Within science classes any number of issues may be structured as academic controversies. A few of the topics we have used in our classes are **Acid Rain** (more research is needed vs. we know enough to act now), **Electrical Power Generation** (coal vs. nuclear vs. renewable), **Hazardous Waste** (more regulations needed vs. fewer regulations needed), **Land Use** (preservation vs. economic/business planned utilization), and **Endangered Species** (endangered vs. protected). Faculty interested in these controversies may want to write the Cooperative Learning Center at the University of Minnesota for more complete descriptions and supporting materials.

Summary

Our...advantage was that we had evolved unstated but fruitful methods of collaboration....If either of us suggested a new idea, the other, while taking it seriously, would attempt to demolish it in a candid but nonhostile manner.
Politeness is the poison of all good collaboration in science.

Francis Crick, Nobel Prize Winner (codiscoverer of the double helix)

To promote students' higher-level reasoning and critical thinking, as well as metacognition, requires the two steps of carefully structuring (a) cooperation among students and (b) academic controversy within the cooperative groups. Cooperation, controversy, cognition, and metacognition are all intimately related. Cooperative learning provides the context within which cognition and metacognition best take place. They are stimulated by the interpersonal exchange within cooperative learning groups. To ensure that higher-level reasoning, critical thinking, and meta-cognition take place, however, students need the intellectual challenge resulting from conflict among ideas and conclusions (i.e., controversy).

Cooperative learning needs to be carefully structured to include positive interdependence, face-to-face promotive interaction, individual accountability, the appropriate use of interpersonal and small group skills, and processing how effectively the group has functioned. Under these conditions, cooperative learning results in higher achievement, more frequent use of higher quality reasoning strategies, the generation of new ideas and solutions, and more frequent meta-cognitive thinking than do competitive or individualistic learning situations. Within cooperative learning groups there is a process of interpersonal exchange that involves expectations to teach what one learns to groupmates, explaining and elaborating what is being learned, exposure to diverse perspectives and ideas, taking others' perspectives, externalization of ideas and reasoning, and feedback. Perhaps most important of all, is that intellectual conflict occurs within cooperative groups.

Controversy exists when one student's ideas, information, conclusions, theories, and opinions are incompatible with those of another, and the two seek to reach an agreement. Controversy, compared with concurrence seeking, debate, and individualistic efforts, results in higher achievement, higher-quality decisions and problem-solving, more creative thinking, more higher-level reasoning and critical thinking, greater perspective-taking accuracy, greater task involvement, more positive relationships among group members, and higher academic self-esteem.

These outcomes occur as a result of the structured process of controversy. Students make an initial judgment, present their conclusions to other group members, are challenged with opposing views, become uncertain about the correctness of their views, actively search for new information and understanding, incorporate others' perspectives and reasoning into their thinking, and reach a new set of conclusions. While this process sometimes occurs naturally within cooperative learning groups, it may be considerably enhanced when teachers structure academic controversies. This involves dividing a cooperative group into two pairs and assigning them opposing positions. The pairs then develop their position, present it to the other pair, listen to the opposing position, engage in a discussion in which they attempt to refute the other side and rebut attacks on their position, reverse perspectives and present the other position, and then drop all advocacy and seek a synthesis that takes both perspectives and positions into account. Participation in such a process requires a set of social and cognitive skills. To promote higher-level reasoning, critical thinking, and metacognitive skills, teachers are well-advised to first establish cooperative learning and then structure academic controversies.

The Teacher's Role
in Controversy

Make Decisions

Specifying Academic and Controversy Skills Objectives. What academic and/or controversy skills do you want students to learn or practice in their groups? Start with something easy.

Decide on Group Size. Unless there are three or four sides to the issue (avoid more than two sides to an issue unless your students are highly experienced and skilled), use groups of four.

Assign Students To Groups. Heterogeneous groups are the most powerful, so mix abilities, sexes, cultural backgrounds, and task orientations. Assign students to groups randomly or select groups yourself.

Plan Materials. Divide materials into pro and con so that each pair of students has the materials needed to complete the task. This includes the position to be advocated, supporting information to be organized, and a guide to further resources.

Assign Roles. In addition to assigning pro and con roles, there are roles that will help students work together, such as perspective-taker, checker, accuracy coacher, and elaborator.

Set The Lesson

Explain The Academic Task. Explain lesson objectives, define concepts, explain procedures, give examples, and ask questions to ensure that students understand what they are supposed to accomplish.

Structure Positive Interdependence. Students must believe that they need each other to complete the group's task, that they "sink or swim together." Use mutual goals, joint rewards, shared materials and information, and assigned roles to create a perception of mutuality.

Structure The Controversy. Students must understand the procedure and the time limits for preparing their position, presenting it, advocating it, reversing perspectives, and reaching a conclusion.

Structure Individual Accountability. Each student must believe he or she is responsible for learning the material and helping his or her groupmates. Frequent oral quizzing of group members picked at random and individual tests are two ways to ensure this.

Explain Criteria For Success. Student work should be evaluated on a criteria-referenced rather than on a norm-referenced basis. Make clear your criteria for evaluating the work of individual students and the entire group.

Specify Desired Behaviors. Clearly explain the constructive controversy rules.

Teach Controversy Skills. After students are familiar with the controversy procedures, pick one controversy skill, point out the need for it, define it by giving students specific phrases they can say to engage in the skill, observe for it, and give students feedback about their use of the skill. Encourage the use of the skill until students are performing it automatically.

Structure Intergroup Cooperation. Having students check with and help other groups and giving rewards or praise when all class members do well can extend the benefits of cooperation to the whole class.

Monitor And Intervene

Ensure All Students Present, Advocate, Criticize, And Synthesize. The beneficial educational outcomes of controversy are due to the oral interaction among students.

Monitor Students' Behavior. This is the fun part! While students are working, circulate to see whether they understand the assignment, the procedure, the material. Give immediate feedback and praise the appropriate use of controversy skills.

Provide Task Assistance. If students are having trouble with the academic material, you can clarify, reteach, or elaborate on what they need to know.

Intervene To Teach Controversy Skills. If students are having trouble with the controversy process, you can suggest more effective procedures for working together on more effective behaviors for them to engage in.

Provide Closure. To reinforce student learning, you may wish to have groups share answers or paper, summarize major points in the lesson, or review important facts.

Evaluate And Process

Evaluate Student Learning. Assess the quality of the group report and give students the individual test on the material being studied.

Process Group Functioning. In order to improve, students need time and procedures for reflecting on how well their group is functioning and how well they are using controversy skills. Processing can be done by individuals, small groups, or the whole class.

Johnson, Johnson, & Smith

CONTROVERSY LESSON PLAN

Title _____

Your Name _____

School and District _____

Subject Area _____ Grade Level _____

Lesson Topic and Summary _____

_____

_____

Instructional Objectives _____

_____

Materials Needed

    Pro _____

    Con _____

Time Required _____ Group Size _____

Assignment to Groups _____

_____

Roles _____

  (Name and _____

  explain) _____

_____

_____

The Lesson

Task _____

_____

_____

_____

_____

_____

Positive Goal/Reward Interdependence _____

_____

_____

_____

Controversy Procedures

   Preparing Positions   _____

_____

   Presenting Positions   _____

_____

   Discussing the Issue   _____

_____

   Reversing Perspectives   _____

_____

   Reaching a Decision   _____

_____

Individual Accountability   _____

_____

_____

Criteria for Success   _____

_____

_____

Expected Behaviors   _____

_____

_____

Monitoring and Processing

Monitor for   _____

_____

_____

Intervene if   _____

_____

_____

Process by   _____

_____

_____

End by   _____

_____

(Attach any materials needed to run the lesson)

⋅§ **Controversy Exercise: Schedule** §⋅

1. **Preparing Positions.** Meet with your partner and plan how to argue effectively for your position. Make sure you and your partner have mastered as much of the position as possible. You have 20 minutes for this.

2. **Exchanging Ideas.** Meet with another pair preparing the same position as you have. Exchange arguments and information and help prepare each other to argue effectively. You have 10 minutes for this.

3. **Presenting Positions.** Present your position to your group of four and listen to their position. Be forceful and persuasive in your presentation. Take notes and clarify anything you do not understand when the opposing pair presents their position. You have five minutes.

4. **Advocating and Refuting.** Argue forcefully and persuasively for your position, presenting as many facts as you can to support your point of view. Critically listen to the opposing pair's position, asking them for the facts that support their point of view. Remember, this is a complex issue and you need to know both sides to write a good report. Work together as a total group to get all the facts out. Make sure you understand the facts that support both points of view. You have 10 minutes.

5. **Reversing Perspectives.** Reverse the roles by arguing your opposing pair's position. In arguing for this position, be as forceful and persuasive as you can. See if you can think of any new facts that the opposing pair did not think to present. Elaborate their position. You have ten minutes.

6. **Reaching a Decision.** Come to a decision that all four of you can agree with. Summarize the best arguments for both points of view. Detail what you know (facts) about each side. When you have consensus in your group, organize your arguments to present to the entire room. Other groups may make the opposite decision and you need to defend the validity of your decision to everyone. To synthesize your group position, write a report. When you are certain your report is as good as you can make it, sign it. You have 30 minutes for this.

7. **Processing.** Process your group's interactions by answering the following questions:

    a. How frequently did we do the behaviors observed for?
    b. What behaviors did we perform particularly well as a group?
    c. What behaviors could we do even better next time?

Rules for Constructive Controversy

1. I am critical of ideas, not people. I challenge and refute the ideas of the opposing pair, but I do not indicate that I personally reject them.

2. Remember, we are all in this together, sink or swim. I focus on coming to the best decision possible, not on winning.

3. I encourage everyone to participate and to master all the relevant information.

4. I listen to everyone's ideas, even if I don't agree.

5. I restate what someone has said if it is not clear.

6. I first bring out all ideas and facts supporting both sides, and then I try to put them together in a way that makes sense.

7. I try to understand both sides of the issue.

8. I change my mind when the evidence clearly indicates that I should do so.

Johnson, Johnson, & Smith

Acid Precipitation:

Pro-Environment Position

You are members of an environmental organization that believes a chemical leprosy is eating away at the face of the United States. It is popularly known as acid rain, but rain is not the only culprit. The true name for this phenomena is acid precipitation, which includes acid rain, acid snow, acid sleet, acid hail, acid frost, acid rime, acid fog, acid mist, acid dew, and "dry" deposits of acid particles, aerosols, and gases. While it is not only a United States problem, the United States needs to recognize the extreme dangers of acid precipitation and to take steps to remedy it before the damage becomes so pervasive that it is irreversible.

Your position is that legislative action is immediately needed to rectify the problem of acid precipitation by controlling emissions of utility plans burning coal and petroleum. You believe that industry policy groups have not accepted responsibility for the damage utility plants are causing. They seem unconcerned about the human and environmental costs of their current practices. Certainly they will not change voluntarily. Whether or not you agree with this position, argue for it as strongly as you can. Use arguments that make sense and are rational. Be creative and invent new supporting arguments. Remember to learn the rationale for both your position and the industrial position. Challenge the industrial position, think of loopholes in their logic, and demand facts and information to back up their arguments.

3. Acid precipitation occurs when sulfur dioxide and nitrogen oxides combine in the atmosphere and change chemically into acid, which falls to the earth mixed with some form of precipitation. The pollutants come primarily from burning coal and petroleum. About 90 percent of the sulfur in the atmosphere of the northeastern United States comes from human-made sources.

2. Acid precipitation can kill fish and other aquatic life outright. In Scandinavia, which is downwind of pollution pumped into the skies of Western Europe, acid precipitation has already destroyed fish life in 5,000 lakes in Southwestern Sweden, in several Atlantic salmon rivers, and in 1,500 lakes in southern Norway.

3. Acid precipitation can have damaging effects on human health through inhalation and through the leaching of toxic materials into drinking water.

These points give you a start in preparing your position. Read the text materials, go to the library, and interview experts to gather additional material to support your position.

Acid Precipitation:
Pro-Industry Position

You are members of an industrial policy group that believes the listed causes of acid precipitation are only hypotheses advanced by scientists to explain certain facts that puzzle them. Acid precipitation includes acid rain, acid snow, acid sleet, acid hail, acid frost, acid rime, acid fog, acid mist, acid dew, and "dry" deposits of acid particles, aerosols, and gases. It is a problem in the United States and elsewhere in the world. Scientists, however, have not conducted experiments tracing acid precipitation from the emission sources. Until cause-and-effect can conclusively be established, stringent controls on industry are presumptuous and costly.

Your position is that legislative action is not needed to increase the controls on emissions of utility plants burning coal and petroleum. You believe that no hard scientific evidence has been presented to justify new controls. In addition, environmentalists are vague about the level of control required and do not mention other remedial measures to control emissions from sources other than utilities. Whether or not you agree with this position, argue for it as strongly as you can. Use arguments that make sense and are rational. Be creative and invent new supporting arguments. Remember to learn the rationale for both your position and the industrial position. Challenge the industrial position, think of loopholes in their logic, and demand facts and information to back up their arguments.

1. Environmentalists are impling causality by association rather than by scientific proof of linkage. If the relationship between power plant emissions and acid precipitation is so overwhelming, then why have investigators been unable to trace acid precipitation back to the source emissions?

2. If both nitrate and sulfate in rain can be halved, the precipitation pH at most changes from 4.2 to 4.5. If sulfate alone is halved, the precipitation pH may change at most from 4.2 to 4.4. Emission controls, therefore, may be ineffective in changing precipitation pH values.

3. If interstate atmospheric deposition were regulated, at a minimum 2,980 mining jobs and 191 million dollars in annual economic input could be affective. The effect on these mines will be dependent on the control scheme adopted.

These points give you a start in preparing your position. Read the text materials, go to the library, and interview experts to gather additional material to support your position.

Bonus Point System

To encourage the interpersonal and small group skills students need to demonstrate during controversies, a bonus point system can be used. Two points may be given for important skills, one point may be given for less difficult skills, and points may be taken away for negative behaviors.

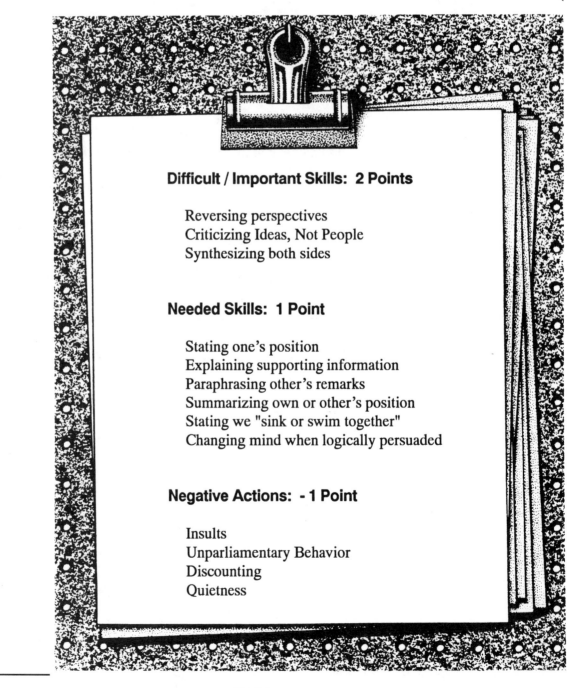

Difficult / Important Skills: 2 Points

> Reversing perspectives
> Criticizing Ideas, Not People
> Synthesizing both sides

Needed Skills: 1 Point

> Stating one's position
> Explaining supporting information
> Paraphrasing other's remarks
> Summarizing own or other's position
> Stating we "sink or swim together"
> Changing mind when logically persuaded

Negative Actions: - 1 Point

> Insults
> Unparliamentary Behavior
> Discounting
> Quietness

Integrated Use of All Types of Cooperative Learning

Introduction

Pull together. In the mountains you must depend on each other for survival.

Willi Unsoeld, Renounded Mountain
Climber

Within Yosemite National Park lies the famous Half Dome Mountain. The Half Dome is famous for its 2000 feet of soaring, sheer cliff wall. Unusually beautiful to the observer, and considered unclimbable for years, the Half Dome's northwest face was first scaled in 1957 by Royal Robbins and two companions. This incredibly dangerous climb took five days, with Robbins and his companions spending four nights on the cliff, sleeping in ropes with nothing below their bodies but air. Even today, the northwest face is a death trap to all but the finest and most skilled rock climbers. And far above the ground, moving slowly up the rock face, are two climbers.

The two climbers are motivated by a shared vision of successfully climbing the northwest face. As they move up the cliff they are attached to each other by a rope (**"the life line"**). As one member climbs (**the lead climber**), the other (**the belayer**) ensures that the two have a safe anchor and that he or she can catch the climber if the climber falls. The lead climber does not begin climbing until the belayer says "go." Then the lead climber advances, puts in a chock (revoval anchor that does no damage to the rock), slips in the rope, and continues to advance. The chocks help the belayer catch the climber if the climber falls and they mark the path up the cliff. The life line (i.e., rope) goes from the belayer through the chocks up to the climber. When the lead climber has completed the first leg of the climb, he or she becomes the belayer and the other member of the team begins to climb. The chocks placed by the lead climber serve to guide and support the second member of the team up the rock face. The second member advances up the route marked out by the first member until the first leg is completed, and then leap-frogs and becomes the lead climber for the second leg of the climb. The roles of lead climber and belayer are alternated until the summit is reached.

All human life is like mountain climbing. The human species seems to have a **cooperation imperative:** We desire and seek out opportunities to operate jointly with others to achieve mutual goals. We are attached to others through a variety of "life lines" and we alternate supporting and leading others to ensure a better life for ourselves, our colleagues and neighbors, our children, and all generations to follow.

Cooperative efforts begin when group members commit themselves to a mutual purpose and coordinate and integrate their efforts to do so. What is true of the real life needs to be true of college life. In the classroom, the mutual purpose and coordinated actions spring from cooperative learning. By structuring cooperation among students faculty remind students that "**None of us is as smart as all of us!**"

Structuring cooperative learning in college classrooms involves integrating the use of the four types of cooperative learning groups. Each course may have a mixture of cooperative formal, informal, and base groups with a periodic structured controversies to spice things up. Given below are two examples of how the different ways of using cooperative learning may be used. The examples are followed by a discussion of grading and personalizing the learning environment of the class. Finally, a sample course syllabus is given to provide an example of what an instructor may wish to hand out to students.

Fifty-Minute Class Session

A typical class session consists of base group meeting, a short lecture and/or a group project, and an ending base group meeting. The instructor formally starts the class by welcoming the students and instructing them to meet in their base groups. The introduction and warmup for the class is provided within base groups. The initial **base group** meeting includes one or more of the following tasks for members: greeting each other, checking to see if all members have completed their homework successfully or need help and assistance, and reviewing what members have read and done since the previous class session. Base group activities must be completed within about 5 minutes. Regularly structuring this time is essential for helping students get into a good learning mood, communicating high expectations about completing homework and helping others, and providing a transition between the student's (and professor's) previous hour and the current class session.

In a 50-minute class session the instructor usually has four choices. The instructor can give a lecture utilizing informal cooperative learning groups, have students complete an assignment in formal cooperative learning groups, conduct a short controversy, or present a short lecture and assign a short group assignment. If a lecture is to be given, it begins and ends with a focused discussion in an informal cooperative learning group and has paired discussions interspersed throughout the lecture (see Chapter 5). During both students would be asked to **formulate, share, listen, create**:

1. **Formulate** an answer to the question or solution to the problem individually (1 to 2 minutes).

2. **Share** your answer with your partner (1 minute each).

3. **Listen** carefully to your partner's answer.

4. **Create** an answer through discussion that is superior to your individual answers (1 to 2 minutes).

Students are slow and awkward at following this procedure initially but once they become familiar with it they work intensely. Again, this is an important time for the professor to circulate among the students, listen in, and learn what they already know about the topic. In the long run it is important to vary the type of informal cooperative learning groups, using simultaneous explanation pairs one day and cooperative note-taking pairs another (see Chapter 5).

If a group assignment is given, it is carefully structured to be cooperative (see Chapter 4). The instructor notes the objectives of the lesson, makes a series of preinstructional decisions, communicates the task and the positive interdependence, monitors the groups as they work and intervenes when needed, and evaluates students' learning and has groups process how effectively members are working together. Formal cooperative learning groups are used when the instructor wishes to achieve an instructional objective that includes conceptual learning, problem solving, or the development of students' critical thinking skills. Formal cooperative learning groups are needed for simulations of first-hand experiences, role playing, or the sharing of expertise and resources among members.

If a controversy is to be structured, it may be a small issue that can be quickly discussed or it may be a complex issue that can last for several class sessions. Each step of the controversy process may be scheduled in consecutive class sessions.

Near the end of the class period summarizing and synthesizing needs to be structured in. In a shorter class period this may simply involve each student working with his or her partner to create a list of three or four major learnings and one or two questions. Periodically these can be collected by the professor. Quickly reading and commenting on these student summaries provides the professor with valuable information about what the students are learning and what questions they have, and sends a message to the students that the activity is important.

At the end of the class session students meet in their base groups to summarize and synthesize what they have learned. Base groups may hand in a written summary of the new concept learned today, or elaborate by relating the new learning to previously learned material, or apply what they have learned to a practical situation. Finally, members of the base groups should celebrate their hard work and success. At the end of the class session, after working cooperatively for 50 minutes, students (and the professor) often have the joyful feeling "We did it." Students leave the class with an empowered sense of, "Since **we** did it, **I** can do it."

Ninety-Minute Class Session

The basic structure of a 90-minute period is essentially the same as for the 50-minute period except it is easier to both lecture and have cooperative learning groups complete an assignment within one class session. Class begins with a base group meeting, the instructor gives a lecture using informal cooperative learning groups to ensure that students are cognitively active while the instructor disseminates information, conducts a formal cooperative learning activity to promote problem-solving and higher-level learning, and closes the class with a second base group meeting.

The base group meetings can be longer (up to 15 minutes) and more varied activities such as "reviewing advance preparation papers" or "progress checks" can be used. Valuable information can be gleaned by eavesdropping on the base groups and noting which parts of the assignment caused difficulty.

A lecture may follow. In using a variety of informal cooperative learning group procedures, faculty need to structure carefully the five basic elements of cooperative learning within the learning situation.

Formal cooperative learning groups become the heart of longer class periods. Students take increasing responsibility for each other's learning, and the professor takes increasing responsibility for guiding this process. Faculty should structure positive interdependence in a variety of ways and give students the opportunity to promote each other's learning face-to-face. It is helpful to use a variety of formal cooperative learning procedures, such as jigsaw, problem- solving, joint projects, and peer composition (see Chapter 4). Occasional reporting by the students to the whole class (by randomly calling on individual students to report for their group, of course) can help the professor guide the overall flow of the class. Carefully monitor the cooperative groups and use formal observation sheets to collect concrete data on group functioning to use during whole class and small group processing.

A 90-minute class period allows adequate time to conduct a quick controversy if it is well planned.

Class ends with a base group meeting. Often base group members sign a contract as to how they will apply what they have learned (see Chapter 5). Longer class periods, such as three-hour sessions, may be structured similarly to the 90-minute class period with the addition of using more than one formal cooperative learning activity during class time.

Giving Students Grades in Cooperative Learning Situations

Grades represent the most common reward given in most classrooms. Current grading systems, however, have created a tragedy within many colleges in America. Almost every student comes to college optimistic about his or her chances for success. Many end up believing they are failures and losers. There are students of average intelligence who refuse to enter college because they believe that they are not smart enough to do so. Their poor academic self-esteem has helped close one door on their future.

One cause is the evaluation and recognition systems used in our classrooms. Some students consistently receive recognition and others never do. If you compare the initial fall test scores in a classroom with final grades in June, there is a high correlation. All year long, the top students are given recognition for being successful. Other students receive little or none. There are winners and there are losers.

The situation is changed dramatically when high-, medium-, and low-achieving students are placed in a cooperative learning group. When the group succeeds, all members are recognized as having contributed to their joint success. Even low-ability students believe **we** can succeed, **we** are successful. Being part of a cooperative learning group empowers each student by increasing his or her **self-efficacy**--the belief that if effort is exerted, success is possible. All students are recognized as contributing to the group's success.

The way grades are given depends on the type of interdependence the instructor wishes to create among students. Norm-referenced grading systems place students in competition with each other. Criterion-referenced grading systems require students to either work individualistically or cooperatively. How to give grades to communicate to students that they "sink or swim together" is one of the most difficult aspects of structuring learning situations cooperatively. Here are a number of suggestions.

1. **Individual score plus bonus points based on all members reaching criterion**: Group members study together and ensure that all have mastered the assigned material. Each then takes a test individually and is awarded that score. If all group members achieve over a preset criterion of excellence, each receives a bonus. An example is as follows:

Criteria for Bonus Points	Group	Scores	Total
100 15 points	Bill	100	110
90 - 99 10 points	Sally	90	100
80 - 89 5 points	Jane	95	105

2. **Individual score plus bonus points based on lowest score**: The group members prepare each other to take an exam. Members then receive bonus points on the basis of the lowest individual score in their group. An example is as follows:

Criteria for Bonus Points	Group	Scores	Total
71 - 75 1 point	Bill	100	103
76 - 80 2 points	Sally	98	101
81 - 85 3 points	Jane	84	87
86 - 90 4 points			
91 - 95 5 points			
96 - 100 6 points			

This procedure emphasizes encouraging, supporting, and assisting the low achievers in the group. The criterion for bonus points can be adjusted for each learning group, depending on the past performance of their lowest member.

3. **Individual score plus group average**: Group members prepare each other to take an exam. Each takes the examination and receives his or her individual score. The scores of the group members are then averaged. The average is added to each member's score. An example is given below.

Student	Individual Score	Average	Final Score
Bill	66	79	145
Sally	89	79	168
Jane	75	79	154
David	86	79	165

4. **Individual score plus bonus based on improvement scores**: Members of a cooperative group prepare each other to take an exam. Each takes the exam individually and receives his or her individual grade. In addition, bonus points are awarded on the basis of whether members' percentage on the current test is higher than the average percentage on all past tests (i.e., their usual level of performance). Their percentage correct on past tests serves as their base score that they try to better. Every two tests or scores, the base score is updated. If a student scores within 4 points (above or below) his or her base score, all members of the group receive 1 bonus point. If they score 5 to 9 points above their base score, each group member receives 2 bonus points. Finally, if they score 10 points or more above their base score, or score 100 percent correct, each member receives 3 bonus points.

5. **Totaling members' individual scores**: The individual scores of members are added together and all members receive the total. For example, if group members scored 90, 85, 95, and 90, each member would receive the score of 360.

6. **Averaging of members' individual scores**: The individual scores of members are added together and divided by the number of group members. Each member then receives the group average as their mark. For example, if the scores of members were 90, 95, 85, and 90, each group member would receive the score of 90.

7. **Group score on a single product**: The group works to produce a single report, essay, presentation, worksheet, or exam. The product is evaluated and all members receive the score awarded. When this method is used with worksheets, sets of problems, and

examinations, group members are required to reach consensus on each question and be able to explain it to others. The discussion within the group enhances the learning considerably.

8. **Randomly selecting one member's paper to score:** Group members all complete the work individually and then check each other's papers and certify that they are perfectly correct. Since each paper is certified by the whole group to be correct, it makes little difference which paper is graded. The instructor picks one at random, grades it, and all group members receive the score.

9. **Randomly selecting one member's exam to score:** Group members prepare for an examination and certify that each member has mastered the assigned material. All members then take the examination individually. Since all members have certified that each has mastered the material being studied, it makes little difference which exam is scored. The instructor randomly picks one, scores it, and all group members receive that score.

10. **All members receive lowest member score:** Group members prepare each other to take the exam. Each takes the examination individually. All group members then receive the lowest score in the group. For example, if group members score 89, 88, 82, and 79, all members would receive 79 as their score. This procedure emphasizes encouraging, supporting and assisting the low-achieving members of the group and often produces dramatic increases in performance by low-achieving students.

11. **Average of academic scores plus collaborative skills performance score:** Group members work together to master the assigned material. They take an examination individually and their scores are averaged. Concurrently, their work is observed and the frequency of performance of specified collaborative skills (such as leadership or trust-building actions) is recorded. The group is given a collaborative skills performance score, which is added to their academic average to determine their overall mark.

12. **Dual academic and nonacademic rewards:** Group members prepare each other for a test, take it individually, and receive an individual grade. On the basis of their group average they are awarded a homework pass or some other valued reward.

Myth: A Single Group Grade Shared by Group Members Is Not Fair

Having students work together on a joint product is viewed by many educators as being less fair to each student than is having each student work alone to produce an individual product for which he or she receives an individual grade. Most students would disagree. It is important that students perceive the distribution of grades and other rewards as being fair, otherwise they may become unmotivated and withdraw psychologically or physically. There have been a number of investigations of students' views of the fairness of various grading systems. There are five major findings:

1. Students who "lose" in a competitive learning situation commonly perceive the grading system as being unjust and, consequently, dislike the class and the instructor (Johnson & Johnson, 1983, 1989a).

2. Before a task is performed, students generally perceive a competitive grading system as being the most fair, but after a task is completed, having all members receive the same grade or reward is viewed as the fairest (Deutsch, 1979).

3. The more frequently students have experienced long-term cooperative learning experiences, and the more cooperative learning was used in their classes, then the more the students believed that everyone who tries has an equal chance to succeed in class, that students get the grades they deserve, and that the grading system is fair (Johnson & Johnson, 1983).

4. Students who have experienced cooperative learning prefer group grades over individual ones (Wheeler & Ryan, 1973).

5. Achievement is higher when group grades (compared with individual ones) are given (Johnson & Johnson, 1989a). The implications of this research for instructors is that group grades may be perceived to be unfair by students before the students have participated in a cooperative learning activity. Once cooperation has been experienced for a while, however, a single group grade will probably be perceived as the fairest method of evaluation.

There are three general systems for distributing rewards within our society: **equity** (where the person who contributed the most or scored the highest receives the greatest reward), **equality** (where every participant receives the same reward), and **need** (where those who have the greatest need receive the greatest reward) (Deutsch, 1975). All three systems operate within our society and all three systems have their ethical rationale. Typically, the equality system assures members of a family, community, organization, or society that their basic needs will be met and that diverse contributions will be equally valued. The need system assures members that in moments of crisis others will provide support and assistance. And the equity system assures members that if they strive for excellence, their contributions will be valued and rewarded. Educators who wish to give rewards in the classroom only on the basis of equity may be viewing "fairness" from too limited a perspective.

In the ideal classroom, at the end of a grading period, each student will have a number of grades resulting from collaborative efforts, a number of grades resulting from individualistic efforts, and a number of grades resulting from competitive efforts. When these grades are added together, instructors we have worked with inevitably find that high-achievers get "A's." Because of the higher achievement found in cooperative learning situations, however, middle- and low-achievers may receive higher grades than they would if the classroom was dominated by competitive or individualistic learning situations. The number of students receiving "B's" and "C's" will tend to grow larger as the positive peer pressure and support raise achievement. The number of "D's" and "F's" will tend to disappear as collaborators refuse to allow unmotivated students to stay that way. In order not to undermine the overall class cooperativeness it is important to use a criterion-referenced evaluation system in determining final grades.

Personalizing The Learning Environment

Learning is a personal experience. The more frequently cooperative learning is used, the more personalized the learning will be. Haines and McKeachie (1967) demonstrated that students in classes stressing competition for grades showed more tension, self-doubt, and anxiety than did students working in cooperative learning groups. There are a number of ways that the learning environment may be personalized.

First, monitor cooperative groups closely. Circulate among the groups, systematically observe, and often stop to (a) join in and interact with group members or (b) intervene within a group . The more attentive instructors are to individual students the more effective and personal the teaching. It is easier to make a direct comment to a student in a small group than in a whole- class setting.

Second, work to establish classroom norms that promote individuality, creativity, and sensitivity to students' needs. All students need to feel respected, free, and motivated to make the maximum contributions of what they are capable.

Third, demonstrate a willingness to learn from students. Every teacher- student interaction carries potential for learning for both the teacher and students. When faculty accept and learn from students' contributions, the learning experience becomes more personal for the students.

Fourth, present students with a realistic assessment of what they have learned and with high expectations as to what they can learn if they make the effort. Faculty offer students a tension between present and future, actuality and possibility. In a detailed and practical study of skills possessed by effective teachers of adults, Schneider, Klemp, and Kastendiek (1981) concluded that effective teachers (a) believe that average students are competent, (b) identify and affirm students' capabilities, (c) express the view that students are capable of change, and (d) accept student suggestions for changes in learning plans when the changes are consistent with the students' learning objectives. Daloz (1987) found that effective instructors were described by students as "giving me confidence in myself," "kept pushing me and telling me I could do it," and "having faith in me even when I did not." Through their expectations of students, faculty can communicate where students are and what they can become without allowing either to eclipse the other.

Fifth, send them out of class feeling happy. John Wooden, the basketball coach at UCLA for many years, wrote out a detailed lesson plan for every one of his practices. At the end of each lesson plan he wrote "Send the players to the showers happy." Similarly, Durward Rushton (a principal in Hattisburg, Mississippi) states that each student should feel personally **secure**, have a sense of **belonging**, and experience some **success** each class session (SBS). Instructors should adopt similar attitudes toward creating a positive atmosphere for each class session. One step to doing so is eliminating put-downs. Being put-down by a instructor is the most common response given to the question "What is your most memorable experience from high school?" (Kohl, personal communication, 1989). Many students are afraid to contribute in class, some for lack of confidence, others because they fear their ideas are not worthy. The simple procedure of saying something positive about every student comment, question, or answer to a question has remarkable power for transforming a classroom.

A simple means for promoting a personalized learning environment is having students (and you) wear name tags to help students learn each other's names. Instructors often comment that for their students, the most important word in the English language is their name. Name tagging is a simple procedure that makes a profound difference in the atmosphere of the classroom. Students immediately "warm-up" to their colleagues and seem to appreciate the opportunity to meet and greet each other. The short time that this activity consumes is more than compensated by the improvement in the learning mood of the students.

On the first day have students complete a name tag. In the center the student (and instructor) places his or her name (actually the way he or she prefers to be addressed) in print large enough to be read 20 feet away. In the corners are placed other information about the student, such as, Birthplace, Favorite place, Hobbies, Favorite artist, Something they're looking forward to, and major or profession. Finally, surrounding their name they are asked to place two or three adjectives that describe them. The students are then given about 10 minutes to meet and learn something about as many other students in the class as possible.

Cooperate And Graduate

The message in many colleges where cooperative learning is being implemented is "Succeeding in this class is hard work, difficult, and takes considerable effort. You do not have to do the work alone. Work together, help each other." Our motto is "Helping and sharing are not cheating during learning time." During testing time, of course, it's a different matter. At testing time we want to see what individuals can do. Students typically perform better on individual tests, however, after they have been prepared by their group. Succeeding academically results from group, not individual, efforts.

SAMPLE COURSE SYLLABUS

THE SOCIAL PSYCHOLOGY OF EDUCATION

Fall 1990

David W. Johnson

202 Pattee Hall, 624-7031

● Overview of the Course ●

This is an introductory course that will cover broad areas in social psychology with specific emphasis in education. Most topics will be teasers in the sense that entire courses could be developed around many of the areas we will discuss in one hour. Hopefully you will leave this course wanting to delve further into specific topics in social psychology. In this course you will be expected to become acquainted with the major theories, research, and "names" in the field. Class sessions will be spent in lectures, discussions, and experiential exercises.

● Textbooks ●

Deaux, K. & Wrightsman, L. (1984). **Social psychology in the '80s**. Monterey, CA: Brooks/Cole, Inc.

Johnson, D. W. (1970). **The social psychology of education**. New York: Holt, Rinehart & Winston.

Johnson, Johnson, & Smith

● **Course Requirements** ●

1. Attend and actively participate in class. This includes being prepared.

2. Read assigned texts.

3. Contract for a grade of C, B, or A (a grade of D or F is available upon request).

4. Participate in a base group that is required to ensure that all group members make satisfactory academic progress in achieving the goals of the course. This includes ensuring that all group members meet the requirements of the class by passing the tests and writing acceptable papers.

5. Pass the quizzes and examinations.

6. Write the papers required for your contracted grade (papers written jointly with other class members are encouraged).

● **Tests** ●

1. The **Group Discussion Test** consists of a meeting of your base group to discuss the content of the assigned reading. Each group will be expected to provide copies of the questions they discussed, an outline of their answers and procedures, and their subjective evaluation of the learning resulting from the experience. A more detailed handout on the group discussion test will be distributed. The test will take place during the next to last class session.

2. The **Basic Concepts Quizzes** will be composed of multiple choice or matching items drawn from readings, lectures, and class discussions. Successful performance is considered to be 90 percent of the questions answered correctly. Any group whose members do not answer 90 percent of the questions correctly will be required to indicate competence on incorrect items. These quizzes will take place weekly.

3. The **Basic Concepts Final Examination** will be given the final day of class. It represents the bottom line of the course. Anyone taking the course has to be able to pass this test at a 90 percent correct level. The test consists of questions taken from the quizzes.

• Papers •

1. **Short Paper**: Take a social issue, such as alienation, racism, sexism, pollution, or corruption in government and write a five or six page paper applying social psychological concepts, research, and theory to its solution. In writing the paper, take a viewpoint (perspective, frame of reference) opposite to your own and construct the paper to support that opposite viewpoint.

2. **Long Paper**: Write a (1) research review in an area of interest in social psychology (required of all MA and PhD degree students) or (2) project applying some aspect of social psychology to a practical situation (alternative for nondegree students). This paper should be approximately 12 pages long.

• Grading •

Grades will be determined on the basis of learning contracts. A certain minimum amount of work is expected of all students in a graduate level course. The alternative learning contracts are:

Grade C: Attend class
 Read assigned texts
 Take Group Discussion Test
 Meet requirements for Basic Concepts Quizzes and Examination

Grade B: Everything for grade of C
 Write the long paper

Grade A: Everything for the grade of B plus
 Write the short paper

All work must meet standards for acceptable performance level. On the final day of classes students must submit a written statement of the contract they are working to fulfill along with the required proof of meeting the contract. Although students will be given grades of "I" if necessary, it is highly discouraged. Absolutely no incompletes will be given for uncompleted group tests.

Class Sessions

WEEK 1: Introduction to the Course

WEEK 2: Systems Theories And Social Organizations

WEEK 3: Social Development

WEEK 4: Social Interdependence Theory

WEEK 5: Conflict Theories

WEEK 6: Attitude Acquisition and Change

WEEK 7: Equity And Attribution Theories

WEEK 8: Social Influence Theories

WEEK 9: Group Discussion Test

WEEK 10: Basic Concepts Test; Summary, Evaluation of Course

● Course Requirements ●

The basic assumption of this course is that learning results from a continuing process of rational discourse. Within the course there are both opportunities and responsibilities. Your **opportunity** is to learn. Your **responsibilities** are to maximize your learning from the course (i.e., improve your intellectual understanding), maximize the learning of your classmates, and to apply what you learn to your work and personal life. To take advantage of the opportunity and to meet your responsibilities you are to:

1. **Master the basic concepts, theories, research studies, and researchers.** You are expected to know more after taking this course than you did before.

2. **Think critically about the course content** and topics to achieve understanding and insights.

3. **Explain precisely to several classmates your learnings, insights, and conclusions.** Your learning is not complete until you teach what you know to someone else and can describe precisely what you have learned.

4. **Ask others to share their knowledge**, conclusions, and insights with you. When they do so, listen carefully, **elaborate by explaining how what you have just learned from them fits in with previous knowledge learned**, and thank them.

5. **Engage in intellectual controversy** by taking positions counter to those of your classmates, developing clear rationales from the material in the texts, challenging their reasoning and conclusions, and arguing the issues until you are logically persuaded. Review the rules for constructive controversy before doing so.

6. **Get your work done on time.** You cannot deprive classmates of their opportunity and obligations to help you improve your understanding, conclusions, and insights.

7. Plan how to apply what you have learned to improve the quality of your work and personal life. **You should be able to describe precisely how you can use what you have learned in this class.**

● **Preparation Papers** ●

To prepare for each class session students may be required to complete a short writing assignment. Even if it is not graded it compels them to organize their thoughts and take some responsibility for how the class goes. Before each class session students:

1. Choose a major theory, concept, research study, or theorist/researcher discussed in the assigned reading.

2. Students write a two-page analysis of it:

   a. Summarizing what the assigned reading had to say about it.

   b. Adding material from another source (research article or book) to enrich their analysis of the theory, concept, research study, or theorist/researcher.

Students bring two copies of the paper to the class. The members of your base group or discussion pair will read, edit, and criticize the paper. The criteria they will use to do so include:

1. An introductory paragraph that outlines the content of the paper.

2. Clear conceptual definition of concepts and terms.

3. Summary of and judgment about what is known empirically. (**R** = Substantial Research Support, **r** = some research support)

4. Description of and judgment about theoretical significance. (**T** = Substantial Theoretical Significance, **t** = some theoretical significance)

5. Description of and judgment about practical significance. (**P** = Substantial Practical Significance, **p** = some practical significance)

6. Brief description of a relevant study that should be conducted.

7. New information beyond what is contained in the assigned readings.

● **Research Review Paper** ●

Write a:

1. **Research review** in an area of interest related to the content of this course (required of all MA or PhD students). The **research review** should move the general to the specific, and may be thought of as a funneling process in which you focus more and more specifically on the topic in which you are interested. As you reach the narrow part of the funnel (research as specific as possible to the topic you have selected), some unanswered research questions should become apparent. These questions can provide direction to further research in this area of inquiry. In the final two pages of the paper, design a research study to answer one of the questions identified.

2. **Practical project** applying some aspect of this course to a practical situation (alternative for nondegree students). The **practical application paper** should demonstrate an understanding of the theory and research covered in the course, but with the purpose of applying that body of knowledge to a practical situation.

Papers should be scholarly, 10 to 12 pages long, and well written. Papers should be typewritten on bond paper (not erasable bond), or done by computer on computer paper. Use APA style, double space pages, with characters per inch no less than 10.

All work must meet standards for acceptable performance level. Students submitting course work that is found to be unacceptable or incomplete will be awarded a grade of "I" with the option of clearing up the course work problems and receiving the grade for which they have contracted, or taking a lower grade. Efforts will be made to contact these students, but the final responsibility lies with the student for these matters.

● **Writing A Research Review Paper** ●

1. **Purposes:**

   a. Review, organize, and synthesize a number of research studies on a specific topic.

   b. Plan a research study that will contribute new knowledge to the topic.

2. **Sections:**

    a. Introduction and statement of the problem.

    b. Summary of relevant theories.

    c. Conceptual definitions of variables.

    d. Review of the relevant research studies, summarizing for each study the:

        1. Conceptual and operational definitions of variables.

        2. Procedures.

        3. Results.

        4. Conclusions.

    e. Overall conclusions and interpretations you make from your reading and thinking.

    f. What is next--a research study that needs to be conducted.

3. **Questions to ask while evaluating a study:**

    a. How do the investigators define the concepts conceptually and operationally?

    b. Are different investigators talking about the same thing, or are they using the same words for different phenomena?

    c. Was the evidence gathered relevant to the problem being investigated?

    d. Were there any sources of bias in the way the data were gathered?

    e. Were there different conditions in the research studies that might explain the differences in findings?

4. **One benefit from understanding the research process** is being able to judge whether a study has been carried out in such a way that (a) you can have reasonable confidence in its findings, and (b) you can apply its findings to the specific situation at hand. In other words, the better you understand the research process, the better able you are to evaluate the validity and applicability of research results.

● **Peer Editing Of Research Review Papers** ●

The research review paper required for this class needs to be written in conjunction with your base group. You are required to hand in a paper revised on the basis of two reviews by members of your base groups. The procedure for writing the paper is as follows.

1. Students are assigned to a base group. Each is individually responsible for writing a paper reviewing the research in an area related to the content of the course.

2. Each member describes to the base group what he or she is planning to write. Base group members listen carefully, probe with a set of questions, and outline the research paper. The written outline is given to the member. This procedure is repeated with every group member.

3. Students search individualistically for the research articles they need to write their papers, keeping an eye out for material useful to the other members of their base group.

4. Base group members work together to write the first paragraph of each research paper to ensure that they all have a clear start on their papers.

5. The students write their compositions individualistically. Cooperative papers are allowed if they clearly reflect twice the work of an individual's paper (if an individual's paper is 10 pages long, a paper written by a pair should be 20 pages long).

6. When completed, the students proofread each other's compositions, making corrections in capitalization, punctuation, spelling, language usage, topic sentence usage, making suggestions for better organizing and conceptualizing the review, and generally making suggestions about how to improve other aspects of the research review.

7. Students rewrite their research reviews, utilizing the suggestions for revisions.

8. Base group members reread each other's research reviews and sign their names (indicating that they guarantee that the review is of high quality).

Students are evaluated in two ways: Does their research review paper meet the criteria for adequacy and do the research reviews of the other members of their base group meet the criteria for adequacy.

Johnson, Johnson, & Smith

When the research reviews are completed, the base group discusses how effectively they worked together (listing the specific actions they engaged in to help each other), plan what behaviors they are going to emphasize in the next peer-editing situation, and thank each other for the help and assistance received.

● Types Of Cooperative Learning ●

In this class cooperative learning will be used to (a) teach specific content (**formal learning groups**), (b) ensure active cognitive processing during a lecture (**informal learning groups**), and (c) provide long-term support and assistance for academic progress (**base groups**). When used in combination, these formal, informal, and base cooperative learning groups provide an overall structure to this class.

Formal cooperative learning groups may last for one class period to several weeks to complete a specific task or assignment. In a cooperative learning group you work together to accomplish shared goals. You have two responsibilities: to maximize your learning and to maximize the learning of all your groupmates. **First**, you receive instructions and objectives from the instructor. **Second**, the instructor assigns you to a learning group, provides needed materials, arranges the room, and may give you a specific role to fulfill in the group. **Third**, the instructor explains the task and the cooperative structure. Any required academic concept, principle, and strategy that you need to complete the assignment is presented at this point. **Fourth**, the instructor monitors the functioning of your learning group and intervenes to (a) teach cooperative skills and (b) provide assistance in academic learning when it is needed. **Finally**, the instructor will evaluate the quality and quantity of your learning and ensure that your group processes how effectively members are working together. If you need help in completing the assignment, first ask your peers for assistance and request help from your instructor second. You are expected to interact with groupmates, share ideas and materials, support and encourage each other's academic achievement, orally explain and elaborate the concepts and strategies being learned, and hold each other accountable for completing the assignment. A criteria-referenced evaluation system is used.

Informal cooperative learning groups are temporary, ad hoc groups that last from a few minutes to one class period. They are used to focus your attention on the material to be learned, set a mood conducive to learning, help organize in advance the material to be covered in a class session, ensure that you cognitively process the material being taught, and provide closure to an instructional session. They are often organized so that you engage in **focused discussions** before and after a lecture and interspersing **turn-to-your-partner**

discussions throughout a lecture. They help counter what is proclaimed as the main problem of lectures: "The information passes from the notes of the professor to the notes of the student without passing through the mind of either one."

Base groups are described in the next section.

During the past 90 years over 600 research studies have been conducted comparing the effectiveness of cooperative, competitive, and individualistic efforts. These studies have been conducted by a wide variety of researchers in different decades with different age subjects, in different subject areas, and in different settings. More is known about the efficacy of cooperative learning than about lecturing, departmentalization, the use of instructional technology, or almost any other aspect of education. From this research you may expect that the more you work in cooperative learning groups the more you will learn, the better you will understand what you are learning, the easier it will be to remember what you learn, and the better you will feel about yourself, the class, and your classmates. A comprehensive review of all studies and meta- analyses of their results may be found in:

Johnson, D. W., & Johnson, R. (1989) **Cooperation and Competition: Theory and Research**. Edina, MN: Interaction Book Company.

● **Base Groups** ●

Base groups are long-term, heterogeneous cooperative learning groups with stable membership whose primary responsibility is to provide each student the support, encouragement, and assistance they need to make academic progress. Base groups personalize the work required and the course learning experiences. During this course you will be a part of a base group consisting of four participants. These base groups will stay the same during the entire course. The members of your base group should exchange phone numbers and information about schedules as you may wish to meet outside of class. **The base group functions as a support group for members that:**

1. Gives assistance, support, and encouragement for mastering the course content and skills and provides feedback on how well the content and skills are being learned.

2. Gives assistance, support, and encouragement for thinking critically about the course content, explaining precisely what one learns, engaging in intellectual controversy, getting the work done on time, and applying what is learned to one's own life.

3. Provides a set of interpersonal relationships to personalize the course and an arena for trying out the cooperative learning procedures and skills emphasized within the course.

4. Provides a structure for managing course evaluation.

You have three major responsibilities:

1. Master and appropriately implement the theories, concepts, and body of knowledge (as well as skills) emphasized in the course.

2. Ensure that all members of your base group master and appropriately implement the theories, concepts, and body of knowledge (as well as skills) emphasized in the course.

3. Ensure that all members of the class master and appropriately implement the theories, concepts, and body of knowledge (as well as skills) emphasized in the course. In other words, if your group is successful, find another group to help until all members of the class are successful.

At the beginning of each session class members meet in their base groups to:

1. Congratulate each other for living through the time since the last class session and check to see that none of their group is under undue stress.

2. Check to see if members have completed their homework or need help and assistance in doing so.

3. Review what members have read and done since the last class session. Members should be able to give a brief, terse, succinct summary of what they have read, thought about, and done. They may come to class with resources they have found and want to share, or copies of work they have completed and wish to distribute to their base group members.

The basic concepts tests and the group discussion final examination will be conducted in base groups. Base group members are responsible for personally completing the tests at a 90 percent correct level and ensuring that all other members do likewise.

Base groups are available to support individual group members. If a group member arrives late, or must leave early on an occasion, the group can provide information about what that student missed. Additionally, group members may assist one another in writing the required papers for the class. The assignments may be discussed in the base groups, papers may be planned, reviewed, and edited in base groups, and any questions regarding the course assignments and class sessions may be first addressed in the base group. If the group is not able to resolve the issue, it should be brought to the attention of the instructor or the teaching assistant.

All members are expected to contribute actively to the class discussions, work to maintain effective working relationships with other participants, complete all assignments, assist classmates in completing their assignments, express their ideas, not change their minds unless they are persuaded by logic or information to do so, and indicate agreement with the base group's work by signing the weekly contract.

Johnson, Johnson, & Smith

• **Group Discussion Test** •

For the **group discussion test** you will meet with your base group and discuss the content of the assigned reading. Find a comfortable spot for your group to meet. The **purpose** of the group discussion test is to have a thorough, intellectually stimulating, creative, fun, and practically useful discussion of the assigned texts. More specifically, the **task** is to demonstrate mastery and deeper-level understanding of the assigned readings. This task is to be accomplished **cooperatively**. You are to generate one set of answers for the group and all members must agree with and be able to explain the answers. During the group test group members should focus on:

1. Integrating relevant theory, research, and practical experiences.

2. Analyzing in depth possible answers to the question in order to achieve insights into the issue.

3. Thinking divergently.

4. Critically examining each other's reasoning and engaging in constructive controversy.

5. Making the examination a fun and enjoyable experience for everyone.

To structure this process a number of discussion questions are attached. These questions are aimed at being **integrative** in the sense that material from many different chapters and books are relevant to answering them. So will be your personal and practical experiences and background. The **responsibilities of each group member** are to:

1. Choose two of the suggested discussion questions. For each question think carefully about the answer. Make sure that your answer combines material from many different chapters of the assigned texts as well as your own relevant personal experiences and background. Learn the answer to the questions thoroughly as you will be the **group expert** on what the text books have to say about the issue highlighted in the question.

2. Plan how to lead a group discussion on the question that will required higher-level reasoning, critical thinking, conceptual integration of material from many different chapters of the assigned texts, and a working knowledge of the specific relevant theories and research findings. In order to do so you will need to prepare for each group member (a) a typed outline of the answer to the question with the relevant page

numbers in the assigned text books and (b) copies of relevant written information to facilitate discussion. As members of your group may be visual rather than auditory learners, **prepare visuals** such as diagrams, charts, and cartoons to help them learn, think critically about, and conceptually integrate the relevant theories, research, and practical experiences.

3. Come to the examination prepared to contribute to the discussion of each question and to learn, think critically about, and conceptually integrate the theory, research, and practical experiences relevant to each question discussed.

The group discussion test should last for at least three hours. Cover at least one question from each member. Since each member will come prepared to lead a discussion on two questions, flip a coin to select which question will be part of the examination. **Guidelines** to follow are:

1. Stick to the questions. It is easy to go off on tangents.

2. Cite specific theories, research, and concepts discussed in the texts. Refer to specific pages. It is easy to make overly broad generalizations and to state personal opinions that are not supported by current knowledge.

3. Refer to personal experiences. Comparing the theories and research findings against your personal and practical experiences is valuable and often allows for integration of several concepts. It is not productive, however, to merely "b.s." about "what happened to me."

4. Set time limits for each question and stick to these limits rigidly.

5. Encourage disagreement and controversy. All viewpoints and positions should be encouraged as long as they can be supported by theory and research. Follow the rules for constructive controversy.

6. Take responsibility for both task and maintenance actions. Your group has a definite task to accomplish (i.e., demonstrate understanding of the field of social psychology), but the discussion should be enjoyable as well as a productive learning experience.

7. All members must participate actively to (a) contribute to the learning of others and (b) demonstrate overtly to the other members of the group that he or she has read the texts and mastered the content of the course.

To document that the group test did take place and that the criteria for passing were met by all group members, each member will be required to sign the certification form. Make sure that there are no "free-loaders." Do not sign off for a group member unless he or she arrived at the examination fully prepared and participated actively in the discussion of each question. If any group member was absent, the group is to determine whether the absence was excusable and what the member has to do to make up the test.

The group will be expected to hand in a **report** consisting of the certification form, a listing of the questions discussed with a summary of the answers and conclusions generated by the discussion, a description of the procedures followed, and a subjective evaluation of the learning resulting from the experience.

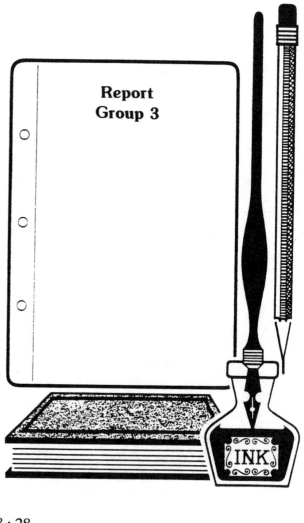

Group Exam Certification Form

We, the undersigned, certify that we have participated in the group discussion examination and have met the following criteria:

1. We understand the basic concepts, theories, and bodies of research presented in the texts and lectures.

2. We know the major theorists and researchers discussed in the texts and lectures.

3. We can apply the theories and research findings to practical situations.

4. We can conceptualize a research question and design a research study to test our hypotheses.

5. We have submitted our choice of questions and a brief summary of each answer we have formulated as a group.

Name (Please Print)	Signature	Date

Basic Concepts Test

This course will cover a body of knowledge that includes concepts, theories, research studies, and researchers. As a result of taking this course there is a mastery of the basic content that is required. Your mastery of this body of knowledge has to be demonstrated. **The basic concepts test** is composed of multiple-choice or matching test items drawn from the readings, lectures, and class discussions. Each student will take the examination individually. **Until all members of the base group complete the examination successfully, however, no base group member will receive a grade for the course.** Successful performance is considered to be 90 percent of the questions answered correctly. Any student who does not score 90 percent or better on the test will be required to meet with their base group and receive remedial help in reviewing the concepts, theories, research studies, or researchers they did not know, until they can indicate competence on 90 percent of the test items.

Student Contract

Name:_____

Please fill out this contract and return it with the completed course requirements.

I have contracted for a **grade** of _____.

_____ Read assigned texts.

_____ Attended class and actively participated.

_____ Completed basic concepts tests at a 90 percent correct level.

_____ Completed the group discussion final examination.

_____ Submitted the long research review or application paper.

_____ Submitted the short paper.

Signature: _____ **Date:** _____

Johnson, Johnson, & Smith

Course_____ Quarter & Year_____

Name_____ Group Number_____

Phone Number_____ Degree Working Towards_____

Present Profession_____

Motivation For Taking This Course:

9 Faculty Working Cooperatively With Colleagues

Introduction

> *To have joy one must share it. Happiness was born a twin.*
>
> Indian Proverb

The college is an organization and, similar to all organizations, it has to achieve its goals, maintain effective working relationships among members, and adapt to changes in its community, country, and world. Like all organizations, colleges must adapt to changes in their environment or risk fading away like the dinosaurs. The dinosaur presumably made good day-to-day adaptations to its environment. It probably made a pretty good choice of what leaves to eat off what trees and selected the most desirable swamps in which to slosh. At a tactical level of decision, we have no reason to believe that these giant beasts were not reasonably competent. But, when faced with major changes in (a) the earth's climate and (b) competition from other animal life, the dinosaur was unable to make the fundamental changes required to adapt to the new environment conditions. Schools may now be faced with new environmental conditions that require them to do what the dinosaur could not.

To adapt to changing conditions in the community, society, and world, and to ensure that the college continuously develops as an organization, individuals within a college must **diagnoses** how effectively the college is functioning and then **intervene** to improve its effectiveness. Fundamental changes in current environmental conditions require fundamental changes in the organizational structure of the college. Structural change requires the redesign of work, a new organizational culture, and changes in the attitudes and competencies of administrators, faculty, and students. The required changes in colleges parallel the changes in organizational structure taking place within business and industry throughout the world.

For decades business and industrial organizations have functioned as "mass manufacturing" organizations that divided work into small component parts performed by individuals who worked separate from and, in many cases, in competition with peers. Personnel were considered to be interchangeable parts in the organizational machine. Such an organizational structure no longer seems effective and many companies are turning to the high productivity generated by teams.

Most colleges have also been structured as mass manufacturing organizations. Faculty work alone, in their own classrooms, with their own set of students, and with their own set of curriculum materials. Students could be assigned to any faculty member because instructors were interchangeable parts in the education machine and, conversely, an instructor could be given any student to teach. Colleges need to change from a mass-manufacturing competitive/individualistic organizational structure to a "high performance" cooperative team-based organizational structure. The new organizational structure is generally known as "the cooperative college."

The Organizational Structure Of Colleges

Two are better than one, because they have a good reward for their toil. For if they fall, one will lift up his fellow; but woe to him who is alone when he falls and has not another to lift him up...And though a man might prevail against one who is alone, two will withstand him. A threefold cord is not quickly broken.

Ecclesiastes 4:9-12

Colleges are not buildings, curriculums, and machines. **Colleges are relationships and interactions among people** (Johnson & Johnson, 1989b). How the interpersonal interaction is structured determines how effective colleges are. There are three ways that faculty relationships may be structured: competitively, individualistically, and cooperatively. Faculty effectiveness depends on the interpersonal interactions being oriented toward cooperatively achieving the goals of the college. Colleges must be cooperative places. The **cooperatively structured college** consists of cooperative learning within the classroom and cooperative efforts within the faculty. In other words, the organizational structure of colleges must change from a competitive/individualistic mass-manufacturing structure within which faculty work alone to a high-performance team-based organizational structure in which faculty work in teams. Such a change will not be easy in many cases as the organizational structure of the college traditionally has discouraged colleagiality among instructors and severely limited their opportunities to cooperate with each other.

Colleges are **loosely coupled** organizations in which instructors and administrators function far more independently than interdependently, with little or no supervision, engaging in actions that do not determine or affect what others do, and engage in actions that seem isolated from their consequences (Johnson & Johnson, 1989b). Instructors have been systematically isolated from one another during most of the college day. And that isolation often results in instructors experiencing an amorphous and diffuse competition with their peers.

A cooperative college structure begins in the classroom. Faculty typically cannot promote isolation and competition among students and be collaborative with colleagues. What is promoted in the instructional situations tends to dominate relationships among faculty. Instructors who regularly tell students, "Do not copy," "I want to see what you can do, not your neighbor," "Let's see who is best," and "Who is the winner," will in turn tend to approach their colleagues with the attitudes of, "Don't copy from me," and "Who is the best professor in our department?" The cooperative context that is necessary for faculty to learn from their colleagues begins in the classroom. Instructors may be expected to:

1. Structure the majority of learning situations cooperatively (see Johnson, Johnson, & Holubec, 1990). Cooperative learning requires that the instructor carefully creates positive interdependence, face-to-face promotive interaction, individual accountability, social skills, and group processing.

2. Teach students the leadership, decision-making, communication, trust-building, and conflict-resolution skills they need to function effectively within cooperative learning groups (see Johnson, 1990, 1991; Johnson & F. Johnson, 1991).

The use of cooperative learning will increase student achievement, build better working relationships among students and between the teacher and the students, and increase the college's ability to respond flexibly to new demands from and changing conditions in the community. In addition, by structuring cooperative learning and teaching students how to work effectively within cooperative teams, instructors themselves learn the skills and attitudes required to work cooperatively with their colleagues.

The second level in creating a cooperative college is to form colleagial support groups,

task forces, and ad hoc decision- making groups within the department and college (Johnson & Johnson, 1989b). The cooperative interaction among faculty should be as carefully structured as is the cooperative interaction among students in the classroom. All faculty should be involved in cooperative teams that meet regularly to work on meaningful tasks. The more faculty use cooperative learning, furthermore, the more likely they are to be productive members of faculty teams.

The third level in creating a cooperative college is to implement administrative cooperative teams within the college (Johnson & Johnson, 1989b). The president should organize administrators into cooperative teams similarly to how faculty organize students into cooperative learning groups. All administrators should be involved in cooperative teams that meet regularly and work on meaningful tasks. If administrators compete to see who is the best, they are unlikely to be able to promote cooperation among faculty. The more the college faculty work in cooperative teams, the easier it will be for faculty to use cooperative learning and vice versa.

What is good for students is even better for faculty. The research that validates the use of cooperative learning in the classroom also validates the use of cooperative faculty teams at the departmental or college level. To increase the cooperation among faculty, faculty members may be organized into three different types of cooperative teams: colleagial support groups to encourage and support each other's efforts to use cooperative learning, task forces to make recommendations about how to deal with collegewide issues such as curriculum revision, and ad hoc decision-making groups to involve all faculty members in the important college decisions. The organizational structure of the classroom, department, and college are then congruent. Each level of cooperative teams supports and enhances the other levels.

Colleagial Support Groups

The success of a college largely depends on the success instructors have in educating students. The success of instructors in educating students depends on (a) how committed instructors are to continually increasing their instructional expertise and (b) the amount of physical and psychological energy instructors commit to their work. The commitment of physical and psychological energy to achieve the goal of improving one's instructional expertise is heavily influenced by the degree to which colleagues are supportive and encouraging. **Instructors generally teach better when they experience support from their peers.** In most colleges, however, such support is hard to achieve. As a result, instructors may feel harried, isolated, and alienated. Yet there is a human need to work cooperatively and intimately with supportive people. Colleagial support groups provide instructors with the opportunity to share ideas, support each other's efforts to use cooperative learning, and encourage each other.

A **colleagial support group** consists of two to five instructors who have the goal of improving each other's instructional expertise and promoting each other's professional growth (Johnson & Johnson, 1989b). Colleagial support groups should be small and members should be heterogeneous. **Colleagial support groups are first and foremost safe places where**:

1. Members like to be.

2. There is support, caring, concern, laughter, camaraderie, and celebration.

3. The primary goal of improving each other's competence in using cooperative learning is never obscured.

The purpose of this colleagial support group is to work jointly to improve continuously each other's expertise in using cooperative learning procedures or, in other words, to:

1. Provide the help, assistance, support, and encouragement each member needs to gain as high a level of expertise in using cooperative learning procedures as possible.

2. Serve as an informal support group for sharing, letting off steam, and discussing problems connected with implementing cooperative learning procedures.

3. Serve as a base for instructors experienced in the use of cooperative learning procedures to teach other instructors how to structure and manage lessons cooperatively.

4. Create a setting in which camaraderie and shared success occur and are celebrated.

Colleagial support groups succeed when they are carefully structured to ensure active participation by members and concrete products (such as lesson plans) that members can actually use. The structure must clearly point members toward increasing each other's expertise in implementing cooperative learning to prevent meetings from degenerating into gripe sessions, destructive criticism of each other, or amateur therapy. Members need to believe they sink or swim together, ensure considerable face-to- face discussion and assistance takes place, hold each other accountable to implement cooperative learning in between meetings, learn and use the interpersonal and small group skills required to make meetings productive, and periodically initiate a discussion of how effective the colleagial support group is in carrying out its mission. Task-oriented discussion, planning, and problem solving, as well as empathy and mutual support, should dominate the meetings.

The three key activities of a colleagial support group are (Little, 1981):

1. Frequent professional discussions of cooperative learning in which information is shared, successes are celebrated, and problems connected with implementation are solved.

2. Coplanning, codesigning, copreparing, and coevaluating curriculum materials relevant to implementing cooperative learning in the classrooms of the members.

3. Coteaching and reciprocal observations of each other teaching lessons structured cooperatively and jointly processing those observations.

Professional Discussions

Knowing is not enough; we must apply. Willing is not enough; we must do.

Goethe

What most instructors find very useful is opportunities to talk to each other about teaching. Within the colleagial support groups there is frequent, continuous, increasingly concrete and precise talk about the use of cooperative learning procedures. Through such discussion members build a concrete, precise, and coherent shared language that can describe the complexity of using cooperative learning procedures, distinguish one practice and its virtues from another, and integrate cooperative learning procedures into other teaching practices and strategies that they are already using. Through such discussions, instructors will exchange successful strategies and materials. They will focus on solving specific problems members may be having in perfecting their use of cooperative learning strategies. Most of all, instructors' comprehension and deeper-level understanding of the nature of cooperative learning will be enhanced by explaining how they are implementing it to their colleagues.

Expertise in using cooperative learning begins with conceptual understanding of what it is. Instructors must conceptually understand (a) the nature of cooperative learning, (b) how to implement the cooperative learning step-by-step, and (c) the results expected from the effective implementation of cooperative learning. Instructors must also think critically about the strategy and adapt it to their specific students and subject areas. They must retain what they have learned, integrate it into their conceptual networks about teaching, and conceptually combine cooperative learning with their existing teaching strategies. Such conceptual understanding is enhanced when instructors **orally summarize, explain, and elaborate** what they know about the cooperative learning to colleagues. Oral reviews consolidate and strengthen what is known and provide relevant feedback about the degree to which mastery and understanding have been achieved. The way people conceptualize material and organize it cognitively is markedly different when they are learning material for their own benefit from when they are learning material to teach to others (Murray, 1983). Material being learned to be taught or explained to others is learned at a higher conceptual level than is material being learned for one's own use. Such discussions, furthermore, enable the listeners to benefit from others' knowledge, reasoning, and skills. The concept of "gatekeeper," for example, was created to explain the process of information flow through an organization. **A gatekeeper** is a colleague who is sought out to explain what a new strategy is and how it may be used. It is within colleagial support groups that faculty exchange understandings of what cooperative learning is and how it may be used within their classes.

Joint Planning and Curriculum Design

Well begun is half done.

Aristotle

Once cooperative learning is understood conceptually, it must be implemented. If faculty are to progress through the initial awkward and mechanical stages to a routine-use, automatic level of mastery, they must (a) receive continual feedback as to the accuracy of their implementation and (b) be encouraged to persevere in their implementation attempts long enough to integrate cooperative learning into their ongoing instructional practice. Thus, productivity hinges on having colleagues to co- plan and co-teach lessons, observe one's implementation efforts, provide feedback, and encourage one to keep trying until the strategy is used routinely without conscious thought. Needless to say, such procedural learning usually does not take place within competitive and individualistic situations.

Members of professional support groups should frequently plan, design, prepare, and evaluate lesson plans together. This results in instructors sharing the burden of developing materials needed to conduct cooperative lessons, generating emerging understanding of cooperative learning strategies, making realistic standards for students and colleagues, and providing the machinery for each other to implement cooperative learning procedures. Instructors should leave each meeting of their colleagial support group with something concrete that helps them implement cooperative learning. The process of planning a lesson together, each conducting it, and then processing it afterwards is often constructive. This cycle of **coplanning, parallel teaching, coprocessing** may be followed by one of **coplanning, coteaching, coprocessing**.

The discussions and coplanning that take place within colleagial support groups ensures that instructors clarify their understanding of what cooperative learning is and create a support and accountability system to ensure that they try it out. The next steps in increasing expertise are to assess the consequences of using cooperative learning, reflecting on how well the lesson went, and teaching another cooperative lesson in a modified way. All of these steps benefit from the input and feedback from supportive colleagues. The more colleagues are involved in your teaching, the more valuable the help and assistance they can provide.

Reciprocal Observations

Members of colleagial support groups should frequently observe each other teaching lessons structured cooperatively and then provide each other with useful feedback. This observation and feedback provide members with shared experiences to discuss and refer to. The observation and feedback, furthermore, have to be reciprocal. **Instructors especially need to treat each other with the deference that shows they recognize that anyone can have good and bad days and that the mistakes they note in a colleague may be the same mistakes that they will make tomorrow.**

Guidelines to follow when observing the teaching of other colleagial support group members include:

1. Realize that you can learn from every other member of the group, regardless of his or her experience and personal characteristics.

2. Make sure observation and feedback is reciprocal.

3. Ask the person you're observing what he/she would like you to focus your attention on. This may include specific students the teacher may wish observed, specific aspects of structuring interdependence or accountability, or some other aspect of cooperative learning.

4. Focus feedback and comments on what has taken place, not on personal competence.

5. Don't confuse a teacher's personal worth with her/his current level of competence in using cooperative learning procedures.

6. Be concrete and practical in your discussions about how effectively members are using cooperative learning procedures.

7. Above all, communicate respect for each other's overall teaching competence. We all have professional strengths and weaknesses. Recognize and respect those strengths in each other.

Working cooperatively with others brings with it camaraderie, friendship, warmth, satisfaction, and feelings of success. These are all to be enjoyed.

Gaining Expertise In Using Cooperative Learning

Colleagial support groups are aimed at increasing faculty expertise in using cooperative learning. The professional discussions, coplanning of lessons, and reciprocal observing of each other's teaching all form a process within which faculty may progressively refine their ability to use cooperative learning procedures competently. More specifically, faculty progressively refine their competence in using cooperative learning by:

1. **Understanding conceptually what cooperative learning is and how it may be implemented in their classrooms.**

2. **Trying cooperative learning out in their classrooms with their students.** Faculty must be willing to take risks by experimenting with new instructional and managing strategies and procedures. Faculty risk short-term failure to gain long-term success in increasing their expertise by experimenting with new strategies and procedures. It is assumed that one's efforts will fail to match an ideal of what one wishes to accomplish for a considerable length of time until the new strategy is overlearned to a routine-use, automated level.

3. **Assessing how well cooperative learning lessons went and obtaining feedback on one's teaching from others.** Although the lesson may have not gone well, from the progressive refinement point of view failure never occurs. There are simply approximations of what one wants and with refining and fine- tuning of procedures and more practice the approximations get successively closer and closer to the ideal.

4. **Reflecting on what one did and how it may be improved.** The discrepancy between the real and the ideal is considered and plans are made about altering one's behavior in order to get a better match in the future.

5. **Trying cooperative learning out again in a modified and improved way.** Perseverance in using cooperative learning again and again and again is required until the instructor can teach a cooperative lesson routinely and without conscious planning or thought. Even at this point feedback should be attained, reflection on how to improve the implementation of cooperation, and refining and fine-tuning should take place until the teacher retires (or beyond).

As part of gaining expertise in using cooperative learning, teachers must:

1. **Take ownership of cooperative learning** and incorporate it into their professional identity. The more faculty use cooperative learning, and the more effort they expend implementing cooperative learning, the greater their feelings of success and the greater their ownership of cooperative learning.

Building

Expertise

2. **Train a colleague.** Expertise is never fully attained until one teaches what one knows to someone else.

Faculty do not become proficient in using cooperative learning procedures from attending a workshop or from reading this book. **Faculty become proficient and competent from doing.** For faculty to develop the expertise in cooperative learning procedures they need to structure a cooperative lesson routinely without conscious planning or thought, they have to use cooperative learning procedures frequently and regularly for several years. **Progressive refinement is not something you do once, it is a way of life!**

Providing Leadership To Colleagial Support Groups

For colleagial support groups to flourish they must be structured, encouraged, and rewarded by administrators. The Department Chair or even the Dean becomes the team leader even though they may attend only periodically. In general, leadership is provided by (Johnson & Johnson, 1989b):

1. **Challenging The Status Quo**: The status quo is the competitive-individualistic mass-manufacturing structure that dominates colleges and classrooms. In the classroom it is represented by the old paradigm that is using operationalized by lectures, whole class discussions, individual worksheets, and tests. Leaders challenge the efficacy of the status quo.

2. **Inspiring A Mutual Vision Of What The College Could Be**: Leaders enthusiastically and frequently communicate the dreams of establishing the new paradigm of teaching throughout the college. The leader is the **keeper of the dream** who inspires commitment to joint goals and objectives.

3. **Empowering Through Cooperative Teams**: This is the most important of all leadership activities. When faculty or students feel helpless and discouraged, providing them with a team creates hope and opportunity. It is social support from and accountability to valued peers that motivates committed efforts to achieve and succeed. In the classroom this means using cooperative learning. In the college this means using faculty teams.

4. **Leading By Example**: Leaders model the use of cooperative strategies and procedures and take risks to increase their professional competence. Actions must be congruent with words. What is advocated must be demonstrated publicly.

5. **Encouraging The Heart To Persist**: Long-term, committed efforts to achieve come from the heart, not the head. It takes courage and hope to continue to strive for

increased knowledge and expertise. It is the social support and concrete assistance from teammates that provides the strength to persist and excel.

Within this general leadership model, there are specific actions that leaders need to take to supervise and enhance the effectiveness of cooperative teams.

1. **Be a coach, not an autocrat.**

2. **Assume that all team members are competent and motivated.** Respect their abilities and respect them as people.

3. **Confront lazy and maladapted members.** One of the surest ways to undermine a team is to ignore its nonperformers. The resentment by other members will quickly destroy the team's effectiveness. When faced with a nonperformer or an obstructor, the leader clarifies what is expected of a team member, notes where changes are needed, gives a timeframe to implement the changes, and sets a clear deadline.

4. **Know how to structure and promote controversy.** Constructive conflict is the key to making team meetings fun, interesting, and challenging. Members must honestly share their points of view which will inevitably result in disagreement and conflict. Leaders help make the conflict a source of creativity and enjoyment.

5. **Be a player.** The leader must be a willing worker, a player, who is ready to take part in team meetings and in the implementation of cooperative learning within the classroom. Be accountable for contributing your share of the work. Coteaching with team members and coplanning of class sessions creates a bond that gives the leader increased influence as well as emotional enjoyment.

6. **Form your own colleagial support group.** You have to want to be a part of a team. Just as students meet in cooperative learning groups, faculty should meet in colleagial support groups. Just as faculty meet in colleagial support groups, administrators should meet with each other to support each other's efforts to implement cooperative procedures and strategies. If you believe in cooperation, be part of a cooperative effort at your own level.

The way to succeed in the old paradigm is to stress personal individual triumphs over peers. The way to succeed in the new paradigm is to provide the support and encouragement peers need to challenge their competencies and gain new levels of expertise. Contributing to team efforts is becoming paramount at every rung of the ladder in modern organizations. Colleges are no exception. Students and faculty have to want to belong to teams, they have to contribute their share of the work, and they must take positions and know how to advocate their views in ways that spark creative problem solving. To be a contributing team member you must be able to win a fair hearing for your ideas. Lone wolves who do not pull with their peers will increasingly find themselves the odd person out.

Colleagial support groups are not the only teams that faculty will belong to. There are also task forces and ad-hoc decision- making groups.

Collegewide Task Forces

For many collegewide issues (such as curriculum revision) task forces need to be organized (Johnson & Johnson, 1989b). Task forces carefully consider and research the issue and make a recommendation to the faculty as a whole. To be effective task forces need to collect valid and complete information about the problem, engage in controversy to ensure that all alternative solutions get a fair hearing, synthesize the best points from all perspectives, and make a free and informed choice of which alternative solution to adopt. Members must have continuing motivation to solve the problem so that a new recommendation may be made if the initial plan does not work.

Ad Hoc Decision-Making Groups

Within faculty meetings, ad hoc decision-making groups consider the recommendations of the task forces and decide whether to accept or modify the proposed solution (Johnson & Johnson, 1989b). Faculty members are assigned to temporary cooperative decision-making triads during a faculty meeting. The ad hoc groups consider the recommendation of the Task Force and decide whether to accept or modify the recommendation. Each ad-hoc group then reports its decision to the entire faculty, a discussion is held, and finally a faculty decision is made by consensus.

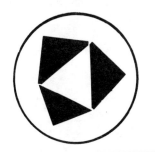

Conclusions

For things we have to learn before we can do them, we learn by doing them.

Aristotle

Traditionally, instructors have not been skilled in working effectively with adult peers. Blake and Mouton (1974) found that instructors and administrators lacked teamwork skills and were too ready to resolve differences by voting or by following the "official leader." They observed that educators were far less competent in working in small problem-solving groups than were industrial personnel. And they found that educators described themselves as being more oriented toward compromising quality of work for harmonious relationships, exerting minimal effort to get their job done, and being more oriented toward keeping good relationships than toward achieving the college's goals. Blumberg, May, and Perry (1974) found that instructors were ill- equipped behaviorally to function as part of a faculty, as they lacked the skills and attitudes needed for effective group problem-solving.

The lack of competence in being a constructive colleague, however, is not primarily the fault of instructors. The competitive/individualistic organizational structure existing in most colleges discourages cooperation among faculty. In order to implement cooperative learning within college classrooms, it may also be necessary to implement cooperative teams among faculty. It is time that the college became a modern organization. In the real world, most of the important work is done by cooperative teams rather than by individuals. When instructors are isolated and alienated from their peers, they will also tend to be alienated from their work and, therefore, not likely to commit a great deal of psychological energy to their jobs or commit themselves to grow professionally by attaining increased expertise. Instead of requiring instructors to engage in quiet and solitary performance in individual classrooms, instructors should be organized into cooperative teams with an emphasis on seeking and accepting help and assistance from peers, soliciting constructive criticism, and negotiating by articulating their needs, discerning what others need, and discovering mutually beneficial outcomes. The structuring of cooperation among faculty would both support the use of cooperative learning and provide a congruent organizational structure throughout the college.

The cooperative college begins in the classroom with faculty use of cooperative learning. **What is good for students, however, is even better for faculty.** In a cooperative college, three types of cooperative groups need to be employed (Johnson & Johnson, 1989b):

1. **Colleagial support groups** to increase instructors' instructional expertise and success. Their purpose is to improve members' professional competence and ensure members' professional growth. Colleagial support groups begin when two or more instructors meet together and talk about their efforts to implement cooperative learning. Participation in the colleagial support groups is aimed at increasing instructors' belief that they are engaged in a joint venture ("**We** are doing it!"), public commitment to peers to increase their instructional expertise ("I will try it!"), peer accountability ("They are counting on me!"), sense of social support ("They will help and assist me!"), sense of safety ("The risk is challenging but not excessive!"), and self-efficacy ("If I exert the effort, I will be successful!").

   The heart of college effectiveness is the faculty's teaching expertise. **Instructors progressively refine their expertise in implementing cooperative learning by being willing to take the risk of teaching cooperatively structured lessons, assessing the consequences of teaching lessons cooperatively, reflecting on how to improve implementation of cooperative learning, and teaching a modified lesson.** Instructors should then share what they have learned about implementing cooperative learning with colleagues. Gaining and maintaining expertise is an interpersonal process that requires supportive and encouraging colleagues.

2. **Task force groups** plan and implement solutions to collegewide issues and problems such as curriculum revisions, recruiting students, and creating more of a learning community. These small problem-solving groups diagnose a problem, gather data about the causes and extent of the problem, consider a variety of alternative solutions, make conclusions, and present a recommendation to the faculty as a whole.

3. **Ad hoc decision-making groups** used during faculty meetings to involve all faculty members in important college decisions. Ad hoc decision-making groups are part of a small- group / large-group procedure in which faculty members listen to a recommendation, are assigned to small groups (usually three members), meet in the small groups and consider the recommendation, discuss the positive and negative aspects of the recommendation, report to the entire faculty their support or questions about the recommendation, and then decide as a faculty what the course of action should be. Such a procedure maximizes the participation and involvement of all faculty members in the college's decision making.

The most important aspect of providing leadership within a college involves empowering faculty by structuring them into cooperative teams. Individual faculty members can feel helpless and discouraged. Having them work with colleagues provides hope and opportunity. It is social support from and accountability to valued peers that motivates committed efforts to succeed. Just as students need to be placed in permanent base groups, faculty need to participate in permanent **colleagial support groups** whose purpose is to increase faculty members' instructional expertise and success.

10 Conclusions

Old Vs. New Paradigm

> *Whether one believes in a religion or not, and whether one believes in rebirth or not, there isn't anyone who doesn't appreciate kindness and compassion...We must build closer relationships of mutual trust, understanding, respect, and help, irrespective of differences of culture, philosophy, religion, or faith.*
>
> The Dalai Lama, 1989 Nobel Peace Prize

Frank Koch, in **Proceedings**, the magazine of the Naval Institute, reported the following: Two battleships assigned to the training squadron had been at sea on maneuvers in heavy weather for several days. I was serving on the lead battleship and was on watch on the bridge as night fell. The visibility was poor with patchy fog, so the captain remained on the bridge keeping an eye on all activities. Shortly after dark, the lookout on the wing of the bridge reported, "Light, bearing on the starboard bow." "Is it steady or moving astern?" the captain called out. Lookout replied, "Steady, captain," which meant we were on a dangerous collision course with that ship. The captain then called to the signalman, "Signal that ship: We are on a collision course, advise you change course 20 degrees." Back came a signal, "Advisable for you to change course 20 degrees." The captain said, "Send, I'm a captain, change course 20 degrees." "I'm a seaman, second class," came the reply, "You had better change course 20 degrees." By that time the captain was furious. He spat out, "Send, I'm a battleship. Change course 20 degrees." Back came the flashing light, "I'm a lighthouse." We changed course.

A faculty member may feel like a captain of a battleship cruising through the seas too powerful to be challenged. When faced with the realities of the modern world, however, it is the faculty member who may find that he or she has to change course to stay afloat.

A **paradigm** is a theory, perspective, or frame of reference that determines how you perceive, interpret, and understand the world. The **old paradigm** of college education views teaching as the transfer of faculty's knowledge to passive students while faculty classify and sort students in a norm-referenced, competitive way. It is based on John Locke's assumption that the untrained mind is like a blank sheet of paper on which faculty write. Quality is assured by (a) selecting only the most intelligent and hard-working students for admission and (b) inspecting them continually to weed out those who prove to be defective. Whether or not colleges "add value" or just serve as a holding ground for students as they mature is unclear.

In college teaching a paradigm shift is taking place. Minor modifications of current teaching practices will not solve the problems with college instruction. A new approach is needed. The **new paradigm** of college education views teaching as helping students construct their knowledge in an active way while working cooperatively with classmates so that students' talents and competencies are developed. Quality is assured by motivating students to exert extraordinary effort to learn, grow, and develop. This is largely done through creating cooperative learning situations in which students care about each other and inspire each other to work hard in actively gaining knowledge and expertise. Adding value becomes an important faculty focus through knowing students personally and being committed to their intellectual growth and general well-being.

The new paradigm is operationalized through the use of cooperative learning within the classroom and the formation of faculty cooperative teams. Cooperative learning is the instructional use of small groups so that students work together to maximize their own and

each other's learning. There is considerable research demonstrating that cooperative learning produces higher achievement, more positive relationships among students, and healthier psychological adjustment than do competitive or individualistic experiences. These effects, however, do not automatically appear when students are placed in groups. To be cooperative, learning groups must be carefully structured to include the five basic elements: positive interdependence to ensure that students believe they "sink or swim together," face-to-face promotive interaction to ensure that students help and assist each other, individual accountability to ensure that everyone does their fair share of the work, social skills to work effectively with others, and group processing to reflect on and improve the quality of group work. There are, furthermore, many different ways to structure cooperative learning. Three broad categories of cooperative learning strategies are **formal cooperative learning groups** that last for several class sessions to complete assignments, **informal cooperative learning groups** that last for only a few minutes for a brief discussion, **cooperative base groups** that last for a semester or more to provide overall academic assistance. One of the most important uses of formal cooperative learning groups in college is through the use of **structured academic controversies**. Cooperation is just as powerful among faculty as it is among students. There needs to be an organizational restructuring from the existing competitive-individualistic college structure to a cooperative team-based college structure.

In order to understand the necessity of adopting the new paradigm to college education it may be helpful to consider in a broader context the issue of colleges providing quality education.

Mission, Product, Customers

The community stagnates without the impulse of the individual; the impulse dies away without the sympathy of the community.
William James, **Great Men and Their Environment**

To determine whether colleges are adding value by giving students a high-quality education, the mission of the college has to be determined. The mission has to specify who the college's customers are and what the product is. There are at least two complementary ways to describe the mission of colleges. **First**, the college may be viewed as an industry that produces and sells knowledge. The college's product is validated theory and its customers are those who need it. The **mission** of the college is to create and test theory through systematic programs of research. Concerns about **quality** focus on high well faculty develop sound theory, conduct systematic programs of reliable research to test the theory, operationalize the results into procedures consumers may use, and convince consumers to implement the procedures.

Second, the college may be viewed as a service organization that functions as a broker between (a) students and (b) employers and graduate schools. While colleges serve both students and the people who hire its graduates, the more important of the two is the student, as the success of a college's graduates will determine the level of demand for future graduates. The "product" of a college is the education it provides and students are its primary consumers. The **mission** of a college, therefore, is to provide quality education to students in order that they will be hired by desirable or prestigious companies or enter prestigious graduate schools. This requires more than intellectual development. Students should also be moral, decent, loving, and loveable people. Concerns about **quality** focus on how well students are educated and trained. The harder it is to get a job or be admitted to graduate school, the more pressure there is on colleges to provide a quality education. In determining the quality of a college's educational program there are at least three factors to consider:

1. Do all instructors provide high-quality teaching? High-quality teaching may be defined as the skillful and effective use of the new (rather than the old) paradigm. Faculty cannot grow by mimicking the past. Cooperative learning must dominate the classroom. Other new instructional methods, processes, procedures, and practices have to be adopted.

2. What is the time it takes to develop and implement improvements in teaching? This may be the most critical factor in a college being successful. In general, cycle time must be continuously reduced.

3. Has a process of continuous improvement in instruction been institutionalized to keep teaching in general and the use of cooperative learning in particular at the state-of-the-art level?

In order to improve faculty's teaching, reduce cycle time, and ensure a process of continuous improvement in instruction, colleges may wish to promote commitment to the new paradigm of teaching, use a benchmarking process to set goals, and adopt a cooperative-team organizational structure.

Changes In Attitudes And Thinking About Teaching

Collaboration operates through a process in which the successful intellectual achievements of one person arouse the intellectual passions and enthusiasms of others, and through a process in which a fact that was at first expressed by only one individual becomes a common intellectual possession instead of fading away into isolation.

Alexander Humboldt

To have high-quality instructional programs, faculty must change the way they think about teaching. The new paradigm must not only be adopted, but faculty must view it positively and be personally committed to implementing it within their classrooms. Faculty must believe that teaching in the old way harder and faster with more bells and whistles will not do. Faculty must believe in their hearts that it is a good idea to give up the "select and weed out" approach to instruction and replace it with the "development" approach. It is only through developing students' talents and competencies that colleges add value through their instructional program.

Benchmarking And Goal Setting

> *Almost every evening, either I went to Braque's studio or Braque came to mine. Each of us* **had** *to see what the other had done during the day. We criticized each other's work. A canvas wasn't finished unless both of us felt it was.*
>
> Pablo Picasso (in a letter to Francoise Gilot)

> *The things Picasso and I said to one another during those years will never be said again, and even if they were, no one would understand them anymore. It was like being roped together on a mountain.*
>
> Georges Braque

The benchmarking process involves establishing operating targets based on best known practices. There are four steps to using the benchmark process to set organizational goals. **First, identify the "best in class" in the world** (search for the practices that will lead to superior performance of students, faculty, and administrators). **Second, set a goal to achieve that level of performance as a minimum** (establish operating targets based on the best possible practices). A college must benchmark its instructional program against the leading instructional programs in the world to determine where the college is today and what the faculty needs to do to maintain or reach "world-class" instruction. Doing so involves examining quality of instruction, its cost, its flexibility, and its speed of delivery. **Third, develop performance measures to evaluate every function's contribution toward reaching the college's goals.** These measures must go beyond student achievement. Ways to measure effort to achieve, team skills, ability to enhance team problem solving, commitment to quality work, and commitment to continuous improvement of competencies need to be developed to supplement the traditional focus on achievement tests. **Fourth, continue to move your benchmark higher as initial goals are reached**. Expertise is not a state, it is a process of progressive refinement of one's use of cooperative formal, informal, and base groups. Either faculty are improving their skills in implementing cooperative learning or else their skills are gradually deteriorating. Their expertise in using cooperative learning cannot stand still. Perfection is never reached but should be strived for in realistic steps.

The Japanese use the concept **Dantotsu**--striving to be the "best of the best"--to describe the benchmarking process. The steps of dantotsu are:

1. Know who your competitors are, especially internationally.

2. Benchmark.

3. Do not "mimic the past." New methods, processes, practices have to be uncovered and adopted.

4. Identify the "best of the best" in instructional procedures. The strategies and procedures identified have to fit together logically.

5. Conduct research on instructional methods and either adopt what is proven to be effective or adapt the good features of an instructional procedure to fit into your teaching.

An important aspect of the benchmarking process is having faculty see each other teach. Just as a ball-player needs to see other people play in order to form a frame-of-reference as to how good he or she is and where improvement is needed, faculty need to access their use of cooperative learning within a broad **frame-of- reference** based on observing many other faculty members using cooperative learning.

In order to form a frame-of-reference within which to set goals for improvement in one's use of cooperative learning, faculty members must understand (a) what cooperative learning is and (b) the basic elements of a well-implemented cooperative lesson. Otherwise, the fidelity of the implementation of cooperative learning may suffer. Most instructional innovations fade away because their implementation deteriorates and becomes approximate and sloppy. Cooperative learning will be in danger of deteriorating into traditional class-room grouping unless faculty pay attention to the exactness of its implementation. **Fidelity of use** depends on the inclusion of positive interdependence, face-to-face promotive inter-action, individual accountability, interpersonal and small group skills, and group processing. No matter if it is a cooperative formal, informal, or base group, or if the lesson is a structured academic controversy, these basic elements must be operationalized into the assignment.

Once a benchmarking process is established for setting and continually upgrading goals for world-class quality of instruction, colleges will wish to modernized their organizational structure.

Cooperative Learning
Classroom Observation

Johnson, Johnson, & Smith

Teacher Observed: _____   **Date:** _____

Observer: _____

My focus as an observer for this lesson is: _____

		COMMENTS
Subject Matter Objective:		
Social Skills Objective:		
Positive Interdependence	☐ Group goal ☐ Group reward (e.g., bonus points) ☐ Division of labor ☐ Materials shared/jigsawed ☐ Roles assigned ☐ Group celebration of success ☐ Other:	
Group Composition	☐ Homogeneous ☐ Heterogeneous	
Seating Arrangement	☐ Clear view/access to others ☐ Clear view/access to materials	
Individual Accountability	☐ Each student evaluated (own work) ☐ Students check each other ☐ Random student evaluated ☐ Other:	
Teach Social Skill	☐ Rationale ☐ Defining social skill, e.g., T chart ☐ Intervening to correct and/or encourage	
Observation • task help • systematic • focused/systematic	**By:** ☐ Teacher ☐ Student(s) ☐ Observation form used ☐ Informal (anecdotal, etc.)	
Teacher Feedback: Social Skills	**To:** ☐ Class as a whole ☐ Group by group ☐ Individual	
Group Processing • first appears • specific processing	**Of:** ☐ Observation data ☐ Social skills ☐ Academic skills ☐ Positive feedback ☐ Goal setting (for next time)	
General Climate	☐ Group products displayed ☐ Group progress displayed ☐ Aids to group work displayed	10 : 7

Modernizing Organizational Structure

> *Nothing new that is really interesting comes without collaboration.*
> James Watson, Nobel Prize Winner (codiscoverer of the double helix)

Ford Motor Company knew it had to do something different, dramatically different, to gain back market share from imports. A new mid-sized car was conceived to be Ford's best chance to do so. For years Ford had operated within a mass-manufacturing structure whose motto was "any color as long as it is black." Designers etched out sketches and gave them to manufacturing with the order "build it!" Sales inherited the car and had to figure out how to sell it. That was the way Ford had always built cars. But not this time. An interdisciplinary team was created made up of designers, engineers, manufacturing and financial executives, and sales and marketing people. Together they created the Taurus, a car whose sales neared one million units in its first four production years and which has consistently won praise from both auto experts and consumers.

Ford is not the only company to switch to cooperative teams. While there is an American myth of progress being spurred on by Lone Rangers, in today's corporations that image is about as current as bustles and spats. From Motorola to AT&T Credit Corporation, self-managing, multi-disciplinary teams are in charge of keeping the company profitable. And they are succeeding. Teams get things done.

Team development is at the core of the changes necessary to alter the way faculty and students think and work. It is the best way of developing the educating students the right way the first time. That does not mean that reorganizing students and faculty into teams will be easy. Changing the college culture while getting all faculty working together to educate students right the first time may be the biggest challenge facing any college.

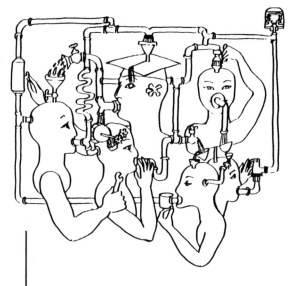

There are two steps in moving from a competitive-individualistic mass-manufacturing organizational structure to a high-performance cooperative-team structure. The first step is using cooperative learning procedures extensively within the college's courses. The second step is organizing faculty into colleagial support groups that focus on the continuous improvement of the use of cooperative learning and instruction in general. These steps are taken not because they are popular, but because it is rational to do so. Currently available data indicates that a cooperative team-based organizational structure is more desirable for many reasons (see Chapter2) than is a competitive- individualistic mass-manufacturing organizational structure.

Data-Driven Change And Gaining Expertise

The amount of research data and the consistency of the findings provide irrefutable evidence that a team-based organizational structure will be more effective in producing quality instruction and achieving the college's mission. Barry Bennett (personal communication) summarizes the research as follows: "Imagine you are a doctor conducting heart surgery. You realize that if you use procedure "A" the patient has a 50 percent chance of survival and if you use procedure "B" the patient has a 75 percent chance of survival. Which procedure do you use? That difference is the difference in achievement between cooperative learning and competitive or individualistic instruction." Once a faculty member knows about cooperative learning, it is difficult not to use it.

Knowing from the research that cooperative learning is more effective than are competitive and individualistic instruction is the first step to change. The second is gaining expertise in using cooperative learning in your courses. To be an expert in cooperative learning you have to use it long enough to:

1. **Be able to take any lesson in any subject area and structure it cooperatively.**

2. **Use cooperative learning at the routine-use level** where it is implemented automatically without a great deal of conscious thought or planning. Cooperative learning then becomes a central part of a faculty member's professional identity and faculty members become willing to share their expertise with interested colleagues.

3. **Use cooperative learning at least 60 percent of the time.** A cooperative context needs to dominate the classroom and college. At least 60 percent of a student's day should be spent in cooperative learning experiences. Up to 40 percent of instruction should probably be individualistic and competitive experiences.

Gaining and maintaining such expertise is a long-term process requiring up to two years or more of hard work. Simply putting students in groups is not enough. The five basic elements of cooperative efforts (positive interdependence, face-to-face promotive interaction, individual accountability, social skills, and group processing) have to be implemented.

This is not easy. **Gaining expertise in using cooperative learning takes at least one lifetime.** Faculty development programs are needed in order to ensure that cooperative learning (rather than traditional classroom grouping) is being used.

Programs to develop faculty expertise in structuring learning situations cooperatively requires procedural learning (very similar to learning how to perform brain surgery, how to fly an airplane, or how to play tennis) and being a member of an ongoing colleagial support group. **Procedural learning** exists when you study cooperative learning to:

1. Learn conceptually what cooperative learning is.

2. Translate your conceptual understanding of cooperative learning into a set of operational procedures appropriate for your students and subjects taught.

3. Teach cooperatively structured lessons regularly.

4. Eliminate errors in using cooperative learning so that you move through the initial awkward and mechanical stages of skill mastery.

5. Attain a routine-use, automated level of use of cooperative learning.

Procedural learning differs from simply learning facts and acquiring knowledge. It relies heavily on feedback about performance and modifying your implementation until the errors of performance are eliminated. Usually your efforts will fail to match the ideal of what you wish to accomplish for a considerable length of time until cooperative learning is overlearned at a routine-use, automated level. **Failure is part of the process of gaining expertise. Success is inevitable when failure is followed by persistent practice, feedback, and reflection on how to use cooperative learning more competently.** To gain expertise you need a colleagial support group made up of peers you like and trust. Gaining expertise takes learning partners who are willing to trust each other, talk frankly about their teaching, and observe each other's performance over a prolonged period of time to help each other identify and eliminate the errors being made in implementing cooperative learning. Unless you are willing to reveal your lack of expertise to obtain accurate feedback from trusted colleagues, teaching expertise cannot be gained. In order to commit the effort required to gain such expertise in the use of cooperative learning (which usually takes from one to two years of hard work) teachers need considerable support and help from colleagues. **Gaining expertise is not a solitary activity. It is a social process requiring a colleagial support group.**

Faculty Development And The State-Of-The-Art Use Of Cooperative Learning

More and more companies, as they move into global competitiveness, see that the one thing that can make a difference in the world market is people. Raw material, technology, and systems are available to everybody. The right people can be a unique commodity. To be a world-class college and provide a world-class education, each faculty member must be developed to his or her highest potential as a teacher. To do so requires that faculty maintain a state-of-the-art use of cooperative learning.

The term **state-of-the-art** is an engineering concept that involves the set of heuristics describing best available practice. Like most heuristics it is difficult to define but easy to recognize. Take sound reproduction technology, for example. The current state-of-the-art is digital-audio tape (DAT), the previous "best available practice" and currently commercially available technology is Compact Disk. Before that it was phonograph record. Best available practice usually persists for a limited period of time, and is eventually replaced by a superior approach. The changes that have occurred in the development of cooperative learning represent a progressive refinement in the state-of-the-art. Improvement is expected to continue, since cooperative learning is a dynamic area in education and the research investigating its nature and use is continuing.

Approaches to implementing cooperative learning may be placed on a continuum with direct applications at one end and conceptual applications at the other. **Direct applications** consist of packaged lessons, curricula, and strategies that are used in a lock-step prescribed manner. Direct applications can be divided into three subcategories. Teachers can adopt a strategy (such as groups-of-four in intermediate math) that is aimed at using cooperative learning in a specific subject area for a certain age student (**the strategy approach**), they can adopt a curriculum package that is aimed at a specific subject area and grade level (**the curriculum package approach**), or they can replicate a lesson they observed another teach (**the lesson approach**). In essence, faculty are trained to use a specific cooperative activity, lesson, strategy, or curriculum package in a Step 1, Step 2, Step 3 manner without any real understanding of cooperation. Some of the more powerful strategies include the jigsaw method developed by Elliot Aronson and his colleagues (Aronson, 1978), the coop/coop strategy developed by Spencer Kagan (Kagan, 1988), the group project method developed by the Sharans (Sharan & Sharan, 1976).

The **conceptual approach** is based on an interaction among theory, research, and practice. The two conceptual approaches to cooperative learning have been developed by

Elizabeth Cohen (1986) and the authors of this book (Johnson & Johnson, 1975/1991; Johnson, Johnson, & Holubec, 1984/1990). Cohen bases her conceptual principles on expectation-states theory while we base our conceptual principles on the theory of cooperation and competition Morton Deutsch derived from Kurt Lewin's field theory. Teachers are taught a general conceptual model of cooperative learning (based on the essential elements of positive interdependence, face-to-face interaction, individual accountability, social skills, and group processing--**the essential elements approach**) which they use to tailor cooperative learning specifically for their circumstances, students, and needs. Faculty are taught to apply a conceptual system to build cooperative activities, lessons, strategies, and curricula. Using the five basic elements of cooperation, faculty can (a) analyze their current curricula, students, and instructional goals and (b) design cooperative learning experiences specifically adapted for their instructional goals and the ages, abilities, and backgrounds of their students. Becoming competent in implementing the basic elements is a requirement for obtaining real expertise in cooperative learning. In essence, teachers are taught an **expert system** of how to implement cooperative learning that they use to create a unique adaptation to their specific circumstances, students, and needs. The resulting expertise is based on a metacognitive understanding of cooperative learning.

At the Cooperative Learning Center of the University of Minnesota we have focused on five interrelated activities: reviewing and synthesizing the research, developing theory, conducting systematic research to validate or disconfirm the theory, operationalizing the research into "state-of-the-art" cooperation procedures, and implementing cooperative learning and faculty teams in a network of colleges and school districts throughout the United States and other parts of the world.

The state-of-the-art use of cooperative learning has changed substantially since the initial conceptualization of the theory by Morton Deutsch in 1949. Deutsch's theorized that positive interdependence was the central feature of cooperation. Our understanding of positive interdependence has increased as the different ways of structuring it have been investigated (see Johnson & Johnson, 1989a). The other mediators of the effectiveness of cooperative learning are continually being redefined and calibrated, modifying how cooperative learning is best structured within classrooms. While the authors used formal, informal, and base groups in their college teaching in the 1960s, the definition of each has been considerably refined and many of the specific operationalizations have been updated and fine-tuned in the 1970s and 1980s.

The dynamic nature of cooperative learning requires faculty development programs that last for several years. As a rule it takes at least three years of training and experience to become proficient in the integrated and flexible use of all types of cooperative learning. Our training programs are divided into training in the fundamentals of cooperative learning the first year, training in more integrated, refined, and advanced use of cooperative learning in the second year, and training in the use of structured academic controversies the third year (Johnson, Johnson, & Holubec, 1988, 1991; Johnson & Johnson, 1987). For administrators there is an additional year of training (Johnson & Johnson, 1989b). And since the theory and research are continually progressing, refresher training is recommended every few years.

Looking Forward

I couldn't have done it without the boys.
Casey Stengel (after winning his ninth American League pennant in ten years)

Now that you have reached the end of this book you are at a new beginning. Years of experience in using cooperative learning in your classroom are needed to gain expertise in its use. While you are using cooperative learning there is much more to learn about its use. The addition of informal cooperative learning activities and long-term permanent base groups will increase the power and effectiveness of cooperation in your classroom. Teaching students more and more sophisticated social skills will improve how well they work together to maximize their learning. Supplementing the use of cooperative learning with appropriate competitions and individualistic assignments will further enrich the quality of learning within your classroom. Structuring academic controversies within your cooperative learning groups will move students to higher levels of reasoning and thinking while providing a considerable increase in energy and fun. Teaching students how to negotiate their differences and mediate each other's conflicts will accelerate their skills in managing conflicts within cooperative learning groups. Finally, moving cooperation up to the college level by organizing faculty into cooperative teams will create a congruent organizational structure within which both faculty and students will thrive.

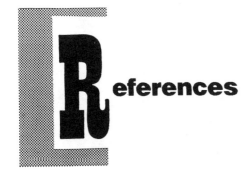

References

Anderson, T., & Armbruster, B. (1982). Reader and text studying strategies. In W. Otto & S. White (Eds.), **Reading expository material**. New York: Academic Press.

Annis, L. (1979). Effect of cognitive style and learning passage organization on study technique effectiveness. **Journal of Educational Psychology, 71**, 620-626.

Armento, B. (1977). Teacher behaviors related to student achievement on a social science concept test. **Journal of Teacher Education, 28**, 46-52.

Aronson, E., Blaney, N., Stephan, C., Sikes, J., & Snapp, M. (1978). **The jigsaw classroom**. Beverly Hills, CA: Sage

Association of American Colleges (1985). **Integrity in the curriculum: A report to the academic community**. Project on redefining the meaning and purpose of baccalaureate degree. Washington, D.C.

Astin, A. (1977). **Four critical years: Effects of college on beliefs, attitudes, and knowledge**. San Francisco: Jossey-Bass.

Astin, A. (1985). **Achieving educational excellence**. San Francisco: Jossey-Bass.

Astin, H., Astin, A., Bisconti, A., & Frankel, H. (1972). **Higher education and the disadvantaged student**. Washington, DC: Human Science Press.

Atkinson, R., & Shiffrin, R. (1971). The control of short-term memory. **Scientific American, 225**, 82-90.

Ausubel, D. (1963). **Psychology of meaningful verbal learning**. New York: Grune & Straton.

Bargh, J., & Schul, Y. (1980). On the cognitive benefits of teaching. **Journal of Educational Psychology, 72**, 593-604.

Barnes, C. (1980). **Questions: The untrapped resource**. Paper presented at the annual meeting of the American Educational Research Association, Boston.

Barnes, C. (1983). Questioning in the college classroom. In C. Ellner and C. Barnes (Eds.), **Studies in college teaching** (pp. 61-81). Lexington, MA: Lexington Books.

Blake, R., & Mouton, J. (1974). Designing change for educational institutions through the D/D Matrix. **Educational and Urban Society, 6**, 179-204.

Blanc, R., Debuhr, L., & Martin, D. (1983). Breaking the attrition cycle: The effects of supplemental instruction on undergraduate performance and attrition. **Journal of Higher Education, 54**, 80-90.

Bligh, D. (1972). **What's the use of lectures.** Harmondsworth, England: Penguin.

Blumberg, A., May, J., & Perry, R. (1974). An inner- city school that changed--and continued to change. **Education and Urban Society, 6**, 222-238.

Bok, E. (1986). **Higher learning.** Cambridge, MA: Harvard University Press.

Bovard, E. (1951a). Group structure and perception. **Journal of Abnormal and Social Psychology, 46**, 398-405.

Bovard, E. (1951b). The experimental production of interpersonal affect. **Journal of Abnormal Psychology, 46**, 521- 528.

Bowers, J. (1986). Classroom communication apprehension: A survey. **Communication Education, 35**(4), 372-378.

Boyer, E. (1987). **College: The undergraduate experience in America.** New York: Harper & Row.

Boyer, E. (1990). **Scholarship reconsidered.** Lawrenceville, NJ: Princeton University Press.

Broadbent, D. (1970). Review lecture. **Proclamations of the Royal Society, 1,** 333-350.

Brown, J., Collins, A., & Duguid, P. (1989). Situated cognition and the culture of learning. **Educational Researcher, 18**(1), 32-42.

Bruner, J. (1960). **The process of education.** Cambridge: Harvard University Press.

Campbell, J. (1965). **The children's crusader: Colonel Francis W. Parker.** PhD dissertation, Teachers College, Columbia University.

Chickering, A., & Gamson, Z. (1987). Seven principles for good practice. **AAHE Bulletin, 39**(7), 3-7.

Cohen, E. (1986). **Designing groupwork.** New York: Teachers College Press.

Collins, B. (1970). **Social Psychology.** Reading, MA: Addison-Wesley.

Cooper, J. (May 1990). Cooperative learning and college teaching: Tips from the trenches. **The Teaching Professor, 4**(5), 1-2.

Costin, F. (January 1972). Lecturing versus other methods of teaching: A review of research. **British Journal of Educational Technology, 3**(1), 4-30.

Daloz, l. (1987). **Effective teaching and mentoring.** San Francisco: Jossey-Bass.

Dansereau, D. (1985). Learning strategy research. In J. Segal, S. Chipman, and R. Glaser (Eds.). **Thinking and Learning Skills (Vol. 1, Relating instruction to research).** Hillsdale, NJ: Lawrence Erlbaum.

Dansereau, D. (1987). Transfer from cooperative learning to individual studying. **Journal of Reading, 30,** 614- 618.

Davison, M. (1991). Personal communication.

Deutsch, M. (1958). Trust and suspicion. **Journal of Conflict Resolution, 2,** 25-279.

Deutsch, M. (1960). The effects of motivational orientation upon trust and suspicion. **Human Relations, 13,** 123- 139.

Deutsch, M. (1962). Cooperation and trust: Some theoretical notes. In M. R. Jones (Ed.), **Nebraska symposium on motivation** (pp. 275-319). Lincoln, NE: University of Nebraska Press.

Deutsch, M., & Krauss, R. (1962). Studies of interpersonal bargaining. **Journal of Conflict Resolutions, 6**, 52-76.

DeVries, D., & Edwards, K. (1973). Learning games and student teams: Their effects on classroom process. **American Educational Research Journal, 10**, 307-318.

DeVries, D., & Edwards, K. (1974). Student teams and learning games: Their effects on cross-race and cross-sex interaction. **Journal of Educational Psychology, 66**(5), 741-749.

DiPardo, A., & Freedman, S. (1988). Peer response groups in the writing classroom: Theoretic foundations and new directions. **Review of Educational Research, 58**, 119-150.

Eble, K. (1983). **The aims of college teaching.** San Francisco: Jossey-Bass.

Eison, J. (1990). Confidence in the college classroom: Ten maxims for new teachers. **College Teaching, 38**(1), 21-25.

Gabbert, B., Johnson, D. W., & Johnson, R. (1986). Cooperative learning, group-to-individual transfer, process gain and the acquisition of cognitive reasoning strategies. **Journal of Psychology, 120**(3), 265-278.

Gagne, E. (1985). **The cognitive psychology of school learning.** Boston: Little, Brown.

Goldschmid, M. (1971). The learning cell: An instructional innovation. **Learning and Development, 2**, 1-6.

Good, T., & Brouws, D. (1977). Teaching effects: A process-product study in fourth grade mathematics classrooms. **Journal of Teacher Education, 28**, 49-54.

Guetzkow, H., Kelly, E., & McKeachie, W. (1954). An experimental comparison of recitation, discussion, and tutorial methods in college teaching. **Journal of Educational Psychology, 45,** 193- 209.

Haines, D., & McKeachie, W. (1967). Cooperative versus competitive discussion methods in teaching introductory psychology. **Journal of Educational Psychology, 58**(6), 386-390.

Harkins, S., & Petty, R. (1982). The effects of task difficulty and task uniqueness on social loafing. **Journal of Personality and Social Psychology, 43,** 1214-1229.

Hartley, J., & Marshall, S. (1974). On notes and notetaking. **Universities Quarterly, 28,** 225-235.

Hartup, W. (1976). Peer interaction and the behavioral development of the individual child. In E. Schloper & R. Reicher (Eds.), **Psychology and child development.** New York: Plenum Press.

Helmreich, R. (1982, August). **Pilot selection and training.** Paper presented at the annual meeting of the American Psychological Association, Washington, D.C.

Helmreich, R., Beane, W., Lucker, W., & Spence, J. (1978). Achievement motivation and scientific attainment. **Personality and Social Psychology Bulletin, 4,** 222-226.

Helmreich, R., Sawin, L., & Carsrud, A. (1986). The honeymoon effect in job performance: Temporal increases in the predictive power of achievement motivation. **Journal of Applied Psychology, 71,** 185-188.

Helmreich, R., Spense, J., Beane, W., Lucker, W., & Matthews, K. (1980). Making it in academic psychology: Demographic and personality correlates of attainment. **Journal of Personality and Social Psychology, 39,** 896-908.

Hill, G. (1982). Group versus individual performance: Are N + 1 heads better than one? **Psychological Bulletin, 91,** 517-539.

Hwong, N., Caswell, A., Johnson, D. W., & Johnson, R. (1990). **Effects of cooperative and individualistic learning on prospective elementary teachers' music achievement and attitudes.** University of Minnesota, manuscript submitted for publication.

Ingham, A., Levinger, G., Graves, J., & Peckham, V. (1974). The Ringelmann effect: Studies of group size and group performance. **Journal of Personality and Social Psychology, 10,** 371-384.

Johnson, D. W. (1970). **The social psychology of education.** New York: Holt, Rinehart & Wilson.

Johnson, Johnson, & Smith

Johnson, D. W. (1971). Role reversal: A summary and review of the research. **International Journal of Group Tensions, 111,** 318-334.

Johnson, D. W. (1973). Communication in conflict situations: A critical review of the research. **International Journal of Group Tensions, 3,** 46-47.

Johnson, D. W. (1974). Communication and the inducement of cooperative behavior in conflicts: A critical review. **Speech Monographs, 41,** 64-78.

Johnson, D. W. (1979). **Educational psychology.** Englewood Cliffs, NJ: Prentice-Hall.

Johnson, D. W. (1980). Constructive peer relationships, social development, and cooperative learning experiences: Implications for the prevention of drug abuse. **Journal of Drug Education, 10,** 7-24.

Johnson, D. W. (1990). **Reaching out: Interpersonal effectiveness and self-actualization** (4th ed.). Englewood Cliffs, NJ: Prentice-Hall.

Johnson, D. W. (1991). **Human relations and your career** (3rd ed.). Englewood Cliffs, NJ: Prentice-Hall.

Johnson, D. W., & Johnson, F. (1991). **Joining together: Group theory and group skills** (4th ed.). Englewood Cliffs, NJ: Prentice-Hall.

Johnson, D. W., & Johnson, R. (1974). Instructional goal structure: Cooperative, competitive, or individualistic. **Review of Educational Research, 44,** 213-240.

Johnson, D. W., & Johnson, R. (1978). Cooperative, competitive, and individualistic learning. **Journal of Research and Development in Education, 12,** 3-15.

Johnson, D. W., & Johnson, R. (1979). Conflict in the classroom: Controversy and learning. **Review of Educational Research, 49,** 51-70.

Johnson, D. W., & Johnson, R. (1981). Effects of cooperative and individualistic learning experiences on interethnic interaction. **Journal of Educational Psychology, 73**(3), 454-459.

Johnson, D. W., & Johnson, R. (1983). The socialization and achievement crisis: Are cooperative learning experiences the solution? In L. Bickman (Ed.), **Applied Social Psychology Annual 4** (pp. 119-164). Beverly Hills, CA: Sage.

Johnson, D. W., & Johnson, R. (1985). Classroom conflict: Controversy vs. debate in learning groups. **American Educational Research Journal, 22,** 237-256.

Johnson, D. W., & Johnson, R. (1987b). **Creative Conflict.** Edina, MN: Interaction Book Company.

Johnson, D. W., & Johnson, R. (1989a). **Cooperation and competition: Theory and research.** Edina, MN: Interaction Book Company.

Johnson, D. W., & Johnson, R. (1989b). **Leading the cooperative school.** Edina, MN: Interaction Book Company.

Johnson, D. W., & Johnson, R. (1975/1991). **Learning together and alone: Cooperative, competitive, and individualistic learning.** Englewood Cliffs, NJ: Prentice-Hall.

Johnson, D. W., Johnson, R., & Holubec, E. (1984/1990). **Circles of learning: Cooperation in the classroom.** Edina, MN: Interaction Book Company.

Johnson, D. W., Johnson, R., & Maruyama, G. (1983). Interdependence and interpersonal attraction among heterogeneous and homogeneous individuals: A theoretical formulation and a meta-analysis of the research. **Review of Educational Research, 53,** 5-54.

Johnson, D. W., Johnson, R., Ortez, A., & Stanne, M. (1990). **Impact of positive goal and resource interdependence on achievement, interaction and attitudes.** University of Minnesota, manuscript submitted for publication.

Johnson, D. W., Johnson, R., & Smith, K. (1986). Academic conflict among students: Controversy and learning. In R. Feldman, (Ed.). **Social psychological applications to education.** New York: Cambridge University Press.

Johnson, D. W., Johnson, R., Stanne, M. & Garibaldi, A. (1990). The impact of leader and member group processing on achievement in cooperative groups. **The Journal of Social Psychology, 130,** 507- 516.

Johnson, D. W., Maruyama, G., Johnson, R, Nelson, D., & Skon, L. (1981). Effects of cooperative, competitive, and individualistic goal structures on achievement: A meta-analysis. **Psychological Bulletin, 89,** 47-62.

Johnson, D. W., & Matross, R. (1977). The interpersonal influence of the psychotherapist. In A. Gurman & A. Razin (Eds.), **The effective therapist: A handbook.** Elmsford, NY: Pergamon Press.

Johnson, D. W., & Noonan, P. (1972). Effects of acceptance and reciprocation of self-disclosures on the development of trust. **Journal of Counseling Psychology, 19**(5), 411-416.

Johnson, D. W., Skon, L., & Johnson, R. (1980). Effects of cooperative, competitive, and individualistic conditions on children's problem-solving performance. **American Educational Research Journal, 17**(1), 83-94.

Kagan, S. (1988). **Cooperative learning.** San Juan Capistrano, CA: Resources for Teachers.

Karp, D., & Yoels, W. (1987). The college classroom: Some observations on the meanings of student participation. **Sociology and Social Research, 60,** 421-439.

Keppel, G., & Underwood, B. (1962). Proactive inhibition in short-term retention of single items. **Journal of Verbal Learning and Verbal Behavior, 1,** 153-161.

Kerr, N., & Bruun, S. (1981). Ringelmann revisited: Alternative explanations for the social loafing effect. **Personality and Social Psychology Bulletin, 7,** 224-231.

Kerr, N. (1983). The dispensability of member effort and group motivation losses: Free-rider effects. **Journal of Personality and Social Psychology, 44,** 78-94.

Kiewra, K. (1985a). Investigating notetaking and review: A depth of processing alternatives. **Educational Psychologist, 20**(1), 23-32.

Kiewra, K. (1985b). Providing the instructor's notes: An effective addition to student learning. **Educational Psychologist, 20**(1), 33-39.

Kiewra, K. (1987). Notetaking and review: The research and its implications. **Instructional Science, 16,** 233- 249.

Kiewra, K., & Benton, S. (1988). The relationship between information-processing ability and notetaking. **Contemporary Educational Psychology, 13,** 33-44.

Kohn, A. (1986). **No contest: the case against competition.** Boston: Houghton-Mifflin.

Kohn, A. (1990). **The brighter side of human nature.** New York: Basic Books.

Kouzes, J., & Posner, B. (1987). **The leadership challenge.** San Francisco: Jossey-Bass.

Kuhn, T. (1962). **The structure of scientific revolutions.** Chicago: University of Chicago Press.

Kulik, J., & Kulik, C.L. (1979). College teaching. In P.L. Peterson & H.J. Walberg (Eds.), **Research on teaching: Concepts, findings, and implications.** Berkeley, CA: Mc-Cutcheon.

Lamm, H., & Trommsdorff, G. (1973). Group verses individual performance on tasks requiring ideational proficiency (Brainstorming): A review. **European Journal of Social Psychology, 3,** 361-388.

Langer, E., & Benevento, A. (1978). Self-induced dependence. **Journal of Personality and Social Psychology, 36,** 886-893.

Latane, B., Williams, K., & Harkins, S. (1979). Many hands make light the work: The causes and consequences of social loafing. **Journal of Personality and Social Psychology, 37,** 822- 832.

Lave, J. (1988). **Cognition in practice: Mind, mathematics and culture in everyday life.** Cambridge: Cambridge University Press.

Levin, H., Glass, G., & Meister, G. (1984). **Cost- effectiveness of educational interventions.** Stanford, California: Institute for Research on Educational Finance and Governance.

Lew, M., Mesch, D., Johnson, D. W., & Johnson, R. (1986a). Positive interdependence, academic and collaborative-skills group contingencies and isolated students. **American Educational Research Journal, 23,** 476-488.

Lew, M., Mesch, D., Johnson, D. W., & Johnson, R. (1986b). Components of cooperative learning: Effects of collaborative skills and academic group contingencies on achievement and main streaming. **Contemporary Educational Psychology, 11,** 229-239.

Light, R. (1990). **The Harvard assessment seminars.** Cambridge, MA: Harvard University Press.

Little, J. (1981). **School success and staff development in urban desegregated schools.** Paper presented at the American Educational Research Association, Los Angeles, April.

Mackworth, J. (1970). **Vigilance and habituation.** Harmondsworth, England: Penguin.

Masqud, M. (1980). Effects of personal lecture notes and teacher notes on recall of university students. **British Journal of Educational Psychology, 50,** 289-294.

May, M., & Doob, L. (1937). **Competition and cooperation** (Social Science Research Council Bulletin No. 25). New York: Social Science Research Council.

Mayer, A. (1903). Uber einzel und gesamtleistung des schul kindes. **Archiv fur die Gesamte Psychologie, 1,** 276-416.

McKeachie, W. (1951). Anxiety in the college classroom. **Journal of Educational Research, 45,** 153-160.

McKeachie, W. (1954). Individual conformity to attitudes of classroom groups. **Journal of Abnormal and Social Psychology, 49,** 282-289.

McKeachie, W. (1967). Research in teaching: The gap between theory and practice. In C. Lee (Ed.), **Improving college teaching** (pp 211-239). Washington, D.C.: American Council of Education.

McKeachie, W. (1986). **Teaching Tips: A guidebook for the beginning college teacher** (8th ed.). Boston: D.C. Heath.

McKeachie, W. (1988). Teaching thinking. **Update, 2**(1), 1.

McKeachie, W., & Kulik, J. (1975). Effective college training. In F. Kerlinger (Ed.), **Review of Research in Education.** Itasca, IL: Peacock.

McKeachie, W., Pintrich, P., Yi-Guang, L., & Smith, D. (1986). **Teaching and learning in the college classroom: A review of the research literature.** Ann Arbor, MI: The Regents of the University of Michigan.

Menges, R. (1988). Research on teaching and learning: The relevant and the redundant. **The Review of Higher Education, 11**(3), 259-268.

Mesch, D., Johnson, D. W., & Johnson, R. (1988). Impact of positive interdependence and academic group contingencies on achievement. **Journal of Social Psychology, 128,** 345-352.

Mesch, D., Lew, M., Johnson, D. W., & Johnson, R. (1986). Isolated teenagers, cooperative learning and the training of social skills. **Journal of Psychology, 120,** 323-334.

Moede, W. (1927). Die richtlinien der leistungs- psycholgie. **Industrielle Psychotechnik, 4,** 193-207.

Motley, M. (1988, January). Taking the terror out of talk. **Psychology Today, 22**(1), pp. 46-49.

Murray, F. (1983). **Cognitive benefits of teaching on the teacher.** Paper presented at American Educational Research Association Annual Meeting, Montreal, Quebec.

Murray, H. (1985). Classroom teaching behaviors related to college teaching effectiveness. In J.G. Donald and A.M. Sullivan (Eds.), **Using research to improve teaching** (pp. 21-34). San Francisco: Jossey-Bass.

National Center for Educational Statistics. (1984). **Two years after high school: A capsule description of 1980 seniors.** Washington, DC: U.S. Department of Education.

National Institute of Education. (1984). **Involvement in learning. Study group on the conditions of excellence in higher education.** Washington, DC.

Neer, M. (1987). The development of an instrument to measure classroom apprehension. **Communication Education, 36,** 154-166.

Noel, L. (1985). Increasing student retention: New challenges and potential. In L. Noel, R. Levitz, & D. Saluri (Eds.), **Increasing student retention: Effective programs and practices for reducing the dropout rate** (pp. 1-27). San Francisco: Jossey-Bass.

Pascarella, E. (1980). Student-faculty informal contact and college outcomes. **Review of Educational Research, 50**, 545-595.

Pelz, D., & Andrews, F. (1976). **Scientists in organizations: Productive climates for research and development.** Ann Arbor: Institute for Social Research, University of Michigan.

Penner, J. (1984). **Why many college teachers cannot lecture.** Springfield, IL: Charles C. Thomas.

Pepitone, E. (1980). **Children in cooperation and competition.** Lexington, MA: Lexington Books.

Petty, R., Harkins, S., Williams, K., & Latane, B. (1977). The effects of group size on cognitive effort and evaluation. **Personality and Social Psychology Bulletin, 3**, 575-578.

Rosenshine, B. (1968, December). To explain: A review of research. **Educational Leadership, 26**, 303-309.

Rosenshine, B., & Stevens, R. (1986). Teaching functions. In M. Wittrock (Ed), **Handbook of research on teaching** (3rd ed.) (pp. 376-391). New York: Macmillan.

Ruggiero, V. (1988). **Teaching thinking across the curriculum.** New York: Harper & Row.

Ruhl, K., Hughes, C., & Schloss, P. (1987). Using the pause procedure to enhance lecture recall. **Teacher Education and Special Education, 10**(1), 14-18.

Salomon, G. (1981). Communication and education: Social and psychological interactions. **People & Communication, 13**, 9-271.

Schoenfeld, A. (1985). **Mathematical problem solving.** Orlando: Academic Press.

Schoenfeld, A. (1989). Ideas in the air: Speculations on small group learning, peer interactions, cognitive apprenticeship, quasi-Vygotskean notions of internalization, creativity, problem solving, and mathematical practice. **International Journal of Educational Research**, in press.

Scully, M. (1981, October 21). One million students at U.S. colleges; triple present number seems likely by 1990. **The Chronicle of Higher Education,** p. 1.

Sharan, S. (1980). Cooperative learning in teams: Recent methods and effects on achievement, attitudes, and ethnic relations. **Review of Educational Research, 50,** 241-272.

Sharan, S. & Sharan, Y. (1976). **Small group teaching.** Englewood Cliffs, NJ: Educational Technology Publications.

Sheahan, B. & White, J. (1990). Quo Vadis, undergraduate engineering education? **Engineering Education, 80**(8), 1017-1022.

Sheingold, K., Hawkins, J., & Char, C. (1984). I'm the thinkist, you're the typist: The interaction of technology and the social life of classrooms. **Journal of Social Issues, 40**(3), 49-6.

Skon, L., Johnson, D. W., & Johnson, R. (1981). Cooperative peer interaction versus individual competition and individualistic efforts: Effects on the acquisition of cognitive reasoning strategies. **Journal of Educational Psychology, 73**(1), 83-92.

Slavin, R. (1980). Cooperative learning. **Review of Educational Research, 50,** 315-342.

Slavin, R. (1983). **Cooperative learning.** New York: Longman.

Slavin, R., Leavey, M., & Madden, N. (1982). **Team-assisted individualization: Mathematics teacher's manual.** Johns Hopkins University, Center for Social Organization of Schools.

Smith, D. (1977). College classroom interactions and critical thinking. **Journal of Educational Psychology, 69,** 180-190.

Smith, D. (1980). **Instruction and outcomes in an undergraduate setting.** Paper presented at the annual meeting of the American Educational Research Association, Boston.

Smith, L., & Land, M. (1981). Low-inference verbal behaviors related to teach clarity. **Journal of Classroom Interaction, 17,** 37-42.

Starfield, A., Smith, K., & Bleloch, A. (1990). **How to model it: problem solving for the computer age.** New York: McGraw-Hill.

Stones, E. (1970). Students' attitudes to the size of teaching groups. **Educational Review, 21**(2), 98-108.

Stuart, J., & Rutherford, R. (1978, September). Medical student concentration during lectures. **The Lancet, 2**, 514-516.

Terenzini, P. (1986). **Retention research: Academic and social fit.** Paper presented at the meeting of the Southern Regional Office of the College of Entrance Examination Board, New Orleans.

Tinto, V. (1975). Dropout from higher education: A theoretical synthesis of recent research. **Review of Educational Research, 45**(1), 89-125.

Tinto, V. (1987). **Leaving college: Rethinking the causes and cures for student attrition.** Chicago: University of Chicago Press.

Treisman, P. (1985). A study of the mathematics performance of Black students at the University of California, Berkeley. (Doctoral dissertation, University of California, Berkeley, 1986). **Dissertation abstracts international, 47**, 1641-A.

Triplett, N. (1898). The dynamogenic factors in pacemaking and competition. **American Journal of Psychology, 9**, 507-533.

Verner, C., & Dickinson, G. (1967). The lecture: an analysis and review of research. **Adult Education, 17**, 85-100.

Vygotsky, L. (1978). **Mind and society.** Cambridge, MA: Harvard University Press.

Wales, C., & Sager, R. (1978). **The guided design approach.** Englewood Cliffs, NJ: Educational Technology Publications.

Watson, G., & Johnson, D. W. (1972). **Social psychology: Issues and insights.** Philadelphia: Lippincott.

Waugh, N., & Norman, D. (1965). Primary memory. **Psychological Review, 72**, 89-104.

White, R., & Tisher, R. (1986). Research on natural sciences. In M. Whittrock (Ed.), **Handbook of research on teaching** (3rd ed.). New York: Macmillan.

Williams, K. (1981). **The effects of group cohesiveness on social loafing.** Paper presented at the annual meeting of the Midwestern Psychological Association, Detroit.

Williams, K., Harkins, S., & Latane, B. (1981). Identifiability as a deterrent to social loafing. Two cheering experiments. **Journal of Personality and Social Psychology, 40,** 303-311.

Wilson, R. (1987). Toward excellence in teaching. In L. M. Aleamoni (Ed.), **Techniques for evaluating and improving instruction** (pp. 9-24). San Francisco: Jossey-Bass.

Workplace basics: The skills employers want. (1988). American Society for Training and Development and U.S. Department of Labor.

Wulff, D., Nyquist, J., & Abbott, R. (1987). Students' perception of large classes. In M. E. Weimer (Ed.), **Teaching large classes well** (pp. 17-30). San Francisco: Jossey-Bass.

Yager, S., Johnson, D., & Johnson, R. (1985). Oral discussion, group-to individual transfer, and achievement in cooperative learning groups. **Journal of Educational Psychology, 77**(1), 60-66.